Poetry and Drama

in the

York Corpus Christi Play

Poetry and Drama in the York Corpus Christi Play

RICHARD J. COLLIER

ARCHON BOOKS
1978

First Published 1977 as an Archon Book,
an imprint of THE SHOE STRING PRESS, INC.
Hamden, Connecticut 06514

Printed in the United States of America

Library of Congress Cataloging in Publication Data

Collier, Richard J 1943–
Poetry and drama in the York Corpus Christi play.

Bibliography: p.
Includes index.
1. York plays. 2. Mysteries and miracle-plays, English—History and criticism. 3. English drama—To 1500—History and criticism. I. Title.
PR644.Y6C6 822'.1 77-21348
ISBN 0-208-01611-2

To Marilyn

CONTENTS

In quoting from printed editions of Middle English works, I have normalized the use of "u" and "v" in accordance with modern practice. Although a new edition of the York Corpus Christi Play is much needed, and has long been promised, the 1888 edition by Lucy Toulmin Smith is still the only modern edition. In quoting from it, I have frequently repunctuated the text without comment.

INTRODUCTION

Thirty-five years ago, the medieval English Corpus Christi plays were being confidently dismissed as, in general, "pretty sorry stuff." Just twenty-five years ago, the "workmanship" of the plays was still widely considered to be "never far from crude." But in recent years, critics have offered very different evaluations of the artistic quality of this early drama. Now the Corpus Christi plays are compared favorably with the splendid Gothic cathedrals of medieval England. In both, one critic has found, "there is magnificence in their design and life in their detail. Despite occasional flaws and inconsistencies," he concludes, "these plays are unlike anything else in the history of English drama, and the sympathetic reader . . . will find they repay any attention he may give."[1]

What has brought about this change? In large part it is due to theatrical revivals of the plays. Since the staging of an abbreviated version of the York cycle during the Festival of Britain celebrations in 1951, increasingly frequent performances have revealed the remarkable theatrical vitality of these plays to increasingly large audiences. In the twenty years following that early experiment at York there were more than twenty-six productions of the four extant cycles of plays in England, and now the regular stagings of the York and Chester cycles are among the most popular of the many British dramatic festivals.[2] I first saw the cycle plays performed in San Francisco—not in a small church, acted by experimentally inclined amateurs, but in the city's largest theater, acted by the professional repertory company. The audience received the old religious plays quite as enthusiastically as they had done the more predictable *The Doll's House.* No doubt modern audiences enjoy these plays in different ways from the original audiences, for whom, on a day of liturgical and civic festival, they served to celebrate communally held beliefs. But it no longer seems surprising that in medieval England the Corpus Christi plays attracted audiences year after year for more than one hundred and fifty years.

The restoration of the Corpus Christi plays to the stage has established them as substantial and powerful works of dramatic art. It has also taken them out of the province of the literary historian and inspired modern critics to take a fresh look at them. For a long time, attempts to evaluate the accomplishment of the plays had been disabled by various unexamined assumptions—by an anti-Catholic prejudice, for example, or by the assumption that the plays' religious function precluded artistic deliberateness, or by an evolutionary sense of the development of drama which looked to the plays of the Middle Ages primarily for anticipations of the great achievement of Shakespeare and his contemporaries.[3] In this light the Corpus Christi plays were found to be, with few exceptions, naive and unimaginative, written by unskillful versifiers for an audience strangely tolerant of pious doggerel and easily pleased by crude farce. The rejection of these judgments, and of the assumptions that led to them, is now almost complete. The Corpus Christi drama now rightly commands attention as one of the most significant artistic achievements of the later Middle Ages in England, one which, in its distinctive aims and qualities, can tell us much about the age, the people, and the cultural traditions that produced them. Yet these plays are more than monuments. They represent a fascinating experiment in the history of drama, one which in many ways—their nature as popular and communal art, their resourceful use of a symbolic stage, their fusion of diverse tones and forms—suggests what the theater and drama can do, and has even directly inspired some twentieth-century experiments.[4]

It is with the Corpus Christi plays as a distinctive form of drama that this study is concerned, and in examining the plays to see how they work as drama I have tried to see them without preconceptions about how they *should* work. In this, my approach coincides with that of all the recent studies of the medieval religious drama. But my focus differs from that of previous studies in two important respects: in its almost exclusive attention to a single cycle of plays, and in its concentrated examination of the poetry of those plays. Both need some explanation.

All the major studies of the Corpus Christi drama, whether historical or critical, have tried to deal with all the extant plays. For example, V. A. Kolve's ground-breaking study of ten years ago was concerned with what the plays have in common: Kolve examines separate aspects of the drama (the form and structure of the cycles, their use of comedy, their characterizations), but he does so in order to establish a generic integrity for "the Corpus Christi *kind*."[5] Rosemary Woolf's more recent study also surveys all the cycles, though she is concerned with the detailed differences between them: her major effort is to describe the various possibilities open to the dramatists for the presentation of a given episode, and to evaluate the plays in terms of the choices that have been made.[6] Inevitably, the broad scope of these studies forces some selectivity and can fragment our view of each of the cycles as a whole. Questions still remain—do any of the cycles reward sustained examination of their details, do they achieve any kind of dramatic unity?[7] These questions are not my explicit concern, but by limiting myself to the study of a single cycle I have been able to pay attention both to the particulars of all the plays of that cycle and to the larger designs that give them shape and point.

My choice of the York cycle was at first simply the result

of my finding it more interesting as a whole than the other cycles. Since then, however, I have come to think that in their considerable variety, the plays of this cycle fully demonstrate the possibilities of the Corpus Christi drama's form and purpose, that some of the most skillful of the Corpus Christi playwrights worked on these plays, and that in the consistent quality of their dramatic art they can fairly stand as the highest achievement of the cycle "kind" of drama. The York plays survive in a single manuscript, probably an official Register of the plays kept by the city council, compiled toward the middle of the fifteenth century.[8] At the time of compilation, a number of plays were not copied into the Register. Subsequently, at different times, all but two of the missing plays were copied on leaves that had been left blank for them. In the middle of the sixteenth century, at the time the plays were beginning to arouse the suspicion of the new religious leaders of the community, the Register seems to have been thoroughly checked against the copies of the individual plays in the hands of the guilds responsible for producing them. A large number of small alterations and corrections in the Register date from this time, as do the frequent marginal notations that a speech or a scene has been "remade." Although attempts to establish specific stages in the "growth" of the cycle have proved inconclusive, it is clear that the cycle, as it has survived, is the work of different playwrights writing at different times, that it was always subject to revision, and that it is incomplete. But it is also clear that the plays in the Register are, with only minimal differences, those that were performed during the one hundred years of the cycle's greatest popularity—roughly from 1425 to 1525. So, however tautologically, I have here treated the cycle as a whole to show that it can be treated as a whole. It is also to be hoped that what I have to say about one cycle will provide a basis for comparisons with the other extant cycles.

The second respect in which my study diverges from previous studies—its examination of the poetry of the plays—will be more surprising to readers familiar with modern criticism of medieval drama. One of the most enduring judgments about the Corpus Christi plays is that their writers were not very good poets. In fact, that I use the word "poetry," with its implications of artistic deliberateness and complexity, to refer to the verbal dimension of the plays, runs counter to an established feeling that the plays offer at best "verse." Some still influential studies ask us to believe that as far as the Corpus Christi plays are concerned, "Whereas the craftsmen of the Middle Ages had mastered stone for their particular purposes—words proved for them too hard a medium"; or that "Much is crude, some is even doggerel. It is understandable that most of the plays have been rejected as poetry even before they have been considered as drama."[9] Exceptions are often made for the poetry of the Wakefield Master and, more relevantly, for the work of the York "Alliterative Poet." Hardin Craig, for instance, has found "great skill, genuine vigor, and no small amount of poetic beauty in the alliterative plays of the York cycle," and even "much else in other metres that is poetically admirable throughout the cycle."[10] But praise, and even consideration, of the poetry has come grudgingly: "We can recognise," one critic concludes a brief survey of the verse of the plays, "that not all the unknown versifiers whose efforts gave us the scriptural drama of medieval England were incompetent hacks."[11]

Almost no attempts have been made to go beyond such impressionistic responses to examine the kinds of poetry in the plays or to clarify the bases on which we can fairly evaluate it. Thirty-five years ago, Henry W. Wells, claiming "a genuine rhythmical sense" and an "aesthetic sensitivity to language" for the Corpus Christi playwrights, offered a preliminary description of certain stylistic patterns found in the plays and of the traditions behind them;[12] but his suggestions were never developed in a full study, and they have rarely been acknowledged in subsequent studies of the drama. Among recent critics, only Rosemary Woolf has paid consistent attention to the quality of the poetry: her comments are constantly fresh, responsive, and fair, but they are necessarily restricted by the scope of her study to isolated passages and effects. So far, the reconsideration that has allowed us to see the traditions, nature, and aims of the Corpus Christi drama more clearly has not been extended to include the poetry of the plays.

What has prevented such a reconsideration has been the tendency of critics to deal with the poetry in very limiting terms and to regard it as an isolable element of the drama. Thus Eleanor Prosser, for example, has stated:

> The critic is beaten before he starts if he approaches the mystery playwrights first as poets. It is my hope that by approaching them first as dramatic craftsmen, we may side-step what has seemed to be an insurmountable barrier. If, by turning first to the more important elements of plot, characterization, and over-all effect, we may find a given play to be potentially good drama, the qualified scholar may be encouraged to take a new look at the verse.[13]

In reducing the poetic art of the plays to a matter of prosody, and refusing to allow even the prosodic effects any place in the "over-all effect" of a drama written throughout in verse, Prosser aligns herself with a long tradition. A standard approach of early studies, one still followed by Hardin Craig only twenty years ago, was to examine the cycles first of all in terms of the verse forms used, because, it was believed, they held clues for determining the development of the cycles and the relationships among them.[14] The assumption here, clearly, is that the use of a particular verse form is determined by historical rather than artistic considerations. As a result, comments on the dramatic appropriateness or effectiveness of the verse are only incidental in these studies and even then tend to be undermined by accompanying historiographical assumptions—for example, that simplicity of form is a necessary sign of early composition and hence, too, a sign of artistic primitiveness.

The unembarrassed sidestepping proposed by Prosser may well have been further encouraged by modern experiments with "poetic drama," in which the use of verse rather than prose is seen as an option allowing the dramatist more or less distinctly identifiable effects. For the medieval playwright, it almost certainly was *not* an option. On the contrary, he would have thought of himself *as* a poet, not a dramatist, though he no doubt recognized that he was a poet working with opportunities not allowed, say, the composer of lyric poems. If the sheer variety of the verse forms in the plays is any indication, or the fact that the two most distinctive playwrights (the Wakefield Master and the York Realist) both chose to work with original and demanding verse forms, then it seems reasonable to think that the playwrights considered their skills as poets as fundamental to their task. Such an assumption asks us to reconsider the usual conclusion that "the authors found it possible to do what the play demanded despite the verse forms which they used,"[15] and to think of the verse as "the authors" must have thought of it—as a natural and valuable resource.

It was the verse forms of the York plays that first prompted this study. Noting the variety and frequent complexity of the forms, I was interested in finding out what impulses lay behind the use of verse, what precedents there were for the various forms, what criteria determined their use. At an early stage, I found—not surprisingly—that I could not answer these questions by concentrating exclusively on prosody. The poetry of the York plays, like any other poetry, is as much a matter of language and style as of meter. Moreover, it is also a matter of distinct kinds of poetry, and of traditions in which those kinds had been developed. As has often been noted, the medieval dramatists borrowed extensively from the vernacular poetic traditions developed in the hundred years or so preceding the compilation of the cycles, adapting what they borrowed to meet the new needs and demands of the drama. And to acknowledge this last point is to acknowledge that consideration of the poetry of the plays necessarily involves consideration of the nature and aims of the drama as a whole. What poetic traditions were borrowed from, and why? How were they adapted for use in the drama? What part do verbal and poetic effects play in the effectiveness of individual plays and of the cycle as a whole? We can properly answer these questions, which are the most inclusive questions I ask in this study, only in the light of what we now understand to be the characteristics of the medieval drama. At the same time, these questions can, I believe, help us to see these characteristics even more clearly. The Corpus Christi drama *is* a poetic drama, and before dismissing the poetry as unworthy of our attention, we should be clear about what criteria we are using to judge it.

This study attempts to provide such clarification. It calls for, and depends upon, one basic adjustment in our expectations of the poetry of the York Corpus Christi plays.

We naturally expect poetry in plays to work dramatically. We tend to look first of all at the ways in which the poetry is used to create characters and the settings in which they act, to articulate the plot of the play, to define the play's action, and so on. That is, we look most closely at the internal world of the play and examine the poetry in that context. This is how commentators on the Corpus Christi plays have generally gone about evaluating the effectiveness of the poetry, both when they have praised it and when they have condemned it. I am not suggesting that the criterion of dramatic appropriateness is irrelevant to a consideration of the poetry of medieval drama. On the contrary, the York plays, like any other drama, depend for their effectiveness in large part upon the creation of a fictionally coherent and compelling world in which the play's action is clearly realized. One of my concerns in this study is to explore the extent to which the dramatists are alert to the dramatic possibilities of their poetic medium.

Yet it also must be granted from the start that, judged by a strict criterion of dramatic appropriateness, the poetry of medieval drama often seems strangely undramatic. It seems to serve functional rhetorical ends rather than mimetic or aesthetic ends. Many modern critics have deplored this aspect of the poetry. But to do so is to wish that the poetry—and the drama as a whole—were something other than what they were trying to be. For example, it may be true that the frequent passages of straightforward explanation and exhortation, at times addressed directly to the audience, seem dull when isolated from their context or obtrusive if we are expecting the self-contained dramatic world of a later drama. But looked at in another way, these passages in their very overtness can be taken as an indication of just how important to the drama's concerns are the need to explain and the access to the audience. My study grants this rhetorical poetry its place in the Corpus Christi drama, and argues not only that it has an *essential* place in the drama, but also that the poetry is not as simply rhetorical as critics' embarrassed comments about its "didacticism" might suggest.

In judging the poetry of the York plays, then, we must initially allow rhetorical effectiveness as much weight as dramatic effectiveness. This is to be expected. First, because the traditions of poetry the dramatists drew from were themselves basically rhetorical. Verse that states and explains points of doctrine, verse that moves its hearers to meditation and repentance, verse that tells the stories of the Bible so that its hearers might remember and associate themselves with those stories—these are the kinds of poetry available to the dramatists. We should be more surprised that they are so frequently and so skillfully made dramatic. The second reason we should expect rhetorical efficiency as well as dramatic inventiveness in the handling of the poetry is that the drama as a whole is itself rhetorical. Its aims are frankly pragmatic rather than aesthetic: "the augmentation and Increase of the holy and Catholick faith of our Saviour Iesu Christ and to Exort the minds of Common people to good devotion and holsome doctrine ther-of"—thus one manuscript of the Chester plays defines the religious aims of the Corpus Christi drama.[16] In this drama, persuading the audience is a more urgent goal than entertaining it. The Corpus Christi drama makes no attempt to exclude its audience as a later, more "realistic" drama might. Nor, on the other hand, does it assume the participation of its audience as the liturgical drama, as part of the ritual of the church, can do. In a variety of ways, more often subtle than overt, the Corpus Christi drama acknowledges its audience to elicit and direct its involvement in what it sees and hears.

This strategic handling of the audience is one of the most

distinctive features of the Corpus Christi drama. It is the result of the drama's distinctive action. Unlike other drama, in which the individual dramatist invents the particular action of his play and reveals it through a plot that is limited in space and time, the Corpus Christi drama, imitating the Scriptures, dramatizes the action of God. Its scope is all of time, its setting is the universe of heaven, earth, and hell. Its focus is an event which joins time with eternity, the world with heaven, and men with God. Necessarily, then, the audience and its present moment are understood as being as much a part of the action of the plays as are the historical characters and events actually depicted. The drama aims above all at making this understanding explicit. Every aspect of these plays—staging, plotting, characterization, music, and poetry—works to reveal the action of God and to persuade the audience to believe in and conform themselves to that action. The Corpus Christi drama, in bringing man and God together, imitates the Incarnation it also celebrates.

In this context, my distinction between "dramatic" and "rhetorical" aspects of the Corpus Christi plays breaks down, for this drama aims at and depends upon a constant interaction of the world of the play and the world of the audience. And it is in the poetry of the plays, I believe, that we can see this interaction most fully created and can recognize it as a deliberate, thorough-going, and usually skillfully managed aspect of the dramatic art of the plays. This at least is the claim that sustains the following chapters in their close examination of the verbal art of the York plays. In the first chapter I deal with the poetry in general terms, discussing the verse forms and the kinds of poetic language found in the plays and establishing the poetry as a crucial dimension of the drama's theatrical effectiveness. In the following chapters, I examine what I consider to be the predominant modes of the poetry—the homiletic, lyric, and narrative modes—discussing each in terms of the tradition from which it is derived, of the effects it aims at, and of the ways in which it is integrated with the dramatic action of the cycle. In isolating these modes, however, and in isolating passages to illustrate them, I have inevitably misrepresented the ways in which they work in the plays. They are not mutually exclusive, and they are always dependent for their effectiveness upon the details in which they are realized and upon contexts created for them by the action of individual plays. With this in mind, I have included as part of these three later chapters a commentary on a particular and complete play which, while concentrating on the features of the poetry discussed in the chapter, allows me to take into consideration every aspect of the drama and to show how the various modes can be worked together.

There is still a great reluctance among critics of the Corpus Christi drama to grant the plays any verbal sophistication or even any sustained verbal interest. Thus Rosemary Woolf, for example, in what I consider to be the most valuable of the recent studies of the plays, concludes that "the mystery plays, more than any other kinds of drama, are meant to be seen. The dialogue has not the richness of texture that would make a constant rereading of the words rewarding. It is not coincidence that the present recognition that the plays are both moving and powerful began with their widespread revival on the stage."[17] Like all drama, the Corpus Christi plays have a life greater than that recorded in the texts of the plays—and I have tried not to forget that in examining the poetry of the York plays. But my constant rereading of the plays has convinced me that the dramatists did pay perhaps their greatest attention to the words. Implicit in this study is the argument that we should do likewise.

I

The Poetry of the Play

The York Corpus Christi Play opens on a note of awesome dignity as God the Creator announces Himself from the center of the stage: "*Ego sum Alpha et O, vita, via, veritas, primus et novissimus.*" Even when the resonant Latin phrases give way to an extended vernacular paraphrase, the Creator's speech remains elevated to sustain the image of splendid authority:

> I am gracyus and grete, god withoutyn begynnyng,
> I am maker unmade, all mighte es in me,
> I am lyfe and way unto welth wynnyng,
> I am formaste and fyrste, als I byd sall it be.
> My blyssyng o ble sall be blendyng,
> And heldand fro harme to be hydande,
> My body in blys ay abydande
> Unendande, withoutyn any endyng.
>
> (I, 1–8)

One critic has recently said about this stanza: "It paraphrases the Scriptures, and is meant to be uttered in ringing tones; it is written in an alliterative verse form, and derives its strength from a series of words beginning with the same letter or containing the same vowel sounds, and shows a certain crude strength of purpose and inflexibility of will such as one might associate with the Apocryphal Old Testament God if one were an illiterate and untravelled peasant living in feudal Yorkshire six hundred years ago."[1] He finds no trace of poetic skill or dramatic complexity in the stanza. But, concerned to prove that "medieval drama is not poetic drama,"[2] he is not looking for any.

Of course the general impressiveness of the stanza is important in suggesting God's power and hierarchical supremacy: these are the premises of the action of the whole cycle. In support of it, however, and of the visual image of the Creator, the stanza's poetic effects are ordered to more precise ends. In announcing Himself, God both details the attributes of the Creator and, at the same time, affirms His absoluteness. The stanza form reflects the paradox in a subtle interplay between the whole and its parts: where in the rest of the play the stanza falls into two parts completely separated by a change in rhythm and rhyme scheme, here the two quatrains, though still rhythmically distinct, are linked by rhyme in such a way that the last line returns to the first to lend support to God's statement that He is without beginning or end.[3] Similarly the individual lines of the stanza are distinguished by the alliteration, but linked by the rhymes; and even within the first two lines, the effects of the heavy caesurae are countered by the alliteration which links the two parts. In its metrical features, the stanza itself images a God who is multidimensional yet perfectly one.

Although the Creator remains decorously motionless as He speaks (the decorum will become obvious later as the Devils run around madly in hell), His words, made dynamic by the stanza's prosodic interplay, seem to prepare for action. The syntax and rhythms of the stanza support this suggestion. The imposing anaphora of the first four lines, the weighty monosyllables, the declarative sureness, all create a sense of stability and firmness which builds up to the uncompromising half-line, "als I byd sall it be." Then, in the second four lines, the rhythms become more fluid with the consecutive feminine endings and the frequent participial forms to create an equally strong sense of process, of potential. In the stanza that follows, in fact, a long periodic sentence takes the place of the parataxis of this first stanza as the attributes of the Creator established at the start become the basis of His creation, and as the process of history begins.

There is point, too, to the language of the stanza. We will soon have cause to remember God's repeated use of the first person pronoun when Lucifer tries to usurp it for his own use. "Blyssyng" and "blys" will echo throughout the cycle, for they are what God first creates, what man forfeits, and what God then offers again to those who are faithful to Him. Even the abstractness of the language is noteworthy: surrounding as it does the single concrete noun "body," it both implies the insubstantiality of God and prefigures the Incarnation which, as the Latin formula also suggests, is seen as inhering in the act of Creation.[4]

A comparison can help to clarify the accomplishment of the opening stanza of the York Creation play. The poet of the *Cursor Mundi* begins his account of the history of the world by explaining the nature of the Creator:

Alle men owe þat lord to drede
þat made mon to have mede
þat ever was and ever sal be
Wiþouten end in trinite;
he þat lorde boþ god and mon
Al maner þing of him bigan;
þouȝe he bigan al oþere þing
Him self hadde never bigynnyng:
of him coom al, in him is al,
al holdeþ he up fro doun fal.
He holdeþ hevene & erþe studfaste
wiþouten ende may no þing laste.
þis lorde þat is so mychel of myȝte
Purveide al in to his siȝt
and þat he ordeyned wiþ his witt

he multiplied & governeþ hit;
þerfore he is þe trinite
þat is o god & persones þre.[5]

Perhaps the dramatist turned to a statement like this for help with his presentation of the Creator. If he did, he has transformed what he found. The differences are not simply those resulting from the dramatist's more ambitious verse form, for the forms themselves are determined by what the poetry is trying to do. In the narrative poem, the poetry's only function is to explain: syntactical and metrical units coincide as the couplets struggle to reduce paradox and mystery to simple statement. Few heightened verbal or rhythmical effects interfere with the practical purpose of the lines. Even in the most careful couplet ("of him coom al, in him is al, / al holdeþ he up fro doun fal"), the balance and repetitions serve to make the statement more memorable rather than to illustrate or imitate the nature of the Creator. The verse here is at best functional; in general, its effects are as arbitrary as the logic of the lines.

The dramatic verse is more complex and careful in every way. We can still hear an expository impulse in the simple language and epigrammatic forcefulness of the opening lines of the play. Part of the function of the stanza is to offer the audience (even though they are not directly addressed) an explanation of *how* God is at the center of all things as well as an assertion that He is. Yet it *is* God who speaks—not some anonymous expositor—and the poetic effects of the stanza give definition to the visual image. The words God speaks are not merely appropriate to the image of God; they *are* an image of the infinite, ineffable God, the one and the many, motion and stillness, whose order, beauty, and might can be known only through finite expressions of them. Drawing upon the theatrical actuality of the moment, the poetry of the opening stanza of the York cycle allows the audience to contemplate God as His action begins to unfold.

Not all the poetry of the York Corpus Christi Play sustains the detailed examination this opening stanza deserves—

mainly because it is not often called upon to do as much as in the cycle's opening moments. But this stanza should raise our expectations about what we will find elsewhere—deliberateness, skill, rhetorical appeal, dramatic point. And whether or not all the details of meter and language I have pointed to would be caught by an audience, they are there in the poetry to be drawn upon by a skilled actor speaking from a stage that provided few distractions. It is to this stage as a setting for the poetry of the York plays that I turn first.

Poetry on the Stage

The medieval playwright wrote with one of two basic kinds of staging in mind.[6] One, now generally referred to as the "place-and-scaffold" method of staging, involved a large open playing area containing a number of raised scaffold platforms which could be given precise identity through stage sets or through association with a particular group of characters. Since both the scaffolds and the unlocalized area could be used by the actors, this kind of staging allowed movement, variety of scene, large-scale action. The other kind of staging was that provided by a fixed stage, often a pageant-wagon which could be drawn through the streets of a city in procession. A development from *tableaux vivants* presentations widely used in civic and liturgical displays, it called for fewer actors and less movement, and was best suited to episodic action that was concentrated rather than dispersed.

Civic records and stage directions in surviving manuscripts indicate that both kinds of staging were used for the Corpus Christi plays. The York plays, however, seem to have been designed exclusively for the pageant-wagon stages.[7] Such wagons, we know, were amongst the possessions of the trade guilds at York as early as 1376. The members of the guilds maintained these wagons at great expense, stored them when not in use in a "pageant-house," and, on days of festival, brought them out to take part in colorful processions through the streets of York. For the celebrations on Corpus Christi day, the guilds used these stages to present familiar scenes from the Old and New Testaments before large audiences gathered at specific locations along the streets. At first the Corpus Christi procession probably offered only static tableaux. Later, more fully dramatic plays supplemented and then supplanted the liturgical procession, but the guilds seem, naturally enough, to have used the wagons and stage sets they already possessed to present these plays.

What were these pageant-wagon stages like? Unfortunately, the pertinent records are so sparse and so cryptic that any detailed reconstruction is impossible. They were small: Stanley Kahrl has recently endorsed Arnold Williams' estimate "that the overall dimensions . . . could not exceed eight feet by twenty feet."[8] Since some of the York plays call for fifteen or more actors, these stages, even with the additional space provided by the adjacent street, must often have been crowded. Moreover, besides the actors the stage had to accommodate properties—and they could be substantial. A recently discovered indenture of 1433 lists the properties used by the wealthy Guild of Mercers in its pageant presentation of the Last Judgment: they include an elaborate structure of iron and wood, decorated with stars, "sunne bemes of gold," and red and blue clouds, representing heaven; an iron swing on which the actor playing Christ could be lowered and raised; a hell-mouth; "ij peces of Rainbow of tymber"; and a string of mechanical Angels, painted red, "to renne about in þe heven."[9] The quaintness of some of these descriptions for a long time fostered the sense that the pageant stages were generally crude and simplistic; a fairer consideration encourages us to see them as colorful, substantial and often complex in their mechanical devices—to see them, in fact, as the guilds' most valuable and carefully protected possessions.

Few aspects of the medieval religious drama have received as much attention in recent years as the staging of the plays, not just because more and more records are coming to light, but because it is on the stage, as the experience of modern performances confirms, that the plays come most vividly to life. But in stressing the visual appeal of the plays, critics have not explored the findings of modern producers that in production the plays also have considerable verbal appeal.[10] They have been reluctant to entertain the possibility that what the audience heard during the long day's dramatic activity was quite as important and compelling as what they saw, or even to examine the effect of the staging on other aspects of the plays such as their poetry. We might imagine, for example, that the tableau-like presentations of the pageant stage would encourage a static poetry of set speeches. It frequently does. But there also are advantages: the limited movement allowed by this stage eliminates the need for passages to cover the extensive movements of the place-and-scaffold stage, and the concentration of focus allows more intense and even more delicate verbal effects than those achieved in the poetry of plays written for the larger stage. In fact, the restriction on movement on the pageant stage used at York means that the poetry itself frequently has to sustain theatrical interest and even, when the action is vast in its dimensions and significance, to perform the actions for which it substitutes.

The opening play of the York cycle, the Creation play, fully illustrates the kinds of demands made of the poetry by the pageant stage—and the kinds of possibilities created for it. There are no records or even stage directions to tell us how the stage was set for this play, how the actors were costumed, or what their movements on the stage were. But given the nature of the action in the Creation play, effects of staging would inevitably be symbolic. They could only suggest what the play had to make real for its audience—the wonder of God's immensity, the splendor of heaven, the universal import of Lucifer's disobedience and its consequences. Therefore, throughout the play, as in the opening stanza I have already described, it is the poetry, what the audience hears, that carries the action of the play. After the opening words in which He announces Himself, God declares the first act of His creation: "Baynely in my blyssyng I byd at here be / A blys al be-ledande abowte me" (I, 20–21). The terms are vague enough almost to preclude visual representation—in the *Ludus Coventriae* Creation play, in contrast, God first creates a "hevyn with starres of lyght."[11] But the insistent alliteration calls attention to the words: God is heard to create "at a worde" (I, 42). Through His words, too, He now brings into being the nine orders of Angels simply by "bidding" them "to be here" (I, 22). Suddenly the stage is filled with the Angels grouped around the Creator and singing His praises in the Latin hymn *Te deum,* creating a solemn aural image of the harmony of God's Creation, and its sublimity.[12] Now God proceeds to create heaven, earth, and hell. Again, in this play He simply names them:

> Here undernethe me nowe a nexile I neven,
> Whilke ile sall be erthe; now all be at ones
> Erthe haly, and helle, þis heghest be heven.
>
> (I, 25–27)

At this moment, the whole stage is constituted as an image of the created universe, dominated by God, its various levels brought into meaningful existence by God's words as the inclusive setting for the action He initiates.

In the Creation plays of the other extant cycles, Lucifer acts out his defiance of God by sitting in the throne which God has temporarily vacated. In the York play, however, there is no indication that God ever leaves His central, elevated position. He remains the central figure on the stage, asserting His control over the action and providing a focus against which Lucifer's pretensions can be judged. Nor in this play is there any indication that Lucifer ever physically approaches God. His act is rather a verbal act, a statement of intention. As the increasingly obtrusive alliteration in his words expresses his growing pride, Lucifer imagines himself "On heghte in þe hyeste of hewven" (I, 88), imagines himself even usurping God:

> Ther sall I set my selfe, full semely to seyghte,
> To ressayve my reverence thorowe right o renowne:
> I sall be lyke unto hym þat es hyeste on heghte.
>
> (I, 89–91)

Quickly and irresistibly, his intentions are frustrated. The unspoken judgment of God makes itself felt in the sudden disruption of the verse form as Lucifer preens himself for the last time:

Owe! what I am derworth and defte! Owe! dewes! all
goes downe!
My mighte and my mayne es all marrande!
Helpe, felawes! in faythe I am fallande!

(I, 92–94)

No doubt the actor at this point did tumble from heaven, but the physical fall from one level of the stage to another could only hint at the great impact of the moment. Here, too, much of the action is in the words. A tumult of unstressed syllables and participles verbally acts out the fall, while the words themselves comment on it. Lucifer's screams assert his transformation from angel to devil, his plea to his "felawes" for help pathetically undercuts the isolated preeminence he has just insisted upon, the simple statement "I am fallande" recalls God's promise that the Angels would remain "stable" in the bliss of heaven as long as they remained obedient to Him. And when the Second Fallen Angel picks up Lucifer's cries—"Fra heven are we heledande on all hande / To wo are we weendande, I warande" (I, 95–96)—the participles carry on the tumbling fall while the rhythmically underlined words "Fra heven . . . To wo . . ." define the terrifying consequences of their rebellion.

That the Angels fall "To wo" and not "To hell" is a small but indicative point. Hell has been identified as a locus on the stage and no doubt some stage effects were used to make it vivid (the dialogue calls for smoke). But this hell is most importantly a verbal one. A neat chiasmus describes the consequences of the fall: "We þat ware beelded in blys, in bale are we brent nowe" (I, 107). The high style of heaven is juxtaposed to the colloquial coarseness of the devils' oaths, celebration and praise give way to laments and accusations. Heaven is the harmony of the Latin hymn, hell the screaming and gibbering of the devils as they turn on Lucifer:

Lucifer: Walaway! wa es me now! nowe es it war thane it was.
Unthryvandely threpe ȝhe–I sayde but a thoghte.
Secundus diabolus: We, lurdane–þou lost us.
Lucifer: ȝhe ly! Owte, allas!
I wyste noghte þis wo sculde be wroghte.
Owte on ȝhow, lurdans, ȝhe smore me in smoke.
Secund. diab: This wo has þu wroghte us.
Lucifer: ȝhe ly, ȝhe ly!
Secund diab.: Thou lyes–and þat sall þu by!
We, lurdans, have at ȝowe, lat loke.
(I, 113–120)

Lucifer *had* "sayde but a thoghte"–and those words have produced this cacophonous chaos in which even the stanza form is shattered.

The stanzas that follow take the audience's attention back to God and His Angels in heaven. In a more somber mood than at the start of the play, the Angels interpret what they have seen and God reiterates the point of what the audience has seen:

Those foles for þaire fayre-hede in fantasye fell,
And had mayne of mighte þat marked þam and made þam;
For-thi after þaire warkes were, in wo sall þai well:
For sum ar fallen into fylthe þat evermore sall fade þam,
And never sall have grace for to gyrth þam.
So passande of power tham thoght þam
Thai wolde noght me worschip þat wroghte þam,
For-þi sall my wreth ever go with þam.
(I, 129–136)

Even in this expository stanza, we can hear the poetry supplementing and commenting on the stage action: the repeated pronouns hanging over the ends of the lines seem to embody the isolation of the devils and the finality of their separation from God even as they draw admonitory attention to them.

In the final movement of the play, God completes the first day of creation by naming light and darkness, day and night. Throughout the play the dramatist has been building up associations between light and heaven and darkness and hell, and now these associations are focused as day and night become metaphors for the attitudes of obedience and arrogance that the play has juxtaposed, and for the community with God or exile from Him which are the consequences of those attitudes.[13] At the same time, the very familiarity of the terms extends the metaphor—in ways that no symbolic stage effect could do—into the everyday experience of the audience to give them an ever-present reminder of the options they have seen displayed.

The inevitably nonrepresentational staging of the Creation play makes special demands of the poetry, but it fulfills them without strain. Just as the central figure of God is created primarily through the words He speaks in the opening stanza, so are the important actions of the play, the creating, the overreaching, the judging, accomplished in large part in the poetry. So, too, are even the crucial settings of the action: heaven and hell may be places on a stage, but they are more urgently the acts of worshiping God, or boasting, of singing hymns of praise, or swearing at your neighbor.

We should not be surprised that the Corpus Christi dramatists are capable of such adept handling of verse in the theater, for the traditions from which the poet-playwrights were working were ones of orally delivered, public poetry for which the stage supplied a natural setting. But the features of drama which can be resources for the poet—variety of speakers and situations, the movements of players on the stage, the visual aspects of the settings in which they move, the constant action—also impose severe discipline upon him. The Elizabethan dramatists, we have often been told, thrived on such demands. Can we say the same consistently for the anonymous writers of the York plays? Glynne Wickham has suggested that just like its successor, the medieval theater was one of "poetry and visual suggestion"[14]—and the York Creation play bears out this claim. I believe that if we constantly ask of the poetry of the York plays "What is the effect?" as well as "What does it say?" we will find countless moments when the dramatists show a sure awareness of the theatrical potential of their verse. I will be pointing to many of these moments in subsequent chapters. Here I want only to suggest ways of responding to the poetry as a theatrical dimension of the drama by examining the ways in which poetry and staging interact to define the movements and gestures of the actors, to give point to the settings in which the actors move and to amplify visual stage sets, and to create the theatrical world in which the stage and the audience are brought together in the comprehensive action of the drama.

In much of the early religious drama, the words that accompany an actor's movements frequently provide little more than an explanatory description of those movements. That is, speech and action are coextensive.[15] For example, the York Creator describes in detail what He does on the second, third, fourth, and fifth days of Creation as He does it: "Of my gudnes now will I ges, so þat my werkis no harmes hent, / Two lyghtis, one more and one lesse, to be fest in þe firmament" (II, 47–48). Although the convention may well seem to a modern reader to be a naive way of adapting narrative sources to dramatic action, in the York plays this kind of verbal commentary, though frequent, is rarely gratuitous. In the example just referred to, there is an appropriateness to the verbal descriptions of action since God does create "noght by [his] strenkyth, but by [his] stevyn" (II, 16). Or in the Creation play, as I have already suggested, the use of the convention to make intentions explicit underlines the fact that in that play God fulfills what He sets out to do, but Satan is frustrated.

As a result of this convention, there is little dissembling in the Corpus Christi plays. Even Satan clearly announces his intention to tempt Eve—and this time he succeeds. At times, however, the dramatists work into this self-exposition a judgment on the actions that it helps to fill out. One stanza from the York play of Christ's Judgment by Pilate can provide an illustration. At the end of the play, Pilate's soldiers enthusiastically set about scourging the condemned Christ:

ii Mil: Swyng to this swyre, to swiftely he swete.
iii Mil: Swete may þis swayne for sweght of our swappes!
iv Mil: Russhe on this rebald and hym rathely rehete!
i Mil: Rehete hym, I rede you, with rowtes and rappes!
ii Mil: For all oure noy, þis nygard he nappes!
iii Mil: We sall wakken hym with wynde of oure whippes.
iv Mil: Nowe flynge to þis flaterer with flappes.
i Mil: I sall hertely hitte on his hippes
and haunch.
ii Mil: Fra oure skelpes not scatheles he skyppes.
iii Mil: Ȝitt hym list not lyft up his lippis
And pray us to have pety on his paunch.
(XXXIII, 361-372)

This is only one of a series of stanzas accompanying the scourging of Christ, but in the ways in which the poetry enhances and comments on the visual spectacle, it is the most carefully worked. The rhythm of the first four lines—an anapaestic rhythm with an additional stress at the head of each line—rains blows relentlessly down on the subdued Christ. Even the alliterating sounds are vivid: in the repeated "sw" sounds we can perhaps hear the swish of the whips, in the trilled "r's" the sting of the blows. The words of action are repeated and rhythmically highlighted as the syntax forces them to the beginning and ends of the lines. Then, as the rhythm shifts into the three-stress lines, the pace of the beating quickens to a climax in the First Soldier's hearty extra effort in the tag line. But even that effort does not end the beating. The blows continue until the Third Soldier pauses at last in the bewildered exhaustion of the last lines.

With the actors only feigning the scourging, such skillfully managed aural effects can usefully literalize and complete their gestures.

For the audience that watches and hears, however, this verbal commentary directs the response to the beating which it helps to make more vivid. The colloquial epithets are clearly ironic: Christ is a "rebald," a "nygard," a "flaterer" only to these blindly vengeful Soldiers. The irony becomes grotesque as they talk about "reheating" Christ with their blows and call His near-unconsciousness a "nap." The Soldiers want to be admired for their efficiency, but they can only be condemned for their viciousness. Of course Christ does not ask them for mercy; Christ is the one who makes mercy available, for those humble enough to ask. The Soldiers' words thus undercut their actions at the same time as they theatrically reinforce them.

In trying to analyze the second theatrical function of the poetry I have pointed to—its amplification of visual stage sets—we will be frustrated by the sparsity of records for the York plays which makes it impossible to reconstruct how the stages were decorated or what properties were available. The dialogue of the plays provides some clues, although, interestingly, there is never any extensive reference to the settings in which the actors moved. Places are often constituted merely by the presence of a particular figure or by a brief verbal reference: the action of the Baptism play, for example, is localized by the Angel's announcement to John the Baptist that Christ will come "Fro Galylee un-to þis flode / ȝe Jourdane call" (XXI, 53–54). Many of the plays seem to call for an interior setting of some kind—Mary's house (Play XIII), the stable (Play XIV), the temple (Plays XX, XLI), the halls of Pilate and Herod (Plays XXX–XXXIII)—and some specify the presence of a hill (Plays X, XIII, XXIII, XXXVI). In general, the precise nature of the setting does not seem important. But when a particular stage effect *is* important to the action of a given play, it is the poetry that makes it so. Many of these effects have to do with light and darkness, effects which, as we have seen, are given metaphorical importance from the very opening of the cycle. A bright light shines at Christ's Nativity, at His Transfiguration, the Harrowing of Hell, and Pentecost; the Trial scenes, on the other hand, take place at night. Torches carried in the Corpus Christi procession may have been used to suggest these effects, but for the most part the dramatists rely upon the language of the plays to actualize them and bring them into the action.

By far the most successful use of poetry to amplify stage effects in the York plays occurs in the beautiful Nativity play. Stanley Kahrl has recently praised this play as the one that makes most effective use of the limited potential of the pageant-wagon stage.[16] But he does not note the ways in which the poetry both focuses and expands upon the staged action. At first, the weariness and despondency of Mary and Joseph are reflected in the setting they describe: Joseph complains about the stable they have been forced to stay in—its walls are falling down and the roof is in ruins (XIV, 17–18)—and about the cold weather and the darkness (41–42). As he leaves to find the fuel and light they need, Christ is born—Christ, the maker of "Merknes and light" (63). From outside the stable, Joseph now notices a bright light shining. Bewildered, he returns to Mary and finds the stable no longer dark but filled with light. The hole in the roof which had imaged their despair now lets in the light of the star that shines to betoken the birth of the Savior. Joseph's despondency disappears as he celebrates the birth of the "lemer of light" (111)—he has found a source of light far more wonderful than the one he sought. The coldness of the stable, too, is transformed into warmth by the breath of the animals, and Joseph's bewilderment is transformed into understanding as he confidently explains this effect to be the fulfillment of Habbakuk's prophecy. In a joyful harmony which replaces their earlier lonely complaint, Mary and Joseph worship the Son of God, their child. The stable has become an image of "þis worlde" (113), transformed by Christ and His Incarnation, the light that lights the stable radiating as a brilliant metaphor for the Incarnation which brings the light of understanding to men as it brings the Light of the World to those who seek it. There are few Corpus Christi plays in which visual and verbal effects interact quite as intensely as they do here.

Perhaps by giving the scene of the Nativity so precise a setting on the small stage, the dramatist was trying to express the familiar paradox of the Incarnation that in coming to the world God who is infinite was nonetheless contained in a manger in a stable. Such a suggestion would be consistent with the "meaning" given to stage space in the cycle. For the most part, the stage focuses rather than encloses the action of the plays, suggesting always the universal dimensions of the action no matter how local the particular scene. In the Creation play, as we have seen, God's Creation of the world orders vertical space to set heaven, earth, and hell, in an immutable hierarchy. In the very last play of the cycle, the stage is similarly organized as the hierarchy is re-established for eternity. Horizontal stage space, too, is given symbolic import in these plays, again most clearly in the final play where first the Angels and then Christ separate the risen souls in accordance with God's instructions:

> Mi blissid childre, as I have hight,
> On my right hande I schall þame see;
> Sethen schall ilke a weried wight
> On my lifte side for ferdnesse flee.
>
> (XLVIII, 75–78)

Even when the action takes place without reference to this definitive symbolism of stage space, the stage tends to have a significance larger than that of its particular identity in any given play, in part because it is frequently referred to as "this world," partly because it is rarely treated as a completely self-enclosed space. Satan moves amongst the audience shouting "Make rome be-lyve, and late me gang. / Who makis here all þis þrang?" (XXII, 1–2); Christ enters Jerusalem in all probability from the street around the pageant-wagon, and may well have been led to His death with the audience in close attendance; frequently the audience is addressed directly from the stage in an unembarrassed coalescence of the dramatic world with that of the audience. For the most part, the stage is only the temporary focus in a world that reaches out to include the audience. Like the Elizabethan stage, the medieval theater and its stage are an image of the whole world—though in this drama, earth is a place firmly set between heaven and hell.

Martin Stevens has recently drawn attention to the metaphorical significance of the medieval stage, and has added an important observation:

> Such a stage virtually demands a dramaturgy of motion. In a very real sense, the progress of the dramatic action in the medieval play depends on the playwright's manipulation of space, of moving his characters from mansion to mansion. As a result, medieval plays constantly focus on journey, in Langland's terms, on "alle maner of men . . . wandryng as the worlde asketh." Procession, we recall, is the impulse behind the popular religious drama, and it becomes the informing metaphor of the Corpus Christi cycle.[17]

The limited space of the pageant-wagon stage for the most part prevents this crucial metaphor from being acted out in the actors' movements. The metaphor is more obvious—as Stevens implies—in plays designed for the place-and-scaffold stage, like *Everyman*. Nevertheless the metaphor is still important for the York plays, though it is in its poetic handling that it becomes so. Christ describes His life on earth as a "jornay" (XLIII, 155), a journey which begins and ends in heaven. This journey is the paradigm of all movement in the plays, and, just as importantly, of the "journey" of man which the audience is embarked upon. Some of the plays make extensive use of the metaphor. At the start of the Adoration of the Magi Play (Play XVII), each of the three Kings appears at a different place, each brought from his own country by the star which all three follow. Each offers a prayer: the first that God might grant him "happe to have / Wissyng of redy waye" (11–12); the second, vowing that he will not cease from his journey until he has found out the meaning of the star, that God might grant him "goode companye" (20); and the third that "God wisse me with his worthy wille" (30). The guidance they pray for brings them together, and at once the goals of their journey come into view—Jerusalem, "To wisse us als we goo," and Bethlehem, "þer sall we seke alsoo" (57, 60). They proceed to Jerusalem, but there, where they had hoped to find guidance, they find only deception: though Herod tells them "Wendis furth, youre forward to fulfill, / To bedlem, it is but here at hande" (193–194), they find that the star that had been leading them has disappeared. One of the Kings realizes that "In oure wendyng some wrange is wroght" (220), and so they pray once again for guidance on their way. The star reappears, and, led by it, the Kings approach the stable in Bethlehem. There a servant of Mary inquires of them, "Whame seke ȝe syrs, be wayes wilde, / With talkyng, traveling to and froo?" (228–229), and when she is told that they seek the Christ child, she tells them, "Come nere, gud syirs, and see, / Youre way to ende is broghte" (237–238). They have reached the goal of their journey. Rejoicing that they have found what they sought, they adore the Christ child and offer their gifts. At the end of the play, an Angel appears to warn them against returning to Herod and to tell them that "Be othir waies God will ye wende / Even to youre awne contre" (320–321). Their journey is that of all men in the world; like all men, they have been distracted and misdirected, but led by God in whom they put their trust, they have found the goal of their journey in Christ. As if to acknowledge this dimension of their action, the Kings at the end pause to offer a final prayer to God and to address a benediction to the audience that has watched their journey: "He þat is welle of witte / Us wisse—and with yow be" (335–336). For that moment the drama creates a world which extends to include the audience which has come to find the "Corpus Christi."

The theatrical aspects of the poetry of the York plays, as these illustrations indicate, can be complex and detailed. They seem to call for skilled actors and attentive audiences such as we are reluctant to grant the medieval drama.

Shakespeare's picture of "rude mechanicals" stumbling over "points" is too vividly with us, and contemporary complaints about congregations who do everything but pay attention to the preacher, or audiences which "disgraced the play by revellings, drunkenness, shouts, songs, and other insolencies,"[18] encourage us to imagine less than optimal circumstances for a performance of the Corpus Christi plays. But we can afford to be idealistic. There is evidence from the beginning of the vernacular drama that great care was spent on the selection and training of actors.[19] At York, expenses for rehearsals of plays are recorded in guild accounts, and substantial fines were levied on players who failed to appear "well arayd and openly speking."[20] Toward the end of the fifteenth century, in fact, the City council intervened to assure that the actors would be a credit to the city and the plays. In 1476 it ordained that "all þe plaiers and plaies and pagentes thurghoute all þe artificers belonginge to Corpus X[ti] Plaie" be examined by "iiij of þe moste connynge discrete and able players within this Cittie." To these four was given the charge to select the best of the aspiring players, and "all oþer insufficiant personnes, either in connynge, voice, or personne to discharge, ammove, and avoide."[21] Clearly the plays themselves, in their wide variety of verbal styles, call for flexibility and skill on the part of the actors—though modern producers using amateur players at York have found that the verse of the plays is also an immense aid to the actor. And if we can grant the plays skillful writers and responsive players, we can provide the attentive audience.

The Verse Forms

At the time the Corpus Christi plays were written, one entrenched authoritarian attitude was that verse was to be condemned and avoided as a way of communicating God's word. It was "theatrical and unspiritual," a "deadly snare for the fashionable preachers who sought to seduce the ear rather than to convert the soul."[23] Yet the plays are in every case written throughout in verse, many of them in elaborate stanzaic verse. Why? One reason no doubt was that verse *was* theatrical, that it *was* a way of seducing the ear—for the audience had to be persuaded to stay through many hours of the drama. The appeal of rhyme and rhythm, the variety of textures and moods that could come from varied verse forms, these possibilities no doubt recommended verse. There would be other considerations—practical ones (verse was easier to memorize and to recite), and circumstantial (most of the works the dramatists turned to as sources would have been in verse), and perhaps the general aesthetic consideration that only verse would fit the sublimity of the drama's action. If there ever was any debate about verse or prose as the medium for the drama, it was probably inevitable that verse would be chosen.

But it was *not* inevitable that the dramatists in England should choose to work in stanzaic verse. Many of the narrative analogues to the drama were in couplets, like the *Cursor Mundi* or *Northern Passion,* as are some of the early dramatic fragments translated from the Anglo-Norman.[24] And in France, the writers of the *mystères* adopted the couplet as the basic verse form, keeping stanzaic verse for special effects.[25] On the other hand, there were substantial precedents for the use of stanzaic verse in drama. Rhymed, stanzaic verse found a natural place in the liturgical plays which were, of course, sung and chanted—though even here stanzaic verse tends to be reserved for emotionally heightened moments of lamentation or praise. For sustained use of stanzaic verse in drama we must look to the vernacular tradition. Both plays in which Latin and the vernacular were combined, such as the St.-Martial *Sponsus,*[26] and the fully vernacular plays like the *Mystère d'Adam,*[27] are marked by their metrical complexity. This coincidence suggests that the use of stanzaic verse, with many forms being taken over from secular tradition, was prompted like the use of the vernacular itself by the wish to extend the appeal of the drama. It also suggests that the heightened aural effects of rhyming metrical verse might have been felt to compensate for the loss of richness resulting from the substitution of the vernacular for the liturgical Latin. These suggestions are not—as they might seem—contradictory. As David Jeffrey has recently explained, in the religious and aesthetic program of the Franciscans, the goals sit comfortably together: "The Franciscans carried with them a passionate determination to harness popular culture as medium, and to elevate it as value."[28]

It may well prove that the influence of the Franciscans was the determining factor in the adoption of stanzaic verse as the medium for the popular religious drama. Certainly in England, the Franciscans had already produced a body of religious lyric verse marked by its metrical variety. In part this variety is a result of the many different modes in which the lyric poets worked—narrative, celebratory, devotional, didactic—modes which are freely mixed in the drama as they are not, for instance, in the predominantly narrative poems of the fourteenth century. But in part, too, the sense of pleasure in poetic experimentation that prompts such variety can be seen as a manifestation of the lyric poets' sense of themselves as poets. St. Francis saw himself and his followers as the minstrels of God, *joculatores Dei.* For them, song and poetry were a primary means of reaching the heterogeneous audiences they addressed and of encouraging them to participate in the sublime joy and grief of the Christian story. These goals encouraged the kind of poetic experimentation we more readily associate with secular troubadour verse: God called for the finest a poet could offer, and religious poetry had to be attractive to win men away from their enjoyment of worldly songs and bring them to an enjoyment of God's beauty.[29] We have been made suspicious of verse in drama that seems merely ornamental—T. S. Eliot argued, for example, that poetry "should justify itself dramatically, and not merely be fine poetry shaped into dramatic form."[30] But we can imagine that for the religious playwrights the very attractiveness of the ornament, the value of verse as embellishment and entertainment, represented a valuable resource. More precisely, we can approach the verse forms of the Corpus Christi plays with an awareness of the potential of verse for appealing to the ears of the audience and at the same time intimating the splendor and import of the action of God for men in which the audience is encouraged to participate.

Even given such justifications for stanzaic verse, however, the range of verse forms in the plays, and the complexity of many of them, are still remarkable. Especially so in the York plays. More than twenty different forms are used, ranging from a simple quatrain with alternative rhyme (Play III), to the fourteen-line stanza used in the play of the Flood (Play IX) and the play of the Conspiracy to take Jesus (Play XXVI), or the exceptionally complicated twelve-line stanza of the Flight into Egypt play (Play XVIII).[31] This variety received much attention from early commentators on the York plays, for when the historical circumstances of the cycle were being investigated, the verse forms were considered to hold clues to the growth of the cycle and its relationship with other cycles.[32] We need to question some of the assumptions behind the traditional historical analyses of verse forms (simple forms are not *necessarily* a sign of early composition or of lack of artistic deliberateness, one writer need not use just a single verse form), yet there is little doubt that the variety in the York plays is to some extent the result of different writers having worked on the plays at different times. However, at Chester, a series of writers and revisers kept to the same stanza forms—can we find any other possible explanations for the variety of the York plays?

One possible explanation, all too rarely considered, is that the writers were alert to the particular appropriateness of a given stanza form, appropriateness to a character, or an incident, or the predominant mode of a play. The most idiosyncratic writer to work on the York plays is often identified by the distinctive, and demanding, verse form he used as "the York Alliterative Poet": his hand has been seen in the plays which organize heavily alliterated lines into stanzas of varying length and complexity.[33] In many of the plays, notably the plays dealing with Christ's Trials, his vigorous alliterative verse borders on the prosaic in its rhythms. The long, often fragmented stanzas blur together, no matter how intricate the rhyme schemes that define them. It is ebullient, noisy verse, perfect for the excessive display of the court, the pretensions of the Princes, the cruelty of the henchmen, and so on, but little suited to the lyrical tones of lament or the rhythms of intimacy. For these effects, more concentrated stanza forms serve, most noticeably in the moving soliloquy of Judas, where the interruption of the established verse form poignantly captures the intrusion of conscience into a world of cruel obduracy (XXXII, 127 ff.). Whether the poet left an earlier version of this scene intact when he was revising or composed the whole scene himself, he shows himself alert to ways in which different verse forms can achieve different effects. That alertness is further evidenced by the possibility that some of the plays in the cycle that show the greatest sensitivity in the handling of complicated stanza forms—the Creation play (Play I) or the Death of Christ play (Play XXXVI)—were also composed by the "Alliterative Poet," though even if these plays were not the work of the same writer they still testify to the skill with which the alliterative verse can produce a wide range of effects in different stanzaic patterns.

Other plays in the cycle not written in alliterative verse show a similar use of different verse forms to reflect the changing tones of the dramatic action. The editor of the York plays noted that in Play XIII, for example, "the metre of this play changes, like a piece of music":[34] we can be more precise—one verse form is used for the lyrical moments of the play (for the exchanges between Joseph and Mary), another for the more public moments (Joseph's interrogation of Mary's servants, the appearance of the Angel to Joseph). The late play of the Purification of Mary uses many different forms to create a variety of often contrasting tones. Sober quatrains serve for the rehearsal of the Old Law at the start of the play, and for old Simeon's complaints; broken into two-line units, quatrains also serve throughout the play when functional dialogue is called for. There is a complicated nine-line stanza ($abab_4c_3\,ddd_4c_3$) which appears most consistently when intimate personal feelings are being voiced, as in the quiet exchange between Mary and Joseph. The play builds to a climax in the public celebrations of the Prisbeter, Anna, and finally the regenerated Simeon, whose hymns are cast in an ornately decorated four-line stanza (aaa_4b_2) patterned, appropriately, after the form of the liturgical sequence. Throughout the play, various patterns of rhyme shape the stanzas into larger groupings to add to the aural richness of this highly lyrical play. The play perhaps shows signs of the metrical excess that overwhelms much late fifteenth-century verse; E. K. Chambers does in fact find "metrical chaos" in the play.[35] But to hear the play is to appreciate how finely modulated the verse is and how surely it defines and enhances the movements of the play's action.

Unlike the Purification play, most of the York plays—and, unlike the French plays, most of the English plays—do not use different verse forms within a single play. What variety of effects is created comes from the careful handling of a single form. To the extent that such effects are a matter of details, I will be pointing to them in subsequent chapters. But an initial indication that the verse is more deftly handled to dramatic effect than is usually granted can be given by looking at the variety of effects achieved within one stanza form in the York plays. Twelve of the plays make use of the "Northern septenar" stanza—a twelve-line stanza of simple structure and rhyme scheme ($abababab_4cdcd_3$).[36] Sometimes enhanced by alliteration or stanza-linking, it is adapted to create effects as different as the plaintive dialogue between Abraham and Isaac (Play X); the horror of the Egyptians as they report the plagues visited upon them by God (Play XI); the ornate liturgical hymns of the Magi at the Adoration (Play XVII); Christ's expository rehearsal of the Ten Commandments before the Doctors in the temple (Play XX); the laments of Mary and Martha over the death of Lazarus (Play XXIV); the noisy commentary of the Soldiers as they crucify Christ (Play XXXV); and, with Latin verses neatly incorporated into the form, the wonder of the Apostles as they receive the gift of tongues at Pentecost (Play XLIV). It has been suggested that the widespread use of this form in the York plays is the result of a single reviser's using the *Gospel of Nichodemus*, where a similar form is used, as the basis of his revisions.[37] It seems just as likely that a dramatist, or even a number of dramatists, chose this stanza form to work with because it is such a flexible form.

For most of the stanza forms used in the York plays, as for the septenar form, there are precedents in contemporary nondramatic verse. The so-called "Burns' stanza," for instance, a six-line stanza ($aaa_4b_3a_4b_3$) found in four of the plays, is common in lyric and narrative verse in Middle English where it is probably an imitation of an earlier French stanza form.[38] Perhaps there was a common stock of forms from which the dramatists drew. But what has determined the choice of one form over another? Is it, as has usually been implied, mere historical circumstance—or are we justified in thinking that an appreciation for a given form's flexibility or appropriateness determined the selection? Most of the evidence, I have been suggesting, points to aesthetic deliberateness. Such deliberateness is, at least, the only explanation I can find for the three stanza forms in the York plays for which there is no precedent in contemporary verse. They are among the most complicated of the forms in the cycle: one is the twelve-line stanza of the Flight into Egypt play ($ababcc_4dde_2fef_3$); the second is the eleven-line stanza of Play V, the play of the Disobedience and Fall of Man ($abab_4c_2bc_4dcdc_3$); the third is the form in the play of the Appearance of Mary to Thomas (Play XLVI), a thirteen-line stanza ($ababbcbc_4deee_2d_3$) which, like the music in the play, seems to have been composed especially for this play.[39] All three forms combine complexity with flexibility. They are composite stanza forms, and so can serve as wholes for sustained speeches of lamentation, celebration, or explanation, or can readily be broken up into their constituent parts to allow for dialogue. It seems unlikely that dramatists would invent such complicated forms to work with unless they felt they added to the play and unless they were sure of their ability to handle them.

Whatever considerations lie behind the use of particular verse forms in the Corpus Christi plays, the use of stanzaic verse clearly determines the kinds of speeches the dramatists can provide for their characters. Many critics have felt it determines them adversely: "Clearly the writers are fettered by the various rimes and measures in which the dialogue is cast."[40] To a great extent, such judgments seem to be based on anachronistic or inflexible requirements. There are few sustained attempts to create naturalistic speech in these plays; even dialogue—exchanges in which characters interact with each other in their speech—is only one kind of speech the plays call for. To a far greater extent than later drama, the Corpus Christi plays depend upon an alternation of "dynamic" and "static" speech, the latter kind furthering the rhetorical aims of the drama by allowing for lyrical concentration of the action, or for clear explanation of it. Since the York playwrights do for the most part maintain a single form throughout a play, one criterion of their skill in handling the verse forms should be the ease with which they adapt the form to the different demands made of it. There are remarkably few moments of awkwardness or obtrusiveness. One play where we can hear the flexibility very clearly is the play of Christ's being led to Calvary, Play XXXIV. The stanza form is an unusual and difficult one—a ten-line stanza, $aa_4b_3aa_4b_3cbcb_3$—but it is surely handled. Broken up, it allows the unruly Soldiers to make their preparations for the Crucifixion at the start of the play and to taunt Christ as they strip Him at the end. Kept whole, it allows the extended laments of the three Marys and John and the bitter speech in which Christ reproaches the city of Jerusalem. At the heart of the play is the scene where Christ wipes His face, a scene that shockingly brings together the contrasting moods of the play through clever handling of the stanza:

iii Maria: Allas! þis is a cursed cas,
He þat alle hele in hande has
        Shall here be sakles slayne.
A lorde! be leve lete clense thy face.
Behalde howe he hath schewed his grace,
        Howe he is moste of mayne.
This signe schalle bere witnesse
Unto all pepull playne,
Howe goddes sone here gilteles
Is putte to pereles payne.

i Miles: Saie, wherto bide ʒe here aboute?
Thare quenys, with þer skymeryng and þer schoute
Wille noght þer stevenis steere.
ii Miles: Go home, casbalde with þi clowte,
Or be þat lorde we love and lowte
Þou schall a-bye full dere.
iii Maria: This signe schall vengeaunce calle
On yowe holly in fere.
iii Miles: Go, hye þe hense with alle
Or ille hayle come þou here.
(XXXIV, 181–200)

A very similar form ($aa_4b_3cc_4b_3dbdb_3$) is used in the play in which God places Adam and Eve in the Garden of Eden (Play IV). The play as a whole is, fittingly, more formal and ordered than the Calvary play (as yet there is no cause for violence or lamentation), but the stanza is used to image both the harmonious rejoicings of Adam and Eve and, more ominously, the warnings given by God. Here the final quatrain serves in every one of the stanzas spoken by God to focus His warning.

Even in their handling of normal dialogue, the York playwrights take great care to avoid undue regularity. O. B. Hardison has shown how the early attempt in the twelfth-century *La Seinte Resureccion* to represent "the dialectic quality of dramatic speech" produces a highly symmetrical mode of speech in which the "speeches tend to fall into paired units."[41] There are few traces of this uncertain approach to writing dialogue in the York plays. Patterned exchanges are usually used for deliberate effects, as in the Soldiers' torturings of Christ where the ritualistic quality of the ordered sequence of speakers controls their brutality. Instead of symmetry, regularity, and awkwardness—what we have been led to expect by most commentators—we find subtle variation. The lengthy exchange between Abraham and Isaac, for example, is conducted in twelve-line stanzas which could become ponderous were it not that the units of dialogue are never allowed to settle into a fixed pattern. Lines 137–272 (stanzas 12–22) are broken up in the following way between Abraham and Isaac: A:4, I:2, A:6; I:2, A:2, I:4, A:4; I:2, A:18, I:6, A:2, I:2, I:1, A:1, I:6; A:4, I:22, A:28; I:12; A:8, I:4 (Play X). The speeches are still often lengthy ones, as befits the sober mood of the play, but in the variations played with the units of the stanza form we can recognize a careful attempt to fuse formality and naturalness—a fusion which is the mark of the cycle as a whole.

Though there is no call for it in the Abraham and Isaac play, lively and realistic dialogue is well within the reach of the York dramatists. The York Realist shows himself capable of imitating naturalistic exchanges, but they can be found in less immediately striking plays as well. Thus, for example, a bewildered and apprehensive Mary and Joseph prepare to escape to Egypt with the newborn Christ:

Mary: Allas! Joseph, for grevaunce grete,
Whan shall my sorowe slake?
For I wote noght whedir to fare.
Joseph: To Egipte talde I þe lange are!
Mary: Whare standis itt?
Fayne wolde I witt.
Joseph: What wate I?
I wote not where it standis.
Mary: Joseph, I aske mersy—
Helpe me oute of þis lande.

(XVIII, 173–182)

The metrical features of the stanza are hardly noticeable in this exchange—the rhythms and tones of a crabby old man and his helpless wife are brilliantly caught. But in the York plays—as in all medieval religious drama—such naturalistic effects are never an end in themselves. This image of a human family is offered only for a moment, long enough for us to recognize in the historical event a timeless resonance. Then Joseph takes the Christ child from Mary, and as he does, is filled with cheerful confidence:

Joseph: Are was I wayke, nowe am I wight,
My lymes to welde ay at my wille.
I love my maker most of myght,
That such grace has graunte me tille.
Nowe schall no hatyll do us harme
I have oure helpe here in myn arme.
He will us fende
Wherso we lende,
Fro tene and tray.
Late us goo with goode chere!
Fare wele and have gud day!
God blisse us all in fere.
Mary: Amen, as he beste may.

(XVIII, 219–231)

Here the same stanza form supports the sustained expression of joy and hope. It is as if the verse has been healed along with Joseph's spirits, and now Mary's prayer complements Joseph's to resolve the stanza, and the scene, in an image of harmony. Their confidence, we can expect, is shared by the audience which knows that they will be protected from Herod's angry determination to frustrate God's will. In short space we have been taken from the confused and helpless world of men into the harmonious and stable world of God, a movement accomplished in the verse which images both.

This brief sequence from a little-noted play can serve as a paradigm of what I would claim is the most significant potential of the dramatists' use of stanzaic forms in the York plays. Even at its most prosaic and chaotic—in the screaming and cursing of Hell in the Creation play, or the wild shouting of the Trial scenes—the stanza forms imbue the verse with an immanent order which can and always will be restored.

The Language

"A principal consequence of writing drama in verse," it has been claimed, "is that it opens the same resources of language to the dramatist as to the lyric poet. . . . Imagery of all kinds, ambivalences of meaning and suggestion, words made uniquely potent by the circumstances of the context, figures of speech, in particular metaphors—all of these become available to the dramatist to be used as his artistic needs require."[42] We are likely to be disappointed if we approach the Corpus Christi drama with these expectations. The claim is made in connection with the plays of Shakespeare; the expectations it embodies arise from the experience of Shakespearean drama and of traditions of poetic expression alien to the medieval poet. Metaphor, for instance, is clearly an appropriate poetic device where the dramatic aim involves "a pushing of the bounds of apprehension . . . into areas where literal certainty and systematic knowledge do not provide the appropriate answers."[43] But it is not such an appropriate device when the dramatic aim is to reaffirm doctrinal truths and paradigmatic experiences—when, to exaggerate the distinction, systematic knowledge does provide the appropriate answers. By and large, the Corpus Christi drama is of this second kind. Its basic language, consequently, like that of the lyric poets of its time, tends to be public and formulaic rather than idiosyncratic.

This distinction, however, does not mean that the language of the Corpus Christi plays is necessarily crude, or dull, or undisciplined. It means only that it is of a certain kind, perhaps unfamiliar, and that it has its own kinds of poetic and dramatic force which may not be those we have become used to. The point needs stressing at the outset, for comments about the "halting, tedious, undeveloped speech" of the plays all too frequently spring from anachronistic demands.[44] D. S. Brewer has made a similar point: "No poet could stand up in his pulpit before the audience as medieval poets did if he was not prepared to use a poetic language with which his audience was reasonably familiar, and which it could be expected to understand and even to like. Such concepts of a recognizable, indeed conventional style, appropriate to both subject matter and audience, consciously chosen with the desire to communicate interest and pleasure, are remote from most modern theories of poetry. They are the concepts of medieval rhetoric."[45] Brewer is writing about Chaucer, a poet whose imaginative independence, subject matter, and audience allowed him to manipulate the conventional bases of his language and the expectations of his audience to often startling new ends. But with the Corpus Christi dramatists we are not dealing with poets with Chaucer's freedom. Nor are we dealing with a drama like Shakespeare's which, though similarly addressed to a heterogeneous and unsophisticated audience, was the expression of a radically sophisticated vision. We are dealing with writers who remain anonymous and with a drama which is the most popular and communal we know.

These qualities of the drama help to explain, first of all, the fact that they are written in the vernacular. Scholars and critics used to believe that the use of the vernacular was the result of a gradual process of secularization of medieval religious drama, a process that urged the drama out of the church and into the marketplace, out of its somber, ritualistic beginnings into its use of farce, out of the liturgical Latin into the various European vernaculars. Such a view, we now can see, was an inaccurate convenience. Fresh examination of the extant texts and their history has established an extensive tradition of vernacular drama developing independently of the liturgical drama from the early twelfth century.[46] Some of the most accomplished of the early plays come from this tradition, notably the twelfth-century *Mystère d'Adam.* In this light, the use of the vernacular seems more deliberate than we have been led to believe. No doubt it was prompted most immediately by a desire to bring the teachings of the Church to wider audiences—as Richard Axton has recently pointed out, the vernacular plays intended for popular audiences are more overtly didactic than the Latin plays.[47] But the use of the vernacular also coincides with (and perhaps helped to promote) a basic change in medieval spirituality:

> The use of liturgical Latin removed the personae and events of sacred history both from their actual context and from the everyday life of the medieval laity, insisting on the irrelevance of 'personal' motives and dissolving

> the chronological links between events. Gregorian chant, ecclesiastical costume, setting and ceremonial action carried the process of abstraction still further. When homilists, poets and playwrights adopted the vernaculars for the purposes of explaining sacred history to lay audiences, the nature of the everyday language as well as the purpose in hand encouraged a different focus on the divine events as human happenings in the contemporary world.[45]

Besides the practical advantages to using the language of the audience, then, there was a spiritual appropriateness—the Christian story is one that most immediately concerns the people in the audience—and that appropriateness encourages an aesthetic sensitivity to the vernacular. It can be seen in those plays where the vernacular is used to express human emotions in the context of the divine events recounted in Latin verses. It can best be seen in the *Mystère d'Adam*, where the inventive and supple handling of the vernacular works to locate the eternal truths of man's fall and salvation firmly within the world most familiar to the audience.[49]

Records from England are so sparse that it is hard to determine how substantial the tradition of drama written in English was prior to the compilation of the Corpus Christi cycles.[50] From the late thirteenth and early fourteenth centuries there are cryptic fragments translated from Anglo-Norman, lines from "boasting prologues" of a kind later used in the cycle plays but here probably from miracle plays.[51] Other miracle plays are known to have existed from the mid-thirteenth century.[52] A collection of Latin sermons from around 1325 preserves a few lines of English verse constituting a speech in which the devil tempts Eve; the fragment testifies to an early interest in dramatizing biblical stories in English (though it is hardly enough to posit, as Rosemary Woolf has done, "the existence of an English cycle beginning with the Fall round about the year 1340").[53] The fullest piece in English antedating the cycle plays is a morality play, *The Pride of Life*, an isolated experiment that draws exclusively from popular rather than ecclesiastical modes of presentation.[54]

If such incomplete evidence is any reflection of the state of vernacular drama in England in the fourteenth century, it suggests that while there may have been a concept of drama sufficient to give the Corpus Christi playwrights a sense of generic possibilities, the cycle plays were nonetheless a dramatic undertaking unprecedented in scope and size. To a great extent, the dramatists were dependent upon nondramatic material that they could shape into their plays. By the end of the fourteenth century there was available to them a varied and impressive tradition of poetry written in English, and the York plays, making use of a wide range of styles, draw variously from this tradition. Yet there are few traces in the plays of the idiosyncratic uses of language we find in Langland or Chaucer. Only the York Realist, in fact, shows any self-conscious concern for language—and even the poetry of his plays builds from styles used elsewhere in the cycle. For the most part, the language that constitutes the norm of the plays is the traditional language of the homiletic, narrative, and lyric traditions of popular poetry in England. It foregoes strikingness in favor of clarity, privateness in favor of an inclusive generalness.[55] Whatever color it has comes from proverbial and popular similes. Joseph's heart is as heavy as lead (XIII, 15); Noah's cares are as keen as a knife (IX, 7). Simeon, as he receives Christ, is made as light as a leaf on a tree (XLI, 444); the cripple healed by Christ at the Entry into Jerusalem throws away his crutches "als lyght as birde on bowe" (XXV, 388). But that such language is the norm in the plays is thoroughly appropriate to the aims and nature of the drama. It allows the playwrights ready access to their audience as a community, and allows them to tell a story that concerns each and every one of the people in the audience. The language is everyday language—but even God uses it, in all its dialectal familiarity.

I am suggesting that in the past judgments based on taste have tended to determine reactions to the poetry of the Corpus Christi plays, and that if we consider the poetry—specifically here its language—in terms of its appropriateness to the audience and the subject matter of the plays, then we must hesitate before dismissing it as limited or crude. We can test this claim, and our expectations, against one predominant feature of the language, its highly formulaic quality. This quality—found in the use of doublets, repeated words and phrases, general rather than specific terms—is what has earned the poetry such a bad name. It is also a quality that the language shares with all other forms of contemporary vernacular poetry. Recent criticism has allowed us to see the aesthetic possibilities of this formulaic poetic style, and to recognize that while it can be a crude crutch to help a lesser poet struggle along, in the hands of a careful poet it can become—as it does for the Gawain-poet or Chaucer—a creative resource.[56]

Though the writers of the York plays rarely try for the kind of subtle irony that Chaucer is capable of in his handling of formulaic language, their use of formulae is often more careful than might seem. Take, for example, the following stanza from the second play of the York cycle in which God proceeds with the Creation to the fifth day:

> Moo sutyll werkys asse-say I sall,
>   for to be set in service sere:
> Alle ye wateris grete and smalle
>   þat undir hevyne er ordande here,
> Gose togedir and holde yow all,
>   and be a flode festynde in fere,
> So þat the erthe, bothe downe and dale,
>   in drynesch playnly may a-pere;
> Þe drynes 'lande' sall be
>   namyd, bothe ferre and nere;
> And þen I name þe 'se,'
>   geddryng of wateris clere.
>
> (II, 27–32)

There is nothing startling in the language here to accompany God's cosmic act; in fact, the stanza could stand as illustrative of the basic language of the plays in its lack of imagery, its denotativeness, its blandness and abstractness. Read on the page, the doublets "grete and smalle," "downe and dale," and "ferre and nere" seem particularly obtrusive as line fillers. But they are not obtrusive when the stanza is recited, and they are not redundant when the passage is set in context. This particular play is full of such doublets, one for about every three lines: these three all occur in one other place (11. 53, 52, 19 respectively), others include "firth and fell" (1. 63), "more and myn" (1. 65) "se and sande" (1.73), and "more and lesse" (1.82). Cumulatively, these phrases work to express a sense of the vastness of God's creation and His bounty—"Begynnyng mydes and ende / I with my worde hase wrothe," God confirms at the end of the play (1. 80)—something which the limited stage cannot suggest. Similarly in the last play of the cycle, doublets like these will again be used to imply the inclusiveness of the action as God prepares for judgment: "ferre or ner" God finds no sinless man, and so He summons "leerid and lewde, both man and wiffe," and "grete" and "small" (XLVIII, 57–72).

A second example, involving more than mere verbal doublets, comes from Simeon's speech as he presents himself in the Purification play:

> A! blyssed God, thowe be my beylde,
> And beat my baill both nyght and day,
> In hevynes my hart is hylde,
> Unto my self, loo, thus I say.
> For I ame wayke and all unwelde,
> My wealth ay wayns and passet away;
> Where so I fayre in fyrth or feylde
> I fall ay downe for febyll, in fay;
> In fay I fall where so I fayre,
> In hayre and hewe and hyde, I say,
> Owte of this worlde I wolde I were!
> Thus wax I warr and warr alway,
> And my myscheyf growes in all that may.
>
> (XLI, 87–99)

There is no attempt to offer a vivid insight into a distinctive personality as there might be in a later drama. The characterization is broad: Simeon's prayers to God locate him as a servant of God, his complaint establishes him as an old man. He is a patriarch, a "senyour / that is so semely in Godes syght" as the prophetess Anna has just described him (78–79). And that is all Simeon has to be, for he serves in the play primarily as an exemplar of how Christ's presence will regenerate those who faithfully await him. He is a type, not an individual; depth of characterization is not as important as recognizability.[57] Whatever dramatic detail there is—the stumbling repetition of lines 93–95, made more awkward by the alliteration, suggests an old man trying "in hevynes" to collect his thoughts—is meant to bring us closer to the figure in preparation for his transformation at Christ's appearance.

These effects are given further point by the verbal formulae of these lines which, as well as generalizing the characterization, work to associate Simeon with other characters and situations in the plays. The phrase "wayke and all unwelde" has been used twice before, once by Noah, praising God for the strength he has received to enable him to build the ark in which he and his family will be saved (VIII, 93), once by Joseph as he mourned his feebleness and old age (XIII, 6). The phrase is part of a larger formula, the lament of the old man, and their use sets up analogies which are an essential part of the characterization. Like Noah, Joseph has been regenerated in physical strength and spirit by the presence of God; so too will Simeon be restored—he will later rejoice "Nowe am I light as leyf on tree, / My age is went, I feyll no fray" (XLI, 346–347). Moreover, this internal dramatic pattern is extended outwards to give point to the emotional recognition sought of the audience by the typical quality of the characterization. For like Simeon, all men will be restored when they accept Christ, this Simeon intimates when he prays to see the child born "mans myrth to mell" and this he confirms when he celebrates the child ordained to be "The helth for all men that be levand / here for ay" (XLI, 106, 417–418).

There are, to be sure, inactive tags and empty formulaic phrases in a series of plays of this length. Like the contemporary romances, the plays betray their popular and public nature most clearly in their language. But if we grant the plays the universal scope and significance of their action and their aim of bringing this significance home to a largely uneducated lay audience, we can recognize in the formulaic language both a rhetorical and a dramatic usefulness which have usually been denied it. The same can be said for the verbal repetition which is perhaps the most consistent verbal device used in the plays. "Obey," "bliss," "light," "will," "grace"—abstract nouns like these provide the staple vocabulary of the plays. But however obvious their repetition might be as an expository device to keep before the audience the premises of the action, their use serves also to inform the variety of the plays with cohesive patterns and to reflect the universal scope of the action they express. And like the formulaic language of the plays, this abstract language can be precise in its effects. We have seen how the Creation play of the York cycle establishes the "bliss" of heaven as the reward of the obedient—the word is used sixteen times in the play as a simple way of underlining the importance of the idea to the action. In the immediately following plays it remains a crucial term: God creates Adam and Eve to fulfill the bliss marred by Lucifer, and sets them in the bliss of Paradise with the warning that if they eat of the tree of good and ill they will be "brought owte of blysse" (IV, 59). So firmly has the idea been established that by the time Satan comes to tempt Adam and Eve, the word "bliss" is available for ironic use: "Byte on boldly," Satan urges Eve as he points to the apple, "And bere to Adam to amende his mode / And eke his blisse" (V, 80–82). The irony is obvious—for Adam the play ends not in bliss but in "sorowe and care" (V, 175). Thereafter throughout the cycle the word "bliss" will be repeated to express the promise that God makes to men, until God's "blissing" is restored in the very last word of the cycle. Effects such as these, derived from the verbal repetition that marks the style of the plays, may be obvious, but they are also essential in a drama of this kind. Shakespeare has trained us to expect a poetic language that keeps on extending the limits of a literally circumscribed action. The language of the York plays has to do different things: it has to circumscribe, interpret, make accessible the most comprehensive and mysterious action of all.

By concentrating thus far on the basic language of the York plays, I may have fostered the impression that the plays are uniformly formulaic, abstract, ordinary in their language. They are not. The action of the plays is varied and inclusive, and the playwrights respond with a range of styles that images this variety even as it organizes it and expresses its unchanging premises. The opening play defines the stylistic range of the language—it includes the elevated, ornate language of the Good Angels' hymns of praise, the noisy colloquialisms of the devils in hell, the sober style of God's expository speeches at the end of the play. These styles alternate throughout the cycle, with the dramatists showing not just a remarkable proficiency in creating them but also a sure alertness to their dramatic and rhetorical effects.

The most ornate language of the York plays comes at emotionally heightened moments of lyrical celebration or lamentation. The following stanzas provide a good example—they are from the hymn that Simeon sings as he receives Christ in the Purification play:

> Haill! floscampy, and flower vyrgynall,
> The odour of thy goodnes reflars to us all.
> Haill! moost happy to great and to small
> for our weyll.
> Haill! ryall roose, moost ruddy of hewe.
> Haill! flower unfadyng, both freshe ay and newe,
> Haill! the kyndest in comforth that ever man knewe
> for grete heyll.
>
> (XLI, 366–373)

Verbal elaboration characterizes this style. As here, rhetorical figures such as *anaphora, exclamatio, repetitio,* along with heavy alliteration, create often brilliant aural effects. Its colorful imagery comes for the most part from the liturgy—though it is borrowed from the vernacular lyric. Richness and splendor, or, in the laments, intensity and power—these are the effects it aims at. There is often a precision to the profusion, however. In the stanzas above, the flower imagery helps to express the feeling of health and freshness which Christ's presence brings (most clearly to Simeon who sings these lines); it also expresses the sense of paradox that informs this play—the paradox that this child is the "redemptour omnium" (322), the paradox that Simeon reflects in his very act of offering these verses fit for a king to a baby. But such precision is not necessary: the style aims at an emotional appeal through which the audience might be brought closer to the action of the drama.

This ornate style is used sparingly in the York plays. That it is so, however, may be an accident of history. Frequent marginal notes in the Register indicate that some speeches and whole plays have been "made anew" but not copied, and a fragment inserted at the end of the Register in a late hand gives us some indication of what such revision might have been like. In the fragment, the prologue to a play on the Coronation of the Virgin, Christ addresses the Father:

> Hayle! fulgent Phebus and fader eternall,
> Parfite plasmator and god omnipotent,
> Be whos will and power perpetuall
> All things hath influence and beyng verament . . .
> O! sapor suavitatis, O! succour and solace,
> O! life eternall and luffer of chastite . . .

And God replies in kind:

> O lampe of light! O lumen eternall!
> O coequale sonne! O verrey sapience!
> O mediatour and meen, and lyfe perpetuall
> In whome of derk clowedes may have none accidence.
> (pp. 514–515, 11. 1–4, 9–10, 40–43)

Sheer weight of language counts. The classical periphrasis for God, the Latinate diction, the scholastic theological terms—they are self-consciously decorative. Eloquence has become an end in itself, impressiveness has taken over from accessibility as the sign of divinity.

The York Realist frequently affects this kind of verbal extravagance, but in his hands it is justified and controlled by the dramatic context he establishes for it. Here, for instance, one of Pilate's servants warns Pilate that night is coming:

> My seniour, will ye see nowe þe sonne in youre sight,
> For his stately strengh he stemmys in his stremys;
> Behalde ovir youre hede how he holdis fro hight
> And glydis to þe grounde with his glitterand glemys!
> To þe grounde he gois with his bemys,
> And þe nyght is neghand anone.
>
> (XXX, 73–78)

Deliberate, and deliberately ludicrous, this verbal redundancy is part of the image of social display and worldly indulgence that provides the setting for Christ's trials by Pilate and Herod. As such, it has a telling appropriateness: just as the sun loses its brightness, even, perhaps, as the speech itself sinks into banality, so will this court be exposed and the Princes who try so ostentatiously to dominate it be brought low—brought low by a "sonne" who, though bound and silent and soon to be put to death, will rise again to glory.

At times, not insignificantly, the pseudo-high style of the speeches given to the enemies of Christ becomes virtually indistinguishable from the lowest of the styles found in the York plays. The noisy assertions of power readily degenerate into abusive cursing when that power is threatened. "Kyng! in þe devyl way, dogges, fy!" shouts Herod when he learns the mission of the three Kings, and "þe develes of helle ȝou droune!" when he later learns that his plan to kill the Christ child has been frustrated (XVII, 121; XIX, 269). Pharaoh similarly curses Moses—"A dogg, þe devyll þe drowne!" (XI, 240)—with precise ironic anticipations of his own fate. However reluctant Pilate may be to condemn Christ, he too falls to cursing when he hears that Christ claims to be a King:

> Kyng! in þe devyllis name, we! fye on him, dastard!
> What! wenys þat woode warlowe overe-wyn us
> þus lightly?
> A beggar of Bedlem, borne as a bastarde?
> Now, by Lucifer, lath I þat ladde—I leve hym not
> lightly.
>
> (XXXII, 104–106)

"By Lucifer" is right—as we shall see, this kind of language serves dramatically to judge Pilate by aligning him with Satan. The plays are full of vivid, even vicious, expletives: "A! ffalse stodmere and stynkand stroye"—this is one of the Jews accusing the woman taken in adultery (XXIV, 13); "Go home, casbalde with þi clowte"—one of the soldiers screaming at Mary, who has just shown him the Veronica (XXXIV, 194). The York playwrights show themselves just as proficient with abusive epithets as with liturgical.

Between these two extremes lies the basic style of the plays, the norm against which the high and low styles gain their effectiveness. All three levels of style create contact with the audience in their different ways, and rhetorical effectiveness is one criterion we should be aware of in evaluating their use. But there is also a general dramatic appropriateness to the mixture of styles in the plays. As in the Canterbury Tales, the mixture of styles has as one of its effects the imaging of a variety which seems to be the variety of the world in which the people in the audience, sooner or later, come to see themselves reflected. At the same time, however, this variety can also be recognized as the manifestation of God who comes into the world. Responding to a similar variety in the *Mystère d'Adam,* Erich Auerbach has suggested that in all medieval religious drama, "all the heights and depths of stylistic expression find their morally or aesthetically established right to exist; and hence there is no basis for a separation of the sublime from the low and the everyday, for they are indissolubly connected in Christ's very life and suffering."[58] We still can hear this sensitivity to style in the York plays, whatever other considerations have come to affect the handling of the poetry. It allows God to speak in the plainest of language; it sanctions scenes like that of the Flood where the crucial event of salvation history becomes a family squabble. It also produces some of the most beautiful moments in the plays—such as that at the heart of the Nativity play where Mary's prayer fuses the liturgical style and the familiar style in a perfect analogue of the event she celebrates:

> Hayle my lord God! hayle prince of pees!
> Hayle my fadir, and hayle my sone!
> Hayle sovereyne sege all synnes to sesse!
> Hayle God and man in erth to wonne!
>   Hayle thurgh whos myht
> All þis worlde was first be-gonne,
>   merknes and light!
> Sone, as I am sympill sugett of thyne,
> Vowchesaffe, swete sone I pray þe,
> That I myght þe take in þes armys of myne
> And in þis poure wede to arraie þe.
>   Graunte me þi blisse
> As I am thy modir chosen to be
>   in sothfastnesse.
>
> (XIV, 57–70)

Perhaps—to use the effect of these stanzas to extend Auerbach's suggestion—we are to find a similar appropriateness in the art of poetry in the York plays as a whole. Through the use of the vernacular, the mysteries of God's will are brought to the audience in all their immediate relevance, yet through the use of verse, the drama reaches constantly for the beauty and harmony of God. T. S. Eliot was thinking of medieval religious drama as well as his own experiments when he wrote: "What poetry should do in the theatre is a kind of humble shadow or analogy of the Incarnation, whereby the human is taken up into the divine."[59]

II

Poetry and Instruction

The Homiletic Modes

Once there was a time, the English clerk Dan Jon Gaytryge explains toward the end of the fourteenth century, when men like the Angels had known God directly. But now, he continues, "all þe knaweyng þat we hafe in þis werlde of Hym, es of herynge and of lerynge and of techyng of oþer." Hence the need for works like his sermon, which sets out "þe law and þe lare þat langes till Haly Kyrke, þe whilke all creatours þat lufes God Almyghtene awe to knawe and to cun and lede þaire lyfe aftire, and swa come to þat blysse þat never mare blynnes."[1] With justifications like this, countless works of instruction—manuals, treatises, homilies, sermons, moral and doctrinal poems—were produced in England during the fourteenth and fifteenth centuries, all part of an officially promoted program of instruction for clergy and laity alike.

In its didactic aspects, the Corpus Christi drama is to be seen as part of this extensive program.[2] It was inevitable that the drama should have been influenced by it. The playwrights were in all probability clerics, the stories the drama told were important precisely because they were the basis of the faith elsewhere more prescriptively preached, and the understanding of those stories which both playwrights and audiences brought to the plays had been formed directly by such instruction. The marks of this tradition are everywhere on the plays. Some of the plays provide formal expositors who approach the audience directly with explanations of the story being presented. At the end of the Chester play of Abraham and Isaac, for example, a Doctor appears openly announcing his purpose:

> Lordinges, this significacion
> of this deed of devotion
> and you will, you wit mon,
> may turne you to much good.

He proceeds to explain that the event is important as an anticipation of the Crucifixion and, in most manuscripts of the play, to pray that the audience might be granted the obedience to God's word that Abraham has just demonstrated.[3] At other times in the plays, such explanations and exhortations are only slightly less formally offered to the audience. The *Ludus Coventriae* play of Christ's Baptism ends with the figure of John the Baptist appropriately directing to the audience a sermon on the necessity of repentance. In the Towneley play of the Raising of Lazarus, Lazarus hammers out a warning about the horrors of death and its inevitability and imminence before similarly exhorting the audience to repent.[4] Yet however much the plays draw from the sermon techniques, they are not sermons and rarely sound like them. And however much the plays stress the theme of repentance, we cannot reduce the instruction they offer to a single point of doctrine. If we acknowledge as unembarrassedly as the plays themselves do that one of their most important motives is to teach, we can recognize that in fulfilling this motive the playwrights proved themselves to be eclectic and inventive.

In the York plays, the didactic aspects of the drama are particularly unobtrusive. The instruction offered is never erudite or technical—the plays serve rather to confirm basic and familiar truths and to offer simple moral advice. More revealingly, the homiletic motive of the plays has, to a great extent, been integrated with the dramatic action, so that *how* the plays teach seems a more central concern than *what* they teach. Exposition is one way—there are moments of statement and clarification in these as in all medieval religious plays—but it is never as simple as it is in the Chester plays. Invariably we have to respond to the expository passages in their dramatic context. Even the Doctor of the York Annunciation play, the one figure who most closely approximates the role of the Chester expositor, is aligned with the Old Testament patriarchs and prophets to provide a direct link between the two stages of Christian history.[5] More frequently, the contexts are carefully and extensively developed, to such an extent that teaching and understanding, the concerns of the drama in its rhetorical didactic modes, become themselves the basis of richly developed internal motifs. Moreover, the instruction offered by these plays is not just a matter of exposition. Like the contemporary sermon, the plays support their explanations with examples offered to guide the audience in their actions, examples which are more accessible than those of the sermon since they involve human figures actually saying and doing things. What the plays teach, they also demonstrate, and it is this interaction between the two homiletic modes of exposition and exemplification that makes the York plays so varied and so effective as a means of instruction. They present "þe law and þe lare þat langis till Haly Kyrke" in a way that enables the audience fully to respond to the demand that they "knawe and . . . cun and lede þaire lyfe aftire" God's word.

Both these modes involve consideration of distinctive features of the poetry of the York plays. Exposition calls for a certain kind of poetic style, plain and clear. By noting where this style occurs—and also where it does *not* occur—we can see how varied are the ways in which the audience's understanding is addressed. Exemplification affects the poetry more pervasively, for the ways in which the characters speak frequently reinforce the examples of their actions in the plays. By examining the moral significance of styles of speech, we can discover also how subtly the audience is guided in its actions. Yet examination of these modes in the poetry involves more than a discussion of varied rhetorical strategies, for in the York plays there are precise internal correlatives of the rhetorical concerns. The dramatic focus of the instructional aspects of the plays is the figure of Christ, who is both the supreme teacher and the supreme example, and whose example is one in which what He preaches is fully acted out. In the plays as in history, Christ comes to explain God's will and to show man the way of God. And those who watch the plays thus see themselves and what is asked of them reflected within the plays. They, too, are part of the Christian history as it moves toward its end in the Last Judgment, where those who understood Christ and followed His example will be saved.

Teaching and Understanding

In the York plays, the expository aim of clarifying doctrinal truths produces a distinctive style of speech, a particular "voice."[6] Though adopted by a variety of characters throughout the cycle, this voice comes to be recognizable not just through what it says (the doctrines are always familiar) but also through its consistent stylistic features. It is an authoritative voice, formal and plain. Speeches in this style frequently draw attention to their purpose through expository formulae ("For þis skylle . . . ," "Here may men see . . ."), and usually involve explicit acknowledgment of the audience. Its clearest and most extended occurrence in the York plays is in the prologue to the Annunciation play (Play XII), where a Doctor, not involved directly in the dramatic action, approaches the audience to explain for them the Old Testament prophecies he recites. For example:

> *Ero quasi ros et virgo Israell germinabit sicut lilium.*
> Þe maiden of Israell al newe,
> He sais, sall bere one and forthe brynge
> Als þe lelly floure full faire of hewe.
> Þis meynes sa, to olde and ȝenge,

Þat þe hegh haly gaste
Come oure myscheffe to mende
In marie mayden chaste
When god his sone walde sende.
Þis lady is to þe lilly lyke
Þat is by-cause of hir clene liffe,
For in þis worlde was never slyke
One to be mayden, modir, and wyffe;
And hir sonne kyng in heven-ryke,
Als oft es red be reasoune ryfe;
And hir husband bath maistir and meke
In charite to stynte all striffe.
Þis passed al worldly witte
How god had ordand þaim þanne,
In hir one to be knytte
Godhed, maydenhed, and manne.

(XII, 89–108)

The poetry here makes no attempt through elaborate effects to reflect the mystery "þat passed al worldly witte." The paradox of the Virgin Mother, the figure of Mary as the lily—they generate no poetic color as they will do later in the plays which celebrate Mary. As the expository formula "þis meynes sa . . ." announces, the purpose of these lines is to explain the prophecy. The language is simple, appealing to the familiar—the only trace of mystery is in the mention of a husband who is "bath maistir and meke" and of a marriage that is without strife. Likewise, the verse form is straightforward, the most noticeable effect being the use of the four-line cauda to allow succinct, almost mnemonic summaries of what the Doctor explains. The expository function of the speech calls for it to be plain, and it is.

The basis of the style of this speech lies in the popular vernacular homily. There the dramatists would have found not only the material for speeches of exposition but also a tradition of verse used to convey exposition. It rarely tries for poetic sophistication. Like the vernacular itself, verse in the service of instruction is prized more for its potential clarity than for its potential richness, rhythm and rhyme being an aid to the memory rather than an excuse for art.[7] Its purpose is to state, clearly and memorably. The translator of the *Northern Metrical Homilies,* for instance, illustrates his aim as he describes it: he writes "In Ingelis tong that alle may / Understand quat I will say / . . . That thai mai her and hald in hert / Thinge that thaim til God may ert."[8]

It is easy to underrate, even to ignore, poetry of this kind, especially when it occurs in a drama which offers so much that is more immediately engaging in passages of elevated celebratory verse or lively dialogue. Yet precisely because it does occur in this context it comes to have a value of its own—especially if we try to hear the plays rather than merely read them. After the singing of hymns and the squabbling in hell in the Creation play, God's quiet stanzas of explanation are reassuring in their orderliness; they provide an essential relief in which the events of the play can be contemplated as they are explained. So too with the Annunciation prologue after the frantic and spectacular activity of the Exodus play; it seems to usher in the quietness in which Christ will be born. Too often, simple language and simple verse forms in the plays have been associated with lack of sophistication. Hardin Craig, for example, talks about "parts in primitive metres" in the York plays that have "escaped" revision.[9] He also notes that these parts are usually "crucial and original scenes." But he fails to draw the likely conclusion that these parts were left alone because later dramatists prized their clarity and quietness, recognizing that they did very well what they were trying to do. If we acknowledge that these plays are working to confirm the truths and lessons they enact, then we must frequently admire the expository speeches of the plays for their clarity and simple force. Nothing needs to be added to them.

At its most obvious, as in the prologue to the Annunciation play, the expository voice in the plays is almost purely functional and rhetorical, in its poetic style as in the address made to the audience. The appeal is to the audience's understanding; they are asked to learn or reaffirm what is stated. The expository voice never loses its rhetorical quality, but by doing away with the formal Expositor and incorporating whatever instruction the plays offer into the dramatic dialogue, the writers of the York plays make this voice available for dramatic treatment, and add to its clarity the freshness and pointedness of often carefully created dramatic contexts. Thus, for example, as God prepares to create Adam, He pauses to explain:

> Of þe sympylest parte of erthe þat is here
> I shalle make man, and for this skylle,
> For to a-bate his hautand cheere
> Both his grete pride and other ille;
>   And also for to have in mynde
> Howe symple he is at his makynge,
> For als febill I shall hym fynde
> Qwen he is dede at his endynge.
>
> (III, 25–32)

The point is made time after time in contemporary sermons and didactic poems, and here the orderly quatrains, the expository formula, and the straightforward statements clearly identify the homiletic origins and expository mode of the speech. Though God does not address the audience directly, His warning is clearly meant for them—there is no one else to hear it. It haunts the audience during the next few moments of the plays, allowing them a privileged position from which Adam and Eve's pledges of obedience take on an ominous irony, until it is confirmed as a valid and urgent warning for the audience when they see it ignored. Much later in the plays, God will recall this warning as He prepares to bring the world to Judgment:

> Men seis þis worlde but vanite
> ȝitt will no-manne be ware þer-by:
> Ilke a day þer mirroure may þei se
> ȝitt thynke þei noȝt þat þei schall dye.
>
> (XLVIII, 49–52)

Again, the context adds urgency to the clarity of the warning, reminding the audience that the Judgment they are being prepared to see is imminent in their own lives.

That it is God who thus warns man has, of course, its own persuasiveness. Such authoritative pronouncements are always given to characters whom the dramatic action has invested with authority—the Angel of God, Noah, Lazarus, the disciples. But the fact that they accept their authority and do serve as teachers in the plays comes to have a dramatic significance as well as a rhetorical convincingness, for there are other teachers in the plays who try to frustrate the will of God by misinterpreting it—ones whom the audience is also asked to recognize, and reject. That is, "teaching" in these plays is not an extrinsic aspect of the drama, a purely functional concern. It is itself an action, thoroughly integrated with the central action of the drama: to teach is to explain God's wonders to man, to prove them and give witness to them, to provide that understanding of God's will which for men is an essential preliminary to doing that will.

In the plays, as in history, Christ is the supreme teacher, and it is to Him that speeches of exposition are most frequently given. As He explains to the Doctors in the Temple, the Holy Ghost has given to Him "Pleyne poure and might / The kyngdom of hevene for to preche" (XX, 103–104). He demonstrates this power immediately by rehearsing for the Doctors the Ten Commandments. It is clear that we, like the Doctors, are to find something miraculous in the fact that this young boy so confidently recites the Commandments. The teachers become the taught, the student becomes the teacher:

> Sirs, sen ȝe are sette on rowes
> And has youre bokes on brede,
> Late se, sirs, in youre sawes
> Howe right þat ȝe can rede.
>
> (XX, 141–144)

In subsequent plays Christ will continue to preach (notably in the plays of His ministry), His speeches based on Scripture and drawing from contemporary homiletic works. One of the citizens preparing to welcome Christ to Jerusalem neatly describes the effect of His teaching:

> ʒa, Moyses lawe he cowde ilke dele
> And all þe prophettis on a rowe;
> He telles þam so þat ilke aman may fele
> And what þei may interly knowe
>   Yf þei were dyme.
>
> (XXV, 148–152)

In the plays, as in history, Christ's teachings make even the dimmest lessons understandable.

The longest expository speech given to Christ in the York plays is the one at the heart of the Ascension play (Play XLIII). Christ appears to Mary and the disciples and addresses them before He ascends into heaven. He prays that guidance and salvation might be granted to those who continue His work on earth, reproaches the disciples for their lack of faith, explains to them what His Ascension means to man, and prepares to return to His Father in heaven. Christ's speech represents the plain expository style of the York plays at its most accomplished—clear, precise, varied in subtle ways, and hallowed by its closeness to Scripture.[10] The speech is based on two Scriptural passages: the first part, Christ's prayer to God, follows the words of Christ at the Last Supper as given in John xvii, and the second part, His words to the disciples, follows with little elaboration Christ's words in Mark's account of the Ascension (Mark xvi, 15–18). The most noticeable changes in the dramatic version of the speech all make it more like a sermon. Its theme is the "endless liffe" which Christ's Ascension assures for Him and makes available for all those who will follow Him. Expository formulae pick out the topics of the sermon ("Anodir skill for-soth is þis . . . þe thirde skille is trewly to telle . . .", ll. 113, 121); they are assisted by the verse form, a simple double-quatrain stanza, which allows a new idea to be developed in each clearly marked stanza. Logical connectives and paratactic syntax mark the structure of the argument:

Sen they are oures, if þame nede ought,
Þou helpe þem, if it be thy will,
And als þou wate þat I þame boght,
For faute of helpe latte þem not spill.
Fro þe worlde to take þem pray I noght
But þat þou kepe þame ay fro ill,
All þois also þat settis þare þoght
In erthe my techyng to fulfill.

(XLIII, 57–64)

As this stanza also shows, both the plain verse rhythms and the uncomplicated syntax contribute to the clarity of the statements, while the rhyme is well used to highlight the important ideas and their connection. The language, too, like that of the Gospels on which it is based, is plain and familiar, characterized by monosyllabic words and common alliterative phrases and tags. Even when the poetry does rise momentarily above the predominant plain style, its effects are still simple, consisting mainly of verbal repetition and slightly intensified alliterative patterns. Thus Christ capsulizes and explains the vast mystery of the redemption of mankind through the Redemption:

In a tre man was traied thurgh trayne,
I, man, forthy to mende þat misse
On a tree boght mankynde agayne
In confusioune of hym and his
Þat falsely to forge þat frawde was fayne.

(XLIII, 114–118)

The true teaching of Christ redeems the "frawde" of Satan—I will be returning to this idea—and makes available the bliss of heaven to those who follow His teaching. This is the lesson Christ offers to His disciples and also, at the very end of the speech, to the audience as well:

Nowe is my jornay brought till ende,
Mi tyme þat me to lang was lente;
To my Fadir nowe uppe I wende

And youre Fadir þat me doune sente:
Mi God, youre God, and ilke mannes frende
That till his techyng will consente,
Till synneres þat no synne þame schende
Þat mys amendis and will repente.

But for I speke þes wordis nowe
To you, youre hartis hase hevynes;
Full-ffillid all be it for youre prowe
Þat I hense wende, als nedful is.
And butte I wende, comes noght to yowe
Þe comfortoure of comforteles;
And if I wende, ȝe schall fynde howe
I schall hym sende of my goodnesse.

Mi Fadirs will full-fillid have I,
Therfore fareswele, ilkone seere.
I goo make youe a stede redye
Endles to wonne with me in feere.
Sende doune a clowde, fadir, for-thy
I come to þe, my fadir deere.
Þe Fadir blissing moste myghty
Giffe I you all þat leffe here.

(XLIII, 155–178)

Though Christ's words are offered most immediately to the disciples, throughout the speech the terms of address have shifted between those acknowledging the "stage-audience"—"Bot ȝe, my postellis all bedene" (81)—and more generalized terms including the audience proper—"Ilke levand man, here to take yeme" (128). The effect is to fuse the audiences in these quiet moments, to make the audience disciples. The "techyng" that Christ offers, that the way to God is through repentance and those who follow that way will follow Christ in His return to heaven, is meant for all whom He leaves on earth to fulfill His mission. In the last words of the speech, as the audience is incorporated in Christ's blessing, they briefly experience the goal of the journey which Christ encourages them to take after Him by consenting to His teaching.

Christ's words of exposition—and their style—fulfill His historical mission of making clear the way to God. In this crucial moment for the action of the cycle, Christ and the audience are briefly brought together through the teaching He offers. The effect is one of moving confirmation. Both the teaching and the rhetorical effect it accomplishes, however, have more than a momentary significance since they also reflect back into the action of the play in important ways. As Christ acknowledges, His teaching reverses the effects of the Fall of Man and of the deceit of Satan. Christ as teacher is set against Satan as sophist, and for the audience, this thematic opposition is realized in the nature of their relationship to the plays. Where the plays in which Christ teaches confirm the truths and lessons they know, the play of the Fall of Man had pointedly denied them. At the start of the play of the Temptation of Adam and Eve, Satan takes the audience into his confidence: troubled and hurt because God prizes man so much that He will take on his form, Satan appeals for sympathy. As he openly expresses his intention to "founde to feyne a lowde lesynge" (V, 23–24) to frustrate God's intention, his frankness only increases the audience's helplessness, and, no doubt, their fascinated attentiveness. He approaches Eve, elicits from her an explanation of the one prohibition that God has placed on her and Adam, and although it is clear enough to Eve (and to the audience), offers to explain it further to her:

> Yha, Eve, to me take tente,
> Take hede and þou shalte here
> What þat þe matere mente
> He moved on þat manere.
>
> (V, 41–44)

What makes Satan so dangerous is that his pretense is so convincing. Even using God's words as he explains that one of the effects of eating the fruit will be "Of ille and gode to have knawyng" (V, 72; cf. III, 75), he sounds so much like God as he speaks to Eve—and his message is intrinsically more appealing. Although Eve tries to resist him, Satan's repeated assertions that he is telling the truth finally persuade her: "Than wille I to thy techyng traste / And fange þis frute unto owre foode" (V, 78–79). She eats. She offers the fruit to Adam, along with "þe reasonne why" she ate it. Adam's initial suspicions are easily overcome by Eve's claim that "it es trewe / We shalle be goddis and knawe al thyng" (V, 102–103), and he in turn is persuaded: "To wynne þat name / I schalle it taste at thy techyng" (V, 104–105). Immediately he realizes that her "techyng" is really "Ille counsaille" (V, 107), and they both realize that they have been betrayed by a false counselor:

Eve: The worme to wite wele worthy were;
With tales untrewe he me betrayed.
Adam: Allas! þat I lete at thy lare
Or trowed þe trufuls þat þou me saide.
(V, 122–125)

For refusing to trust and obey God's teaching and listening instead to the words of the deceiver, Adam and Eve are driven from Paradise. To a large extent, the effect of this scene relies upon the way the audience's privileged perspective is played upon. Their knowledge is poignantly reinforced as they watch it being ignored. Perhaps, too, the scene would have a familiar ring to it. In the age of Lollards, the audience had been warned against teachers like Satan: "ȝif any swich come to ȝou to preche or to teche ȝe, for Criste sake, her him nawth, but put him away fro ȝe."[11]

Satan as deceiver, Christ as teacher, denial and confirmation—the theme and its involvement of the audience are given varied treatment throughout the cycle. They come together most crucially in the two plays in which Christ and Satan confront each other. At the start of the Temptation of Christ play, one which repeats with a theological precision the structure of the Fall of Man play only to change it, Satan again appeals to the audience. Again he states his intentions openly:

> In glotonye þan halde I gude
>   to witt his will.
> For so it schall be knowen and kidde
> If godhed be in hym hidde
> If he will do as I hym bidde
>   Whanne I come nare.
>
> (XXII, 47–52)

In the Chester play, the Expositor formulates for the audience the typological and moral significance of Satan's temptation.[12] Here, with a magnificent irony, Satan does it himself. Defining his later attempts as temptations through "vayne-glorie" (93) and "covetise" (131), he sets up the terms for his own defeat and for the lesson the play contains. Christ resists the temptations, and at the end of the play confirms what the audience has learned:

> For whan þe fende schall folke see,
> And salus þam in sere degre,
> Þare myrroure may þei make of me
>   for to stande still.
> For over-come schall þei noȝt be
>   bot yf þay will.
>
> (XXII, 193–198)

The clear voice of authority asserts itself.

But the contest is not over. Satan and Christ confront each other in the play of the Harrowing of Hell as Christ's redemptive mission reaches its climax.[13] In the York play, the confrontation produces a finely handled verbal debate in which Satan, alleging "right resoune" (XXXVII, 255), is set against the divine wisdom and truth of Christ. Rosemary Woolf has well described the debate: "In this debate about the nature and justice of the Redemption, Christ's magisterial assertion of the divine plan of redemption meets Satan's impudent misunderstandings of Scripture and theology."[14] They are both skillful debaters, quick and forceful. But Satan's vow that "þis lawe þat þou nowe late has laide / I schall lere men noȝt to allowe" (XXXVII, 329–330), is frustrated. As Christ commands Satan to fall, to "go doune" into his cell where he will be bound in torment, His verbal authority is complete. Woolf notes: "in the York play Christ's verbal defeat of the devil is a far more impressive symbol of the victory of the redemption than his token destruction of the gates of hell."[15] But she does not note that this defeat brings to triumphant resolution a conflict of authority begun in the play of the Fall of Man.

This dramatic treatment of the role of teachers in the plays provides one rich internal focus for the expository aspects of the York plays. Both the false and the true teacher are given access to the audience, and in rejecting or accepting them the audience strengthens its understanding of the Christian truths and doctrines the plays clarify. Other figures in the plays reflect this focus. On the one hand there are the disciples who accept Christ's injunction that they should "preche and bere wittenesse / That he schulde deme bothe quike and dede" (XLIV, 15–16). On the other hand there are the Counselors to Pharaoh, Herod, and Pilate, who play upon the weaknesses of those they should teach, and whose hatred blinds them to the truth. Though they are established as authorities (see especially XXXIII 29–33, 40–47), the interpretations and wisdom they offer so directly contradict what the audience knows to be the truth that they are always exposed.[16]

Necessarily involved in this dramatic treatment of teaching in the York plays is the process of understanding. Since the teachers offer their wisdom (or lies) first of all to the characters within the plays, the responses of these characters become a reflection of what the audience is asked to do by the expository aspects of the drama. Adam and Eve fail to follow God's word and listen to Satan; Pilate—whatever his misgivings—gives in to the lies of his Counselors. Noah, on the other hand, learns the "techyng" and "lessoun" of God (VIII, 104, 123); Moses listens to God's word—"I undirstande þis thyng / With all þe myght in me" (XI, 177–178). From such reflection of the process of understanding within the plays derive some of the drama's richest effects. There are many moments in the plays when what the audience knows to be true or salutary—often from prior explanation or demonstration—is denied by characters in the plays to produce an irony which can be intense. But although this discrepancy and the irony to which it gives rise are at times disturbingly prolonged, always they are resolved in a triumphant acknowledgment and statement of the truth that brings audience and characters together to reward and strengthen the audience's acceptance of what the plays teach them. This pattern is not unique to the York plays among the vernacular cycles,[17] nor is it original with them: the liturgical drama surrounds the events of the Nativity and the Resurrection with scenes which serve to confirm the validity of the truths they celebrate, notably in the Easter plays where the misgivings of the disciples, Mary Magdalene, and the Travellers to Emmaus are voiced to create a dramatic irony in which what the congregation knows to be true is denied before being joyfully reasserted.

The York plays that dramatize these events share the "corroborative evidential nature"[18] of the liturgical plays and work through a similar use of irony. The pattern is most clearly seen in the play about the doubts of Thomas. After one demonstration to the disciples of the fact that Christ has risen from the dead, a demonstration which as well as confirming the disciples' faith within the play also places the audience in a privileged position, Thomas appears mourning the loss of his master. He refuses to believe the claims of the others that they have seen and eaten with the risen Christ and angrily accuses them of playing tricks on him. Christ reappears, urges Thomas to feel His wounds and "be no more so mistrowand / But trowe trewly" (XLII, 179–180). Thomas does as Christ commands, and the resolution of his doubts gains added force by being also the resolution of the discrepancy between his assertions and the awareness of the audience:

A! blode of price! blessid mote þou be!
Mankynd in erth, be-hold and see
  þis blessid blode.

(XLII, 182–184)

The dramatist takes full advantage of the joyful climax to make explicit the point of the play and its demonstrations:

Deus: Thomas, for þou haste sene þis sight,
  Þat I am resen as I you hight.
Þerfore þou trowes it; but ilka wight,
  Blissed be þou evere
Þat trowis haly in my rising right
  And saw it nevere.

(XLII, 187–192)

Christ's Scriptural words may seem incongruous in this context, since the audience He implicitly acknowledges has seen Christ rise from the dead. But the incongruity only underscores the lesson: the audience *has* seen the Resurrection, so there is no reason for them ever to doubt it.[19]

The most imaginative and compelling handling of this pattern in the York plays—the one that derives the most *dramatic* interest out of what is essentially a rhetorical motive—is the play of Joseph's doubts about Mary (Play XIII), which works to confirm belief in the mystery of the Nativity as the Thomas play confirms belief in the mystery of the Resurrection. The cycle plays that dramatize Joseph's doubts have frequently been praised, most recently by Rosemary Woolf who describes them as "amongst the most delicate and masterly works in the cycles."[20] Behind the rich characterization of Joseph as the bewildered and beguiled husband, Woolf recognizes a doctrinal justification: "Joseph's doubts serve by ironic reversal to emphasize that the Virgin is the second Eve."[21] The praise is appropriate to the York Joseph play; the doctrinal point alleged is, however, only dimly seen, if at all. The expository basis of the play is developed to less erudite ends. John Mirk gives as the reason for Joseph's doubts about Mary "þat Ioseph schuld be wytnes to hur of hur maydonhed; for when þe wyfe trespassyþe yn þat degre, þe husbond bysyuþe hym most to knew þe soþe,"[22] and it is more along these lines and with this appeal that the incident is represented. Joseph busies himself to find out the truth about Mary and her son—the truth which Mary and the audience already know. The play draws humor and frustration from the irony, then works toward a reconciliation in truth that is beautiful in its simplicity.

We first meet Joseph after the Angel Gabriel has announced to Mary that she will bear a son who will be God, and after Elizabeth has confirmed and celebrated the announcement. The experience of the Annunciation play will be skillfully drawn upon in the Joseph play. Joseph appears old and tired, lamenting his misfortune. One thing in particular irks him:

> For shame, what sall I saie,
> That þus-gates nowe on myne alde dase
> Has wedded a yonge wenche to my wiff—
> And may noȝt wele tryne over two strase!
> Nowe lorde, how langes all I lede þis liff.
>   My banes er hevy als lede
>   And may noȝt stande in stede
>   Als kende it is full ryfe.
>   Now lorde, þou me wisse and rede
>   Or sone me dryve to dede
>   Þou may best stynte þis striffe.
>
> (XIII, 10–20)

On the one hand, Joseph is funny. This crotchety old man with his popular expressions and his young wife comes straight from the fabliau tradition. The dramatist wants the audience to laugh at him—Joseph even draws attention to his creaky bones—and they do, mainly because they know what he does not know, that the "yonge wench" is the mother of God. Yet the laughter is not at all malicious. Joseph's faith in God is firm, and his prayer that God "wisse and rede" him reinforces the expectation of his inevitable enlightenment.

Joseph's subsequent account of his marriage to Mary makes his helpless lack of understanding clearer, thus widening the discrepancy of understanding between him and the audience. For him, the fact that his "ȝonge wiffe is with childe full grete" (43) means only that he will be put to death for having defiled her—even though he knows, to his greater unhappiness, that the child is not his. He has heard, however, "thurgh prophicie / A maiden clene suld bere a childe" (61–62); but that his wife is that virgin is a possibility he rejects out of hand. In his misery he determines to run away; but first, he will go to Mary to find out whose child she carries.

Joseph's rejection of the prophecy concerning Mary must be seen as a brief parody of the Annunciation play in which all prophecy had been brought to fulfillment in Gabriel's announcement, and a pointed denial of what the audience has had confirmed for them. In the scene that follows, this discrepancy widens further, but the audience's knowledge also keeps irony from becoming bad taste. Joseph finds Mary (whom he unwittingly calls "þat yonge virgine" [77]) praying in her house. Irritably he demands to know how Mary became pregnant: he knows he has been beguiled, he tells his wife, since "With me flesshely was þou nevere fylid" (106). But Mary's attendants insist on her innocence. No one, they tell him, has been near her, except an Angel who "with bodily foode hir fedde" (126)—which means, as they try to explain, that Mary has received the grace of the Holy Ghost. Joseph, however, sees things differently:

Þanne se I wele youre menyng is:
Þe Aungell has made hir with childe—
Nay, som man in aungellis liknesse
With somkyn gawde has hir begiled,
And þat trow I.

(XIII, 134–138)

His certainty is magnificently logical—especially since the audience has just seen "som man in aungellis liknesse" in the figure of Gabriel. But it is precisely that common sense, that natural response, that is being shown to be inadequate—and the audience is complicit in the demonstration. Insistently Joseph asks Mary, "Whose is þe childe þou arte with-all?"; and Mary answers just as insistently, "Youres, sir, and þe kyngis of blisse" (158–159; cf. 102–103, 167–168; 188–189). To Joseph this is a cryptic and evasive answer: "Na, selcouthe tythandis than is þis / Excuse þam wele there women can" (161–162)—even proverbs are exposed as no longer holding the truth. All Mary can do is pray that God might have compassion on Joseph and "þat in his herte might light / Þe soth to ken and trowe" (205–207). The truth, however, is not so readily apparent to her literal-minded husband:

Jos: Who had thy maydenhede Marie? has þou oght mynde?
Mar: For suth, I am a mayden clene.
Jos: Nay—þou spekis now agayne kynde.
Slike þing myght nevere naman of mene,
A maiden to be with childe;
Þase werkis fra þe ar wilde—
Sho is not borne, I wene.
Mar: Joseph, yhe ar begiled:
With synne was I never filid.
Goddis sande is on me sene.

(XIII, 208–217)

Both of them are, of course, right—Joseph when he argues that it is unnatural for a virgin to be with child, Mary when she asserts that Joseph is beguiled (though not in the way he thinks) and that God's messenger is seen in her. This is precisely the paradox that the play aims at confirming, and here the stanza form neatly contains it while juxtaposing the two voices. But Joseph remains unpersuaded. Angry in his bewilderment, he leaves. Mary again prays for him:

Now, grete God be you wisse
And mende you of your mysse
    Of me, what so betyde.
Als he is kyng of blysse
Sende yhou som seand of þis
    In truth þat ye might bide.

(XIII, 231–236)

Mary's concern that Joseph's understanding be guided toward the truth is echoed as Joseph, now on his own, prays that God "Wise me now som redy way / To walke here in þis wildirnesse" (239–240)—a wilderness that is, clearly, more metaphorical than real. He lies down to sleep. Immediately an Angel appears to him in the vision Mary had prayed for, and in spite of Joseph's petulant complaints about being woken up, tells him to return to Mary, explaining to him in simple terms what Joseph has so far been unable to understand:

The childe þat sall be borne of her,
Itt is consayved of þe haly gast.
Alle joie and blisse þan sall be aftir,
And to al mankynde nowe althir mast.
    Jesus his name þou calle,
For slike happe sall hym fall,
    Als þou sall se in haste.
His pepull saff he sall
Of evyllis and angris all
    Þat þei ar nowe enbraste.

(XIII, 267–276)

Now Joseph does see the truth, and his heaviness and feebleness are excitedly cast away. He returns to Mary and asks for her forgiveness, and together they prepare to go to Bethlehem.

In his discussion of characterization in the Corpus Christi drama, V. A. Kolve has described Joseph as "a 'type' of natural man" who fulfills most substantially "the dual role of natural man and servant of God."[23] He sees the presentation of Joseph and similar characters in the plays as an indication that the dramatists were writing from a keen and sympathetic sense of the human condition:

> Because the good people in this drama remain human, they lack the copybook simplicities, but they are meant to reassure us as audience that in our own imperfect lives their example can be found relevant. We are expected to be good, but not good beyond our capacities. This didactic end, so modest and sensible, demanded of the dramatists that they imitate human life in recognizable ways; the result was a religious drama that pays tribute to every man's right to existence and idiosyncracy, while insisting that he serve God.[24]

Kolve underestimates the influence of the expository motive behind the characterization of Joseph. It is undeniable that care has been taken over this characterization, especially in the York play; my summary ignores some wonderful touches, as when Joseph, returning to Mary, wishes that he were not so old so that he could bend his back and his knees. Yet the basis of the characterization is rhetorical rather than mimetic: the play depends for its humor and its final effectiveness upon the audience's recognition of Joseph's limitations, a recognition sought at every point. Joseph is distinctly human to be sure—but that is the point, that the audience asserts the mysterious truth of the Incarnation even in the face of the most familiar and probable questions about it. *We* supply the truth which has to be revealed to Joseph in a vision. In this context the clarity of the expository voice in this play takes on increased forcefulness as the relief of tension, conclusively formulating the simple but profound truth that brings all men together:

> The childe þat sall be borne of her,
> Itt is consayved of þe haly gast.
> Alle joie and blisse þan sall be aftir,
> And to al mankynde nowe althir mast.

The joy that accompanies Joseph's recognition of the truth, or Thomas's, is the joy appropriate to the events they witness to, the Nativity and the Resurrection. During the trials of Christ there are few such moments. There the truth the audience knows is insistently, loudly denied—even though with an inclusive irony the ostensible purpose of the plays is to find out the truth. The evidence presented in the case is substantial: frequent and extended rehearsals of the accusations made against Christ and of the events of His ministry upon which the accusations are based; Christ Himself is questioned and speaks on His own behalf; one of the Beadles supports the people's claim that Christ is Savior; and, movingly, Judas repents of having betrayed his master and pleads that Christ be freed. To this verbal evidence are added the miraculous manifestations of Christ's power in the lowering of the banners and the involuntary rising of the Princes to worship Christ. But in all this evidence, the characters in the plays for the most part find only what they are looking for, justifications for their own actions. They understand Christ to be a traitor, a lawbreaker, an evil magician. Even when Satan appears in a dream to Pilate's wife to warn the Princes and Bishops that Christ is indeed the Son of God who, if He is put to death, will destroy their power, they refuse to listen; for them the dream is the trickery of "some feende" which Christ has sent through "his fantome and falshed and fendescraft" (XXX, 292–297). The irony is intense. At every point the audience is asked to supply a point of view which finds little acceptance from the characters within the plays. The plays work, that is, in an ironic version of the expository mode that both exposes those within the plays who claim to know the truth and inverts the response usually demanded of the audience by this mode. They have to reject the explanations they hear within the plays. But that rejection itself asserts Christ as the Son of God—calls for the understanding elsewhere more directly sought and positively reinforced.

This perseverance in the truth will be rewarded by the events of Christ's death and His Resurrection. The Resurrection play itself, however, does not simply assert the truth that Christ is the Son of God. Though Christ is seen to rise from the tomb, and though the Angels announce the news to the three Marys, little room is created for the joy the event should occasion. The truth is countered first by the continued lament of Mary Magdalene (an effect I will be examining in the next chapter), then more rudely by the soldiers sent by Pilate to guard the tomb. Terrified that their incompetence will be discovered, they agree to tell Pilate that one hundred men stole Christ's body—though one of the soldiers does suggest they should "saie þe soth even as it stoode" (XXXVIII, 330). The truth comes out when they get back to Pilate—but he in turn is terrified of being exposed by it. At the insistence of his advisers he bribes the soldiers to say that not one hundred but ten thousand men stole the body.

Standing by the truth is the controlling concern of this skillful play. At the start, the Centurion who had seen Christ die had vowed to Pilate:

> To mayntayne trouthe is wele worþi:
> I saide ȝou, whanne I sawe hym dy,
> Þat he was Goddis sone almyghty
> Þat hangeth þore:
> Ȝitt saie I soo, and stande þerby
> For evermore.
>
> (XXXVIII, 73–78)

And the play ends with Pilate's words to the soldiers and to the audience:

> Thus schall þe sothe be bought and solde
> And treasoune schall for trewthe be tolde,
> Þerfore ay in youre hartis ȝe holde
> Þis counsaile clene.
> And fares now wele, both younge and olde,
> Haly be-dene.
>
> (XXXVIII, 449–454)

Even Pilate, in spite of himself, is forced to acknowledge "þe sothe" (for me, it is not so much "the satisfied observation of the villain"[25] as the guilty, weary perception of one who knows himself defeated by the truth he came so close to seeing). But his acknowledgment of the ease with which the truth is concealed and forsaken applies also to the audience, with moving irony: will their knowledge of the truth of the Resurrection, so severely challenged by the long second half of the play, be maintained? Pilate's proverbial truth has the ring of others' divine truths in these plays.

Taken in isolation, this Resurrection play might seem to be an unduly indirect way of confirming the central truth of the Christian faith—and an inappropriate example of the expository aspects of the drama. But of course it does not stand in isolation. Its distinctive effects have been well prepared for in the previous play of the Harrowing of Hell. There the magisterial voice of Christ insisted:

> Mi dede, my rysing, rede be rawe,
> Who will noght trowe, þei are noght trewe;
> Unto my dome I schall þame drawe
> And juge þame worse þanne any Jewe.
> And all þat likis to leere
> My lawe, and leve þer bye,
> Shall nevere have harmes heere
> But welthe, as is worthy.
>
> (XXXVII, 317–324)

Although Christ is speaking to Satan, His words at this point reach beyond the immediate dramatic situation as they anticipate the Resurrection. To the clarity of the expository voice is added the urgency of Christ's absolute demand. It is to the audience "heere" that He offers His warning to believe in His Resurrection and to learn and practice what He teaches—a warning they will do well to remember during the play that follows.

If I have stretched the definition of "exposition" in this section, it is because the York plays themselves do. Though the plays take care to clarify the truths and lessons they contain, this aim has been imaginatively assimilated into the dramatic technique of the plays, their structure, language, characterizations, and into their themes. We more accurately see exposition as a mode rather than simply as a function of the drama. Providing one of the ways in which the concerns of the historical action dramatized within the plays are extended to include the audience, it works to create an audience firm in its communal assertion of the truths of the Christian faith, an audience which, understanding the will of God, can be persuaded to fulfill it.

Following Christ in Word and Deed

That some of the characters in the plays, like Moses and Joseph, do come to understand the will of God, while others, like Herod and Pharaoh, do not, is, of course, only in part due to the authority of their respective teachers. It is also the result of their attitude toward God. Even in their bewilderment and grief, Moses and Joseph remain firm in their acknowledgment of God as their guide, while Pharaoh and Herod, misled by a sense of their own authority, deny Him. In demonstrating these attitudes, the figures in the plays serve to instruct the audience in a way that has nothing directly to do with the exposition of the truths they accept or deny. They provide examples of behavior which the audience is asked to imitate or to avoid. The medieval preacher knew well the instructional effectiveness of describing events or people in which the lessons he taught could be recognized as being exemplified, and in the Corpus Christi plays this homiletic motive combines perfectly with the sense of history that informs the drama to find a permanent and practical significance in the particular historical events dramatized.[26]

This is not the only interest the drama has in the Biblical stories it presents, but it is a pervasive one. Sometimes it is explicitly articulated. In a speech added to the Abraham and Isaac play in the Brome Commonplace Book, a Doctor explains to the audience:

Lo! sovereyns and sorys, now have we schewyd
Thys solom story to gret and smale.
It ys good lernyng to lernd and lewyd
And þe wysest of us all
Wythowtyn ony berryng.
For thys story schoyt ȝowe her
How we schuld kepe to owr powere
Goddys commawmentys wythowt grochyng.

He elaborates: how many of you, he asks the audience, would not resist if an Angel came to you and commanded you to slay your child? Look at those women who weep when their children are taken away from them—to complain against God is foolish, for He will never be discomforted. So, he concludes:

. . . groche not aȝens owre Lord God,
In welthe or woo, wether that he ȝow send,
Thow ȝe be never so hard bestad
For whan he wyll, he may yt amend,
Hys comawmentys treuly yf ȝe kepe with good hart
As thys story hath now schowyd ȝow beforne.[27]

The moral drawn here is unusually extended and almost tastelessly explicit; the Chester Expositor more simply prays that God grant obedience to His word "that in the same wee may accord / as this Abraham was beyne."[28] But the Doctor's comments point vividly to the fact that the lessons of the Corpus Christi plays are meant not only to be learned but also to be applied to the lives of the people in the audience.

There is no Expositor in the York plays to draw the exemplary moral from an event, but the dialogue does occasionally point to such a moral. These moments occur most frequently in the plays dealing with the events of Christ's public ministry, where the words of Christ recorded in the Gospels are expanded to establish His acts as examples for all men to follow. After Christ has put to shame the Jews who would prosecute the woman they accuse of committing adultery, and after He has forgiven the woman, He explains to the disciples that what He has done to the Jews was willed by God "to make þam ware þer-by / To knawe þamselffe have done more ill" (XXIV, 81–82). Moreover, He continues,

> . . . evermore of þis same
> Ensample schall be sene
> Whoso schall othir blame
> Loke firste þam-self be clene.
>
> (XXIV, 83–86)

The disciples find further significance in Christ's act, which they express in even more generalized terms:

> A, maistir, here may men se also
> How mekenes may full mekill amende
> To forgeve gladly where we goo
> All folke þat hath us oght offende.
>
> (XXIV, 87–90)

To this lesson Christ adds a final warning, that "He þat will noȝt for-giff his foo / And use mekenesse with herte and hende" (XXIV, 91–92) will never enter the Kingdom of heaven.[29] Similar sequences occur in the Baptism play, where Christ points to Himself as a "mirrour" in which man might see the necessity of his own baptism (XXI, 92–98); and at the end of the play of the Temptation of Christ, where Christ explains to a conveniently inquisitive Angel that the significance of His act is that when men are tempted by the devil,

> Þare myrroure may þei make of me
> for to stande still;
> For overcome schall þei noȝt be
> bot yf þay will.
>
> (XXII, 195–198)

Though their appeal is to action, these passages are purely expository. They parallel the ways in which narrative and homiletic works also draw out the exemplary significance of a story, describing the event, explaining the moral idea or quality it illustrates, and admonishing the reader or congregation to follow the example. But the drama is not limited to a description of the example, and the dramatists frequently derive considerable dramatic interest from such explicit moralizing. In the York play of the Last Supper, for example, Christ's demonstrations of humility, urged on the disciples and on the audience, are made more human by the actions of the disciples who struggle to imitate that humility—or, in the case of Judas, pointedly ignore it (Play XXVII). The scene of Mary's Purification after the birth of Christ provides another example. In homiletic works, this scene was invariably interpreted as exemplifying Mary's humility, and that interpretation has provided the basis of the dramatist's tender representation of the scene in the York plays.[30] As Mary and Joseph approach the temple to make an offering for her Purification, Mary listens patiently to her husband's complaints that the journey is unnecessary since she is a virgin and so exempt from the law. Then she explains:

> That I my madenhede hais kept styll
> It is onely throgh Goddes wyll,
> that be ye bold;
> Yett to fulfyll the lawe, ewysse,
> That God almyghty gon expresse
> And for a sample of mekenesse,
> offer I wolde.
>
> (XLI, 216–222)

Joseph, understanding her words and persuaded by her example, now himself expresses the need to make an offering:

> . . . Mary, go we thyther forthy
> And lett us both knele devowtly
> And offer we up to God meekly
> our dewe offrand.
>
> (XLI, 277–280)

They proceed to the temple where they offer the two birds required by the Law and, in place of the lamb that they are too poor to buy, their son. Reverently, the priest accepts their offering, praying as he does that God will protect "all such folke lyvand in clay / That thus to the mekly wyll heyld" (XLI, 305–306). In generalizing the application of what Mary and Joseph have done, the priest's prayer confirms the relevance of that act for the audience that watches them.

As this last example shows, the homiletic mode of the drama that seeks to teach through example rather than through explanation involves all aspects of the drama. On the stage, for instance, the gestures of the actors would provide a ready way of clarifying and reinforcing the meekness exemplified by Mary and Joseph as they kneel and offer their gifts. Less obviously, the ways in which they speak also image their meekness. Listen to how they address each other: "Joseph, my husbonde and my feer / Ye take to me grathely entent" (187–188); "A, Mary, blyssed be thowe ay" (223); "As thow haist said, Mary, I say, / I will hartely consent there-tyll" (225–226); "Joseph, my spowse, ye say full trewe" (270–271). As husband and wife, they are loving and forbearing, reflecting their humility toward God in their relationship with each other. The verbal element of their "sample of mekeness," though for the most part implicit, is arguably the most effective. For while what Mary and Joseph do is prescribed by the particular narrative situation and hence limited in exemplary significance, in how they speak the people in the audience can hear themselves. Not many of them will be required to offer sacrifices at the temple, but almost all of them will sooner or later speak to their spouses.

The effectiveness of the exemplary mode of the York plays lies in the handling of this cooperation between speech and gesture. The concern for providing examples through the ways in which the characters speak can be found everywhere. Listening to Mary and Joseph, the audience might remember earlier exchanges between husbands and wives—when Adam and Eve had exchanged bitter recriminations after the Fall (Play VI), or when Noah's wife had screamed and cursed at her husband while she beat him about the head (Play IX). Earlier, too, Cain and Abel had been called upon to make an offering to God, and their responses had been vividly imaged in their words:

> *Caym:* We! Whythir now in wilde waneand?
> Trowes þou I thynke to trusse of towne?
> Goo, iape þe, robard iangillande,
> Me liste noȝt nowe to rouk nor rowne.
> *Abell:* A, dere brothir, late us be bowne
> Goddis biddyng blithe to fulfille,
> I tell þe.
> *Caym:* Ya! daunce in þe devilway—dresse þe downe—
> For I wille wyrke even as I will.
> What mystris þe, in gode or ille
> of me to melle þe?
>
> (VII, 45–55)

The contrast is stark. On the one hand Abel's courteous address to his brother, his gentle urging, his eagerness to do God's will, on the other, the surly invective of Cain that spills over the end of the line, the scorn, the impulsive rhythms—in short, the "iangillande" that he so wrongly attributes to Abel. But as with the Mary and Joseph of the Purification episode, more is involved in this exchange than vivid characterization. At the start of the play an Angel had told Cain and Abel of God's commandment that they should offer a tenth of all their goods to God, warning them to take heed to His words since "ilke-a lede þat liffe has lente / Shalle you ensewe" (VII, 32–33). For the audience, Cain and Abel are to be seen in part as examples of those who pay their tithes willingly and unwillingly, examples brought home to the audience most immediately by the familiarity of their ways of speaking.

That the speeches of the characters in the plays can be exemplary is a reflection of a traditional concern in contemporary homiletic works. For the Middle Ages no less than for the Renaissance, the way in which a person spoke was considered to be a sure sign of that person's moral condition. Ben Jonson's well-known dictum, "Language most shewes a man; speake that I may see thee,"[31] is frequently anticipated in English sermons of the fourteenth century, albeit in more schematic and overtly moral terms. "Be oure speche men may knowe what þat we be, wheþur of heven or of hell," warns one preacher.[32] Another explains at greater length:

> Every man may be knawon by is langage, but þan ben þer þre language of þre divers contres. On is þe langage of heven; the second is þe langage of þe world; and þe þird is þe langage of hell. Sir, he þat longeþ to heven woll gladly speke of hevenly þinges and of þe blisse þer of . . . But whan þat þou seist a man have anny ioye to speke of þe soteltee of þe world or of worldely lucre, trewly he is of þe world. . . . The langage of hell useþ þis envious men, þe wiche speken ever slaundur and detraccion of þer neyȝbore owt of charite. Þise men have þe dewell dwellyng with-in hem, and þat causeþ hem to speke so.[33]

Behind such pronouncements lies the authority of the Bible—in particular of Christ's words, "A good man out of the good treasure of the heart bringeth forth that which is good: and an evil man out of the evil treasure of his heart bringeth forth that which is evil: for of the abundance of the heart his mouth speaketh" (Luke 6: 45). Secular, classical authorities like Dionysius Cato had written about the moral significance of speech; but the concern developed by patristic commentary was far more comprehensive and influential.[34]

The relevance of this tradition to the Corpus Christi plays is that of a resource rather than a source. To the extent that the dramatists were concerned with bringing characters to life on the stage, they would find in the homiletic commentaries a precise basis for a dramatic decorum from which they could build appropriate kinds of speeches. But that decorum is more than just dramatic, for whatever its suggestions for mimetic invention, it preserves an instructive significance and rhetorical force through which the exemplary dimension of the action can be brought home to the audience through the characters' speeches. In the speech of Cain, for example, we might want to praise the lively image of coarse contemptuousness his words create; but we should also notice that his angry curses, only too familiar in their contemporary and very local ring, mark him as clearly as the sign on his forehead as one who speaking out of charity has "þe dewell dwellyng with-in hem." In the exemplary mode of the York plays, the poetry serves a crucial function in realizing the characterizations in their dramatic particularity and also in allowing the audience to recognize in them a real and immediate relevance.

The moral dimension of the speeches in the York plays is sustained throughout the cycle by a consistent stylistic paradigm which is reasserted at key moments in the plays to contextualize the variety created by dramatic speech. There is no need for explicit commentary to align Cain with the devil, since all the features of his speech—the loud expletives, the chaotic rhythms, the insistent first person—all have been heard in the opening play of the cycle in Lucifer's speeches both before and, more tellingly, after his fall to hell. It is, in fact, the Creation play that fixes the extremes of the paradigm through which the exemplary moral dimension of speech in the York plays is determined. The most vivid contrast in the play is between the harmony of heaven, imaged in the singing of the liturgical hymns by the Angels, and the chaos of hell, imaged in the angry cursing and manic gibberings of the devils.[35] Both will be heard throughout the cycle. At the same time, a more subtle contrast emerges, one which shows the dramatic possibilities of the basically rhetorical device. After the singing of the antiphonal hymn that marks the creation of the Angels, the Cherubin Angel sustains the mood of celebration in richly wrought verses:

> A! mercyfull maker, full mekill es þi mighte
> Þat all this warke at a worde worthely has wroghte.

> Ay loved be þat lufly lorde of his lighte
> That us thus mighty has made, þat nowe was
> righte noghte. (I, 41–44)

At every point the Angel echoes words used by God in His opening speech in the play, but only to reflect them back to Him in fulfillment of His purpose in creating the Angels. After one stanza, another Angel joins in—the Angel previously identified and praised by God as Lucifer. Though at first he seems to share the attitude of loving praise, by the end of the first line of his hymn he has revealed the attitude of pride that will exclude him from heaven:

> All the myrth þat es made es markide in me;
> Þe bemes of my brighthode ar byrnande so bryghte,
> And I so semely in syghte my selfe now I se.
> For lyke a lorde am I lefte to lande in þis lighte,
> More fayrear be far þan my feres;
> In me is no poynte þat may payre.
> I fele me fetys and fayre.
> My powar es passande my peres.
> (I, 49–56)

As the "me" at the end of the first line reveals, Lucifer sings his hymn of praise to himself. Glorying in the splendor that God has given him, he is not content to be the "mirror" of God's might as God had intended. Instead of reflecting God's glory, he tries to appropriate it for himself, just as he assumes for his own glorification the words of God, most significantly the first person pronoun in which God had expressed His eternal authority at the start of the play. Even the rhythms of the stanza suggest the inflation of his self-glorification, in the unrestrained run-on of the two quatrains or the strutting certainty of the last three lines. Here, dramatically embodied in Lucifer, is the "vauntyng" all the handbooks proscribe, an identification which Lucifer's imminent banishment will openly confirm.

The antiphonal structure of this scene at the heart of the

Creation play allows the dramatist to establish from the start a paradigm of responses to the will of God. They define themselves against each other, obedience against will-fullness, love of God against self-praise, humility against self-assertion. And, to begin with, they define themselves exclusively through the characters' speeches, on the one hand, formal rhythms ordered by regular alliteration, formulae of prayer and praise, on the other, the growing profusion of unstressed syllables, colloquial exclamations, persistent self-reference. Although all the cycle Creation plays present some such contrast, none of the others achieves the York version's skillful combination of mimetic suggestiveness and exemplary clarity. In the other plays, Lucifer's pride is more a matter of assertion by the other Angels, and needs to be demonstrated in Lucifer's physical attempt to usurp God's throne. In the York play, the word "pride" is never mentioned, because it doesn't need to be.[36]

Besides the normative patterns of speech presented in the Creation play, a third mode of speech becomes recognizable as exemplary as the plays progress. It is the speech of Christ. Drawing authority from its Scriptural idiom not from assertive stylistic features, the speeches of Christ are characteristically cast in a plain style that images the meekness so often associated with His actions. Even in the agony of His Crucifixion, He speaks calmly:

> My Fadir, þat alle bales may bete,
> For-giffis þes men þat dois me pyne,
> What þai wirke, wotte þai noght,
> Therfore my Fadir I crave
> Latte nevere þer synnis be sought
> But see þer saules to save.
>
> (XXXV, 259–264)

What Christ does here—praying for salvation, forgiving—is what the Crucifixion accomplishes, and the meekness that enables the Crucifixion seems also to have determined the unadorned poetic style. In their stark contrast with the rowdy, cruel speeches of the Soldiers, Christ's words gain additional impact as the illustration of a familiar lesson about speaking:

> In þi woordys be mylde, & þanne schalt þou ben eyre of heven. . . . Ȝif þou kepe myldenes in þi woordys, þou smytest out of þi mowth stryif, chydyng, & woordys of discord, and nurscheth & kepyth pes in tunge wyth þi neyȝhbours. Þe vyolence of a gunne or of an engyne-stone is qwenchyd whan softe erthe or softe thyng is sette þeraȝens; ryght so, wyth myldenes of softe woordys þou schalt qwenchyn angry and boystous woordys of angry folk. . . . Be fayr of speche, answere swetely! Þanne delvyst þou out wyth myldenes dyspytows woordys. But þou do þus þou shalt noȝt askape þe dredefull ryȝt of doom.[37]

The warning made here, that every man will be held accountable for his words at Doomsday, reminds us that the proper context in which to set examples of speech is the eschatological—a context which the Corpus Christi plays insist on.

These, then, are the verbal styles that control the York plays: singing hymns of praise to God, a sign of heaven; violent swearing and screaming, the mark of hell; blustering self-praise, the sign of Lucifer; simple, humble, prayer and expressions of obedience, the sign of Christ. Their persistence in the plays is remarkable. Abel anticipates Christ as surely as Cain echoes Lucifer. Noah and Abraham identify themselves as servants of God in their prayers, Isaac is linked to Christ in his exemplary humility expressed in plain prayers of obedience and forgiveness. Old Testament history in the cycle ends in the controlling verbal images of heaven and hell as the Egyptians drown in their curses and the children of Israel rejoice in song. The plays surrounding the Nativity rely to a great extent for their theatrical effect as well as for their theological meaning upon variations on these stylistic norms—Mary's quiet obedience, Herod's self-proclaimed glory, the exultation of the Magi. Similarly in the Passion plays, the verbal images of humility, arrogance, and worship focus the meaning of events in more immediately apprehensible ways than any overt exposition could do. And in the climactic Harrowing of Hell play, as the joyful patriarchs in hell celebrate the coming of Christ while the devils scramble around in noisy confusion, the resonances of their speeches reach back through the Exodus play to the opening play of the cycle, and forward to the play of the Last Judgment.

So firm is this stylistic paradigm and its moral associations that it can serve as a kind of dramatic shorthand to identify characters in moral terms even before they are identified by name. A formula of prayer identifies a character as one of God's servants, an oath by the devil or "mahounde" as one of His enemies. At the other extreme, the patterns can be used to define the movement of a whole play—both the play of the Slaughter of the Innocents and the play of Christ's Trial before Herod, for instance, begin with Herod's boasting vanity and end with him swearing in angry frustration at his companions in stylistic repetitions of the dimensions of Lucifer's fall. Moreover, it is not just the major characters who participate in these patterns. In fact a sure sign of their usefulness to the dramatists is that the dialogue of minor characters, which usually has to be invented, is invariably cast according to them. Their speeches thus often establish the predominant moral atmosphere of an episode. Noah's sons in the Flood play echo his response to God in their quiet pledges of obedience to create a background against which Noah's wife's outrageous disobedience stands out all the more clearly (Play IX). In the following play, the servants of Abraham and Isaac, echoing their masters' words and tone, provide a contemporary social analogue of the exemplary obedience acted out in the historical action (X, 110–136). In contrast, the servants and followers of Pharaoh, Herod, and Pilate, imitating the followers of Lucifer, almost outdo their masters in the energy of their expressions of violent contempt.

The presence of these controlling styles in the York plays

has been pointed to by other critics, but usually only for their internal, structural function in ordering the variety of characterizations.[38] We more accurately see them as both dramatic and rhetorical—that is, as an aspect of the internal action and as one of the ways in which that action is extended to the audience. The verbal patterns interpret the moral paradigm with which they are associated. They are constituted of the language of the audience, whether of simple prayers of love or obedience or of colloquial oaths and abuse. Moreover, the efficacy of the examples of speech offered in the plays, and their urgency, are constantly reinforced by the action as it moves toward its fulfillment in the Last Judgment. There, representative souls are brought to judgment before the audience's eyes. The damned souls lament as they find brought forth "þe dedis þat us shall dame bedene," including all "þat eres has herde or harte has þoght, / . . . / That mouthe has spoken or ey has seene" (XLVIII, 162, 163, 166). Their exile from heaven, and the acceptance of the blessed into heaven, confirms the judgments passed on characters throughout the cycle, judgments which the audience has seen to be the inevitable and just consequence of attitudes displayed not just in the actions of the characters, but in their words. Through the plays, sinful and virtuous speaking can be recognized as matters of salvation and damnation.

Explicit traces of the terms in which homiletic works analyzed the moral significance of speech can be found scattered throughout the Corpus Christi plays. In the *Ludus Coventriae* cycle, for instance, besides the appearance of the characters "Raise-Slander" and "Back-Biter" in the play of Mary and Joseph's Trial, the exposition of the Ten Commandments includes the warning, "Wykkyd worde werkhyt oftyn tyme grett ill: / be war þer-fore of wykkyd langage. / Wyckyd spech many on doth spyll, / therefore of spech beth not owt-rage."[39] In the York cycle, the most overt references to this traditional concern occur in the plays dealing with the Trials of Christ—the plays attributed to the York Realist. In the play of Christ's Judgment before Pilate (Play XXXIII), Christ is called upon to defend Himself against the charges which Annas and Caiphas have been making against him. "Speke, and excuse þe if þou can," Pilate urges, and Christ does speak:

Every man has a mouthe þat made is on molde
In wele and in woo to welde at his will:
If he governe it gudly like as God wolde,
For his spirituale speche him thar not to spill.
And what gome so governe it ill,
Full unhendly and ill sall he happe:
Of ilke tale þou talkis us untill
Þou accounte sall, þou can not escappe.
(XXXIII, 301–308)

Though the words are scriptural, there is no authority in the Gospels for Christ's speaking them during the Trials.[40] If we respond to this speech in its context, however, we can see that in displacing it and giving it to Christ immediately before He is judged, the Realist is providing a telling focus for what he has developed as a major theme of the sequence of plays, a concern for the language of men, for what it signifies, and for its consequences. Inventively, the York Realist has drawn from homiletic considerations of speech to make them the very basis of the dramatic action of the sequence.

The art of the York Realist has recently drawn much critical attention and admiration.[41] He has been praised above all for the ways in which he brings the Trial scenes to life in a naturalistic vividness rarely attempted by other medieval dramatists. Part of this vividness lies in his use of language to create subtly detailed characterizations: Caiphas, whose unctuous verbosity cannot hide his cruelty; Herod, fastidious in his vanity; Pilate, who is forced into boasting by his insecurity. Everywhere there is evidence of the skillful use of speech for dramatic effect: none of the other cycle plays, for instance, captures quite as surely the chilling hypocrisy of Judas in his greeting of Christ:

All hayll, maistir in faith, / And felawes all in fere,
With grete gracious gretyng / On grounde be he graied.

> I wolde aske you a kysse, / Maistir, and youre willes were,
> For all my love and my likyng / Is holy uppon ȝou layde.
> (XXVIII, 244–247)

What has not been noticed, however, is how thoroughly self-conscious is the Realist's use of language throughout these plays. That self-consciousness can be seen in his use of the alliterative verse form, itself marking a search for distinctive verbal effects. It can be seen, too, in the verbal satire of the plays—both in general, in the ways in which poetic excess images the extravagance of the world which judges Christ, and, more particularly, in the satirical misapplication of poetic forms of praise or in precise parodies such as Judas' "Do open, porter, þe porte of þis prowde place" (XXVI, 155–156), an ironic anticipation of Christ's breaking down the doors of Hell.

But this self-consciousness about language is most clearly seen, as I have suggested, in the ways in which language becomes itself the theme of these plays. The inclusive issue is power—legal power, physical power, and, most interestingly, verbal power.[42] At the heart of the plays is the contrast, derived from Scripture and developed in other cycles, between the host of vociferous, violent accusers, judges, and torturers of Christ, and the isolated figure of the silent Christ. The dramatist constantly highlights this theatrically vivid contrast by having Christ's enemies loudly threaten Him, scorn Him, and curse Him in an attempt to get Him to speak:

> *ii Fil:* Carpe on knave, cautely, and caste þe to corde here,
> And saie me nowe somwhat, þou sauterell, with sorowe.
> Why standis þou as still as a stone here?
> Spare not, but speke in þis place here.
> þou gedlying! it may gayne þe some grace here.
> My lorde, þis faitour is so ferde in youre face here
> None aunswere in þis nede he nevyns you with none here.

iii Fil: Do, bewscheris, for Beliall bloode and his bonys
Say somewhat or it will waxe werre.
i Fil: Nay, we get nouȝt one worde in þis wonys.
ii Fil: Do crie we all on hym at onys, Oȝes, oȝes, oȝes!
Rex: O! ȝe make a foul noyse for þe nonys!
iii Fil: Nedlyng, my lorde—it is nevere þe nerre.
(XXXI, 309–321)

Mere volubility—idle words, jangling—customarily draws the preacher's scorn, but in this context, with Christ as the butt of their shouting, Christ's enemies surely damn themselves. Not only do they become ridiculous as they try to compel Christ to speak through the power of their own voices—so ridiculous that even Herod complains. Their words judge them, so that even in His silence Christ seems to speak eloquently. For Christ, of course, is the only one who can dispense grace, and Christ's "blode and bonys," not Beliall's, are at this point the audience's concern and should be the concern of those on the stage.

Herod's sons do not recognize the inappropriateness of their speech, the emptiness of their own attempts at power. Nor do they recognize the power and significance of Christ's silence. On the contrary, while they try to assert their verbal power over Christ—and, in their blustering prologues, over the audience as well—they are constantly concerned with finding grounds for accusations in Christ's verbal power. The primary charge brought against Christ is that He has bewitched the people in His preaching, misled them into thinking that He is the Son of God and into forsaking the law of Pilate. In just one of the plays, that of the Conspiracy to take Christ (Play XXVI), Christ is accused of causing strife by His words, of blasphemy, of lying, of perjury, of perverting the people through His preaching. Similar accusations are brought time and time again. The irony is intense. For the audience, those very sins that Christ is accused of are the sins His accusers are committing. In previous plays, the audience has felt the power of Christ quietly persuading them to what they know is the truth and so has been prepared to resist the attempts at authority they are here subjected to. The more Christ's enemies try to justify themselves, the more they are judged guilty.

This conflict for power conducted through words and silence is not restricted in these plays to the conflict between Christ and His judges. It is extended into the struggle between Pilate and the bishops Annas and Caiphas. Pilate's willingness to entertain the possibility of Christ's innocence—one that comes more from his attempt to protect his authority against the bishops than from any real awareness of the truth—is used by the dramatist to allow a critical commentary on the action to run through the plays. Much of this commentary is directed at the speeches of the characters and draws explictly from the terms of the homiletic analyses of the "sins of the mouth."[43] Thus, when Annas and Caiphas first bring their accusations against Christ to him, Pilate accurately judges them: "I here well ȝe hate hym—Youre hertis are on heght. . . . Why are ȝe barely þus brathe?" he asks (XXVI, 35, 37). Later in the same play, as they persist in their accusations, Pilate again notes that he hears only that "To noye him nowe is youre noote" and warns them that "Ȝoure rankoure is raykand full rawe" (XXVI, 67, 93). In all of the plays where Pilate appears, comments like these sustain a critical response to the speeches of the accusers. But in each of the plays, too, Pilate falls prey to the malicious rhetoric of the Priests and, threatened by what he is told are Christ's claims to be King, finally adopts their language himself.

This overt attention to the language and style of the speeches culminates in the play of Christ's Judgment where it is focused in the speech of Christ in which He holds man accountable for the words he speaks. Pilate's opening monologue establishes the concern, at first indirectly, as he appears as usual loudly trying to threaten the audience and his followers into silence, then explicitly as he directs his threats against a whole list of potential troublemakers, notably taletellers, traitors, flatterers, boasters, seditious whisperers, inciters, hypocrites, blusterers—all those who cause trouble through the words they speak. Ironically, every outrage that Pilate here lists follows in quick succession as the audience is treated to an almost programmatic illustration of the perversions of speech. Annas and Caiphas begin by flattering Pilate—he is "pereles prince" and "derworth duke"—though Pilate, rather than punishing them as he had threatened he would, accepts their praise as the truth and plans to reward them. Then the Soldiers bring in Christ from Herod, flattering Pilate with an extravagant "Hail" lyric. Derisively they report that Christ had remained silent during His trial: the implication clearly is that if He had spoken, His words would have provided cause for condemning Him to death!

Relieved that Herod has found no fault with Christ, Pilate now asserts His blamelessness as well. But the bishops insist that He be brought to trial since His "blusterings" have bred unrest. They have witnesses, they say—the only recognizable name is that of Judas!—who will tell the truth that Christ's words are false. Even Pilate sees through this perverse stratagem:

> Ȝa! tussch for youre tales—þai touche not entente:
> Þer witnesse I warande þat to witnesse ȝe wage.
> Some hatred in ther hertis agaynes hym have hent
> And purpose be this processe to putt down þis page.
> (XXXIII, 121–124)

He tells them to cease their suborning of witnesses and their false accusations, and, when Annas urges him to listen to their words, grows even more adamant: "If ȝe feyne slike frawdis I sall felle ȝou, / For me likis noȝt youre language so large" (131–132). Nevertheless, fearful for his own position, Pilate allows Christ to be summoned.

In the following scene, the dramatic emphasis shifts from the verbal to the visual as Christ's miraculous power makes the banners bow and the judges rise at His entrance. But what is for the audience confirmation of Christ's power turns out to be for those on stage only proof of His witchcraft. They are reduced to angry cursing: "Be þe devyllis nese, ȝe ar doggedly diseasid! / A, henneharte, ill happe mot þou hente" (197–198), and to threats: "If ȝou barnes bowe þe brede of an hare / Platly ȝe be putte to perpetuell pyne" (243–244). Their last resort is openly to accuse Christ of witchcraft, the most blatantly blasphemous of their accusations.

It is at this point that Christ speaks, ostensibly to defend Himself against their accusations, and warns them of the consequences of their sinful words. His firm speech, completely free from rancor, stands out in the context of the verbal chaos around Him. Both what he says and the quiet way in which He speaks provide a basis for evaluating how those who have accused Him will themselves be judged. And Pilate seems to recognize what Christ is telling them:

> Why suld I deme to dede þan with-owte deservyng
> in dede?
> But I have herde al haly why in hertes ȝe hym hate.
> He is fautles in faith, and, so god mote me spede,
> I graunte hym my gud will to gang on his gate.
> (XXXIII, 325–328)

But he has only to hear of Christ's claims to be King for all his apparent fairness to disappear. Cruelty and anger mark his last words to Christ, qualities that will be acted out as his orders to "Skelpe hym with scourges and with skathes hym scorne" (338) are carried out by the all too eager Soldiers. Frustrated in their attempts verbally to subdue and convict Christ, His enemies resort to crude physical assertions of power.

It is appropriate, and I am sure not coincidental, that the play of the Judgment of Christ should concentrate the exemplary aspect of the drama that I have been describing. The play achieves an intense local irony by showing the brazen presumption with which the most corrupt of men judge the guiltless Son of God, but that irony also draws into the play the action of the whole cycle. Christ's death is, of course, the means of man's salvation—that paradox is hidden in this play, though subsequent plays will make it clear. Moreover, the one who is judged here is Himself the Judge who will return to earth at Doomsday to judge all men. By dramatizing the Last Judgment, the Corpus Christi plays create an opportunity to make explicit the eschatological dimensions of the action which, while they inform all aspects of the drama, lie most forcefully behind the rhetorical impact of the homiletic modes. All men will be held accountable for their words and deeds—the Corpus Christi plays uncompromisingly confirm this truth. But the plays also offer the reassurance that through Christ men have been given the means of finding grace and salvation when they are summoned to Judgment. In the prologue to the York Last Judgment play, God rehearses the history of the world, explaining how He sent His Son to redeem mankind:

> Sethen in erthe þan gonne he dwelle,
> Ensaumpill he gave þame hevene to wynne;
> In tempill hym-selffe to teche and tell
> To by þame blisse þat nevere may blynne.
>
> (XLVIII, 37–40)

In the figure of Christ in the York plays, the historical action and the homiletic modes that extend that action to the audience come together. As in history Christ came to offer His teaching and His example as the way by which man might come again to heaven, so in the plays—it is to the audience that His words and His example are most urgently offered. And just as in history the life of Christ provides the focus for the words and deeds of all men, so in the plays. By understanding and doing the will of God or by refusing to understand and trying to frustrate the will of God, the characters in the plays are recognized as imitating or rejecting Christ. But by honoring or defying God in the action of the drama, the characters also enable the audience to perceive how they in their turn might fulfill God's will and be restored to the everlasting bliss of heaven which Christ promises to all those who follow Him.

The Play of the Baptism of Christ (Play XXI)

The aspects of the York plays discussed separately in this chapter come together in the Baptism play, to make it a dramatically richer play than its simple structure might lead us to expect. One of the shortest plays in the cycle, it consists mainly of a dialogue between John and Christ composed in relatively plain language and cast in a stanza form which, though not simple, is used more for its clarity than its lyric potential. Apart from the play's solemn climax in the baptism of Christ, there is little stage action. But as an example of how drama can serve instruction in the Corpus Christi plays, this tightly constructed play is full of interest, particularly since it deals self-consciously with the art of teaching. The question of how to teach effectively is the play's controlling concern, one developed both explicitly in the dialogue and characterizations of the play and implicitly in the ways it addresses its audience.

In the Baptism play, this concern for effective teaching is articulated in terms of the necessity to integrate word and deed in the service of God. Christ's expository speeches at the heart of the play define this necessity, with both a general relevance for all men and a specific urgency for those called upon to preach the word of God—in particular John and Christ Himself. But while Christ from the start is presented as an effective teacher who states His precepts forcefully and supports them with the example of His own actions, John's role is treated with a gentle irony. John has to be taught the lesson Christ exemplifies, and his difficulty in learning provides the basis of the play's action. In presenting the relationship between John and Christ in these terms, the dramatist may well have been drawing upon a tradition that saw John as an exemplary preacher, one who justifies his condemnation of sinners by his own "holynes of lyvynge" and who in so doing imitates Christ who also "fyrste lyvede holyly invard and afturward tauthe it forth."[44] But the action implied here is brought to life in the play as John struggles to bring himself to follow Christ.

However, more than the internal action of the play revolves around the motif of supporting precept by example. The play's rhetorical appeal—the ways in which it extends this action to the audience—is also shaped by this motif. The play offers instruction to the audience, directly through John, indirectly through Christ. But as the play develops, every precept offered is supported by exemplary enactment. Christ's Gospel establishing the necessity of baptism is confirmed by His own submitting to baptism, and John's more general commandment that all men be prepared to receive Christ is supported by the dramatic representation of his own preparation. Thus the play itself supports precept by example to make its teaching effective: it, too, can be said to integrate word and deed in the service of God.

Neither the dramatist's self-reflecting concern for his art nor the terms in which that concern is developed should surprise us, for both emerge from contemporary discussions of the responsibilities of those whose obligation is to instruct. In the absence of any firm evidence, we have to assume that the writers of the Corpus Christi Plays were educated clerics—perhaps, it has been suggested, the priests attached to the city guilds responsible for producing the plays.[45] As priests, they would have heard over and over again the requirement that those who instruct should be prepared themselves to act out what they demand of others; John Mirk's *Instructions for Parish Priests*, for instance, begins by establishing this requirement.[46] It is, of course, traditional; but in the late fourteenth century, with the Church coming under attack for hypocritically forsaking its own precepts, it is widely rehearsed.[47] From the same handbooks and collections of sermons that assert that teachers should practise what they preach comes another, closely related recommendation: that in their teaching, priests and preachers should make their precepts more available and more memorable by illustrating them with exemplary narratives. "Most opon informacioun is had be ensampull—*optimum genus docendi habetur per exempla,*" the handbooks insist.[48] Again, this is a traditional recommendation for the preacher, but it is one never more widely put into practice than in the popular instruction of the fourteenth and fifteenth centuries.[49] The dramatist would, then, find this concern for what makes teaching effective in the homiletic material to which he no doubt turned as he composed the play. That concern finds a natural place in a play which presents Christ as a teacher and which is itself an attempt to teach.

The play begins with a long monologue by John which immediately introduces the topic of effective teaching:

> Almighty god and lord verray,
> Full woundyrfull is mannys lesyng,
> For yf I preche tham day be day
> And telle tham, lorde, of thy comyng
> þat all has wrought,
> Men are so dull þat my preching
> Serves of noght.
>
> (1–7)

John would probably be identified for the audience in historical terms by his costume, the traditional coat of hair (which the Barbers guild responsible for the play could readily have provided). But his opening words bring him at the same time directly within the audience's experience: John the Baptist is a preacher, complaining like so many other preachers the audience must have heard that his words are having no effect.

This interplay between the historical and the actual is sustained in the rest of John's speech. As he proceeds to rehearse his scriptural prophecy of the coming of Christ, his historical mission is reaccomplished in his immediate practical function of announcing what this play is to present. Similarly, his historical role as preacher is dramatically reaccomplished as the words of Isaiah given to him in the Gospel as his message to the people now provide the text of a sermon addressed directly to "þe folke" in the audience:

> 'Loke þou make þe redy,' ay saide I,
> 'Un-to oure lord god most of myght';
> Þat is, þat þou be clene haly,
> In worde, in werke, ay redy dight
> Agayns oure lord,

With parfite liffe þat ilke a wight
be well restored.

For if we be clene in levyng
Oure bodis are goddis tempyll þan
In the whilke he will make his dwellyng.
Ther-fore be clene, both wiffe and man,
þis is my reed;
God will make in yow haly þan
his wonnyng-steed.

And if ȝe sette all youre delyte
In luste and lykyng of þis liff,
Than will he turne fro yow als tyte
By-cause of synne, boyth of man & wiffe,
And fro ȝou flee.
For with whome þat synne is riffe
Will god noght be.

(29–49)

All the characteristics of the expository voice of the York plays are appropriately found in these stanzas, the plain style, the directness of address and deliberateness of structure, the simple emphasis of antithesis and repetition. As John announces that "Nowe whoso can / may undirstande" (20–21), his clarity underlines a message already familiar to the audience from its frequent rehearsal in other sermons.[50]

Yet the very familiarity of John's words, or rather the fact that his message needs repeating, leaves open an uncomfortable possibility. The message has been ignored in the past—will it be ignored again? "Men ar so dull," John has complained, that mere preaching, no matter how clear, too often "serves of noght." Why should this present audience remember his words? How can his message be brought home? Though the audience is not addressed again until the very end of the play, the rest of the play works to answer these questions.

One answer provided by the play concerns John, for he will be called upon to make his demand of the audience more readily answerable by fulfilling it in his own actions. As an Angel brings to him the tidings that Christ will come that day to be baptized, John is himself asked to prepare for this coming of Christ. "Be gladde," the Angel urges him, "And thanke hym hartely, both lowde and still" (57–58). John does rejoice—but only for a moment:

> I thanke hym evere—but I am radde!
> I am noȝt abill to fulfill
> Þis dede certayne.
>
> (59–61)

In its faltering rhythms of fear and unworthiness, John's response contrasts sharply with his confident opening speech. Faced with the imminent appearance of Christ, he seems immobilized, unable to do what is asked of him. As if to encourage him, the Angel continues to explain the significance of the anticipated event: at Christ's baptism, the Holy Ghost will descend upon Christ and the voice of God will be heard speaking to His son. And for a moment, John seems reassured:

> I will be subgett nyght & day
> as me well awe
> To serve my lord Jesu to paye
> in dede & sawe.
>
> (73–75)

The echo in these words of John's opening address seems to indicate that John is prepared to act out the demand he had made of the audience that they be "In worde, in werke, ay redy dight / Agayns oure lord." But no sooner has he thus professed his willingness to serve Christ than he hesitates, questioning the need. Baptism, he knows, is taken to wash away man's sins—why then should Christ, who is without sin, need to be baptized? His question has no scriptural basis, though it is raised frequently in homiletic treatments of the Baptism.[51] In giving the question to John at this point, the dramatist creates an opportunity for teaching that comes from and adds to his characterization of John. Earlier John had served as teacher for an audience in need of instruction; now, wavering in his willingness to act out his obedience, he stands in need of instruction himself.

It is at this point in the play that Christ appears, as if summoned by John's question, to take over the role of teacher. Rosemary Woolf has described Christ in this play as "an uncharacterised teacher and man of authority";[52] but while He does serve primarily to voice traditional explanations of the significance of His baptism, the characterization is more pointed than Woolf's comment suggests. From the start, the very fact that Christ *is* a teacher is given importance. He comes, He explains to John, to make clear to "kyndly witte" the purpose behind His actions. But He links this role to His "knitting" of Himself to "kynde of man" in the Incarnation (84–88). His humility in teaching John is imbued with the sublimity of the act of Redemption—both serve to make God's will available to man. The Angel had told John that Christ would come "myldely with mode" to be baptized (55), and while the play does not follow contemporary homiletic commentaries in making explicit Christ's exemplary humility, Christ's presence and posture before John, like His words of quiet and patient instruction, signify a humility which will be fulfilled as He submits himself to baptism.[53]

In answering John's question about the necessity of His baptism, Christ also begins to answer the play's larger question about what makes effective teaching. He explains that since He has taken on the form of man to provide men with a "myrroure" for their actions, He will Himself be baptized as an exemplary fulfillment of His own precept that "Mankynde may noȝt un-baptymed go / to endles blys" (90–91). At first John seems to understand what Christ is implicitly asking of him, but he has only to be urged directly to perform the baptism for him once again to protest his unworthiness. He is not yet ready to do Christ's will:

Lorde, save thy grace þat I for-bede
  Þat itt soo be,
For, lorde, me thynketh it wer more nede
  Þou baptised me.

(109–112)

How, and why, he asks, should he "þat is a thrall" baptize Christ who is the "roote of rightwissenesse / Þat forfette nevere" (115, 117–118)? And further:

What riche man gose from dore to dore
To begge at hym þat has right noght?
Lorde, þou arte riche and I am full poure,
Þou may blisse all, sen þou all wrought.
  Fro heven come all
Þat helpes in erthe, yf soth be sought,
  fro erthe but small.

(120–126)

John's questions elaborate upon his scriptural assertions of unworthiness, and they serve in large part to draw attention to the paradox of Christ's humbling Himself in being baptized. But in the context provided for them here, they serve also to express John's incomplete preparation for following Christ. For John, the distance between man and God, expressed in the popular image of the social differences between rich and poor, seems to be absolute. He cannot see that in Christ heaven and earth have been joined, or that by making Christ his "myrroure" in humility he can be restored to God in heaven as he desires. John has professed humility, but he still cannot do what Christ asks of him.

It is precisely to this discrepancy that Christ now points in words not of reproach, as might be expected, but of gentle encouragement:

Thou sais full wele, John, certaynly:
But suffre nowe for hevenly mede
Þat rightwisenesse be noȝt oonlye
Fulfillid in worde, but also in dede,

thrughe baptyme clere.
Cum, baptise me in my manhed
Appertly here.
Fyrst schall I take, sen schall I preche,
For so be-hovis mankynde fulfille
All rightwisenesse, als werray leche.

(127–135)

Now Christ stresses the need for deeds as well as words, as John had earlier done. And from Christ's promise that He will Himself do what He asks of others, John at last draws assurance. His words are quiet but firm:

Lord, I am redy at þi will,
And will be ay
Thy subgett, lord, both lowde and still,
in þat I may.

(137–140)

"Redy" is the important word: he will now show that readiness he had asked of the audience. There is still a moment of fear at touching Christ, but it is quickly overcome as he prays that Christ will help him "to do þis werke" (147). He baptizes Christ:

Jesu, my lord of mightis most,
I baptise þe here in þe name
Of the fadir and of the sone and holy gost.

(151–153)

This is the climax of the play. In being baptized, Christ acts out His own Law, establishes an example of that Law for all men, and "als werray leche" Himself fulfills righteousness in word and deed. And John, his trembling reluctance resolved, in performing the baptism fulfills Christ's will and follows His example in acting out his demand of the audience. No doubt the audience would share in this moment, too, for the words John uses are the words with which those who watch would have been baptized—at this moment,

Christ is truly their "myrroure." As if to confirm the sacramental nature of this climax, the familiar hymn, *Veni creator spiritus*, is heard as the Angels celebrate.

The play continues after the singing of the hymn. Christ has said, "Fyrst schall I take, sen schall I preche," and now He fulfills His words as He emerges from baptism to explain once again the meaning of His act:

> John, for mannys prophyte, wit þou wele,
> Take I þis baptyme, certaynely.
> The dragons poure ilk a dele
> Thurgh my baptyme distroyed have I,
>   Þis is certayne,
> And saved mankynde, saule and body,
>   fro endles payne.
>
> What man þat trowis and baptised be
> Schall saved be and come to blisse;
> Whoso trowes noȝt, to payne endles
> He schalbe dampned sone, trowe wel þis.
>
> (155–165)

The sudden image that makes the devil a dragon asserts the power that Christ has paradoxically displayed in His act of submission. All help does come from heaven as John had earlier stated—Christ makes salvation available for all men—but as John has learned, the fulfillment of God's will also calls for the faithful obedience of man. The Gospel that Christ preaches is quite as binding on the audience He implicitly speaks to as on those whom He had first addressed, and it is made compelling not just by the forceful parallelisms of the vernacular paraphrase but, even more so, by the persuasive effectiveness of Christ's prior enactment of it.

Christ now takes John to Him, acknowledging John's cooperation in the fulfillment of righteousness: "But wende we nowe / Wher most is nede þe folke to wisse / both I & ȝou" (166–168). The situation of the very start of the play is reestablished as John assumes once again his role as teacher preaching to "þe folke." But there is a difference. John has validated his posture as a teacher by demonstrating and confirming his precepts in his own acts. Now, Christ's words to him seem to imply, this audience has learned the lesson he brought, and John and Christ can leave, perhaps to proceed to the audience gathered at the next station. As John leaves the stage with Christ, he pauses to address a prayer to Christ which, in contrast to his opening complaint, is a warm acceptance of his obligation:

> I love þe lorde, as sovereyne leche
> That come to salve men of þare sore;
> As þou comaundis I schall gar preche
> And lere to every man þat lare
>   That are was thrall.
>
> (169–173)

His words echo back into the play: earlier Christ had described Himself as "werray leche" (136) and John had described himself as "a thrall" (115). By following the example of Christ, John has resolved his disabling doubts and hesitations; together they have established the sacrament of baptism through which all men, freed from "the dragons poure," can be restored to God.

At the very end of the play, John turns to the audience to offer them a benediction: "Now, sirs, þat barne þat marie bare / be with ȝou all" (174–175). There is, first of all, a precise dramatic appropriateness to the terms of this benediction: at one point John had expressed his sense of distance from Christ by describing Him as a rich man; now, in acknowledging Christ as the child born to Mary in the stable, he acknowledges the supreme enactment of that humility which he has imitated and which has, consequently, brought him and Christ together. Yet even as the benediction thus resolves the specific action of this play, it extends it into the action of the whole cycle—the fulfillment of the will of God for the salvation of all men which the Incarnation makes possible—and at the same time explicitly incorporates the audience into that action. In the Incarnation, in the sacraments, and in the plays, Christ comes to men that they might forever be with God.

Compared to the Baptism plays from the Towneley and *Ludus Coventriae* cycles (Chester does not have a Baptism play), the York play is straightforward in what it teaches. It contains little trace of the often elaborate typological and iconographic traditions associated with the baptism, which are reflected in the Towneley version, and none of the rather technical directions on penitence offered by John in the *Ludus Coventriae* version. Though Christ's expository speeches certainly do inform the audience of the necessity and significance of baptism, the primary lesson of the York play is a general one: in the words of a contemporary sermon, "The way that ledes us uppe to heven, as the prophete telles, is the way of rightwysnes both in worde and dede in þat þou may."[54] In forsaking more complicated lessons for this inclusive one, the York dramatist perhaps should be seen as responding sympathetically to the heterogeneous audience he was writing for and as acknowledging the difficulties that audience would have in assimilating complex instruction during a performance of the cycle. Perhaps, too, he was aware of the fact that most of the people in the audience would have been baptized and so was more concerned with showing the audience how to sustain the grace of the Holy Spirit which the sacrament instilled in them. In either case, it seems clear that the dramatist shows his concern for making the instruction offered by the play readily accessible.

But the effectiveness of the play lies much more in how it teaches than in what it teaches. In the address the play makes to the audience it can be said to follow the recommended structure of the sermon: a precept is stated and then explained and supported by an example. John's opening speech to the audience establishes the precept: "be clene haly / In word, in werke ay redy dight / Agayns oure lorde." The rest of the play provides the example in its representation of John's preparation to serve his Lord Christ and his fulfilling of Christ's will that "rightwisnesse be noȝt oonlye / Fulfillid in worde, but also in dede." Moreover, in dramatizing this example, the dramatist has internalized the concern it illustrates to make it also the basis of the relationship between the characters in the play. For Christ presents himself to John as a teacher who carries out his own precepts in his exemplary actions. The effect of the play is that as John learns to make Christ his "myrroure," so does the audience come to see John as their mirror wherein they may see reflected what they have to do to be followers of Christ.

III
Poetry and Communion
The Lyric Modes

The program of religious instruction that lies behind the didactic aspects of the Corpus Christi drama was extensive enough to prompt the rather plaintive comment that "There beth so many bokes and tretees of vyces and vertues and of dyvers doctrynes, that this schort lyfe schalle rathere have an ende of anye manne thanne he may owthere stydye hem or rede hem."[1] But the religion of the later Middle Ages in England was not just a matter of treatises and doctrines, of vices and virtues. Just as importantly, it was a matter of the emotions. Pity, fear, love, joy—through these feelings, as the Franciscans most influentially taught, man could readily be brought to an awareness of the wonderful love of God for man and to an acknowledgment of his own sinfulness. The most efficacious stimulus for these feelings lay in the Christian story itself, in the events of Christ's life on earth, in the love and grief of Mary for her son, above all in the suffering of Christ; and with an ever-increasing vividness, sermons, poems, paintings, and sculptures recreated these scenes so that through contemplation of them men might be moved to repent their sinfulness and come again to God. In the fifteenth century especially, the exciting of emotions becomes a more immediate goal of the popular forms of religion than the providing of instruction.[2]

Compiled at the height of this devotional movement, the Corpus Christi drama provides a form in which its affective aim can be accomplished with peculiar richness. In combining the vividness of pictorial representation and the power to move of poetry with the immediacy of enactment, the drama informs the familiar devotional scenes with an unparalleled emotional intensity. It is sometimes difficult for a modern sensibility to appreciate how any spiritual end could be served by scenes as brutal in their detail as the Crucifixion plays of the York or Towneley cycle in which, one critic has felt, "The feelings of the audience are as unsparingly assaulted as the flesh of Christ."[3] But that unsparing assault is precisely the aim of the scenes: "Beholde þe peynes of þy savyour / And crucyfye þyn herte with grete dolour," the contemporary *Meditations on the Passion* urge, "Loþe þou nat hys sorowes to se / Þe whych hym loþed nat to suffre for þe."[4] The rhetorical aim justifies the detailed dramatic recreations. Seeing the scenes of Christ's life brought so vividly to life, the audience could be persuaded that they were present at those scenes; through the emotions elicited—and there are scenes of tenderness and joy as well as grief and suffering—the audience could be brought devoutly to participate in the action of God revealed through the Incarnation, the Death, and the Resurrection of Christ. Instructing and moving are complementary aims in the Corpus Christi drama.

Although the affective intensity of the representations can be sustained throughout long sequences of the plays, it is frequently concentrated in moments when the action on stage is briefly halted to allow the emotional potential of the stage tableau to be clarified and heightened. The effect is analogous to those moments in the expository mode of the drama when the action is similarly suspended to allow clarification of the lesson it contains. Here, however, the appeal is to the emotions rather than to the understanding, and lyrical intensity is its distinctive feature rather than expository clarity. To make this appeal, the dramatists characteristically turn to devotional poetic structures provided in the tradition of the vernacular religious lyric. Only one or two cases can be documented where an independently existing religious lyric has been incorporated into the drama,[5] but the parallels between speeches in the plays and nondramatic lyric poems are extensive.[6] Some of the lyric structures need little adaptation for use in the plays: prayers to God and Christ, hymns of celebration, complaints of an old man, hymns in praise of Mary—the scenes depicted in the drama called for such forms of speech, and the contemporary lyric provided readily assimilable models. Moreover, among the most popular forms of devotion were ones that seem almost to require the context the drama provides for them. In them, as Rosemary Woolf has noted, "the reader is to imagine that he is present at the Nativity and overhears the Virgin comforting her Child, or that he is present at the Crucifixion and that Christ on the Cross appeals to him personally for compassion, or that he is present at the Entombment, and hears the lamentations of the Virgin." Such lyrics "give the effect of being a key speech detached from a whole dramatic scene in which the reader actually takes part."[7] Sermons can provide a descriptive context for these lyrics, sculpted crucifixes can provide a visual focus for them, but for the most part their effectiveness relies upon the ability of each listener to recreate the appropriate scene in his imagination. What the drama loses in intimacy by providing full context for the speeches of Christ from the cross or the laments of Mary, it gains in impact. The lyric forms further the devotional motive of the drama, but the drama frequently fulfills the affective potential of the lyric forms.

So formalized are many of the lyric structures that when they occur in the Corpus Christi plays they are readily recognizable. The tendency of critics of the drama has been merely to identify them and at best to discuss them as isolable passages of poetry which rise above the generally undistinguished level of poetic skill in the plays.[8] The approach is in part justified by the fact that, for instance, the monologues spoken by Christ in the Resurrection plays of the Towneley, *Ludus Coventriae,* and Chester cycles do seem to have been added to already existing plays.[9] In the York plays, however, passages of lyric poetry, though extensive, rarely seem obtrusive. While adaptations of nondramatic lyric structures are still identifiable, they are not isolable aspects of the plays: they are in general set in carefully created dramatic contexts even though their primary impulse remains rhetorical. They may produce moments of stasis as far as the physical action on the stage is concerned, but they invariably serve to promote a dramatic action which includes them and their effects within a developing relationship between the play and the audience.

The first part of this chapter examines some of the most familiar lyric structures as they occur in the plays—the speeches of Christ from the Cross, the laments of Mary, hymns of celebration. Some of the most finely crafted and moving poetry of the cycle is produced by these lyric modes of poetry and I will be concerned with evaluating their poetic effectiveness. But an integral part of that effectiveness is, this examination will show, the way in which the rhetorical, devotional motives behind these structures become the basis of the dramatic action in the plays, enriching and directing the response they seek to elicit from the audience. The emphasis in the second part of the chapter is on a pervasive structure of the dramatic action: in ways analogous to the liturgical drama, the York plays enact a movement from a state of sorrow to a state of joy, a movement which, while it is focused in individual plays and characters, comes to characterize the action of the cycle as a whole. More than a structural pattern, however, it is extended through the lyrical poetry of the plays to become for the audience the definition of their emotional experience as they watch the plays unfold. At the heart of these aspects of the York plays in both their dramatic and rhetorical realizations is the figure of Christ whose humanity demands His suffering and death, but whose divinity enables His triumphant victory over death. By recreating these scenes in all their emotional compellingness, the Corpus Christi drama extends their efficacy to the audience that is made to share in them. A communion in sorrow and joy is established, not only in the audience but more importantly between the audience and the play through which they might be brought to share in the joy and bliss of heaven.

Grieving and Rejoicing

The York play of the Crucifixion of Christ (Play XXXV) is dominated by the four Soldiers who with sadistic relish and painful incompetence nail Christ to the cross and raise it "On heghte þat men mighte see" (156). In brutally energetic two-line speeches, they describe how they beat Christ, stretch His limbs to fit the holes in the cross, tear the sinews of His body, drive the nails into His hands and feet, jar the body as they drop the cross into its socket and drive in the wedges that will hold it upright. Only twice is their frantic activity interrupted, both times by speeches given to Christ. As the Soldiers lead Him to the cross, Christ pauses to pray that man might find favor with God; and later, when the Soldiers finish their work and turn in contemptuous jest to ask Christ how He feels, Christ answers them from the cross:

> Al men þat walkis by waye or strete,
> Takes tente ȝe schalle no travayle tyne.
> By-holdes myn heede, myn handis, and my feete,
> And fully feele nowe or ȝe fyne
> Yf any mournyng may be meete
> Or myscheve mesured unto myne.
> My Fadir, þat alle bales may bete,
> Forgiffis þes men þat dois me pyne.
> What þai wirke wotte þai noght;
> Therfore my Fadir I crave
> Latte nevere þer synnys be sought
> But see þer saules to save.
>
> (XXXV, 253–264)

Contrasting sharply with the Soldiers' abuse, Christ's calm and dignified words draw the audience's attention fully to

Him. Briefly, but unmistakably, He speaks to them from the cross, appealing to them for compassion before emphatically demonstrating *His* compassion by praying for forgiveness for those who cause His suffering. But the Soldiers' cruel ridicule shatters the quietness:

i Mil: We! harke, he jangelis lyke a jay.
ii Mil: Me thynke he patris lyke a py.
iii Mil: He has ben doand all þis day
And made gret mevyng of mercy.
(265–268)

Incapable of understanding Christ, persisting in the blind hatred that marks all their actions, the Soldiers provide a shocking example of how perverse man can be. They are the ones who have been "jangling" like jays and "pattering" like magpies in this play, and even though they now precisely identify the nature of the offer Christ makes to them, they do so only to reject it. But the irony of their response works against them, as do their actions. By denying the response asked for by Christ they only make His appeal more urgent for the audience and His prayer for forgiveness all the more wonderful.

We can be fairly sure that effects such as these were aimed at in this moment in the play, for in other contexts an ideal response to such an appeal from Christ is often explicitly indicated:

> Awake from synne and rise owte of þi fowle lustis and loke abowte and be-hold þi mirrour in þe Cros, and þou may see hym—is bake scourged, þe hede sett with white þornes crowned, þe side perched with a speyre, hondes and feete with nayles pershed and non hool parti in all is bodie but is tounge, with þe wiche he preyed for synnefull men, þat all men þat beleved in hym shuld not perish but have everlastynge liff. And þer-fore Crist seid þus on þe Crosse: "*O vos omnes qui transitis per viam, attendite et videte si est dolor sicut*

> *dolor meus*—all ȝe," he seiþ, "þat goon be þe wey of þis world, a-bide ȝe in hope of mercy, and see my woundes, iff any sorowe for mans synne may be like to myn." And þerfore cri to hym þat stedfastly woke for þe xl dais and xl nythes, and spred is harmes on þe Cros to call þe to hym. He is as plenteous of mercy as þou arte to aske itt.[10]

Christ's speech in the play provides the same impetus for the audience to be moved to respond to Christ's offer of mercy as the sermon, but the action of the play does not yet allow room for its fulfillment. The Soldiers' cruelty reasserts itself, and the audience is left uncomfortably to await the affirmation of their response and the vindication of their faith.

While sermons and narrative poems make frequent and vivid use of Christ's appeals from the cross, it is in contemporary lyric verse that the dramatists found the patterns for these speeches most richly developed and the rhetorical strategies behind them most effectively realized. Versions of the appeals of Christ from the cross are among the earliest of surviving lyric poems in English, and they remain a popular form of devotional verse. Based on one of a number of Biblical verses which, though they are taken from the Old Testament, Biblical glosses and the liturgy had sanctioned as being words spoken by Christ from the cross, they exploit the verses' potential for compelling compassionate meditation on the suffering of Christ by having Christ speak more or less directly to the congregation, describing the marks of His suffering.[11] The following mid-fourteenth century lyric, which uses the verse from Lamentations used in the sermon quoted and in the speech from the Crucifixion play, is representative:

> Abyde, gud men, & hald yhour pays,
> And here what god him-selven says
> Hyngand on þe rode.
> Man & woman þat bi me gase,
> Luke up to me and stynt þi pase:
> For þe I sched my blode.

Be-hald my body or þou gang
And think opon my payns strang,
    And styll als stane þou stand.
Bihald þi self þe soth, & se
How I am hynged here on þis tre
    And nayled fute & hand.

Be-hald me heved, bi-hald my fete,
And of þi mysdedes luke þou lete;
    Behald my grysely face.
And of þi syns ask aleggance
And in my mercy have affyance
    And þou sall gett my grace.[12]

The last three lines make the point of the lyric clear: contemplation of the suffering that Christ endures is meant to evoke in the meditators an awareness of their own sinfulness and to encourage them to trust in the mercy that His Passion makes available. They lyric's primary poetic aim is to force the meditators into contemplation. The words bring to life the visual icon of the Crucifix and, through the insistent imperative "Bi-hald," direct attention closer and closer to the image of the wounded Christ, focusing finally on the "grysely face" in which His agony is most movingly marked. Everything becomes immediate. Through the mediation of the preacher the historical moment of the Crucifixion is brought into the present and the meditators are placed at the foot of the cross, looking, stopping, thinking: their "mysdedes" are the cause of the suffering they see. That "god hymselven" speaks to them adds urgency to the familiar call to repentance; the promise of God comes directly to them. By responding to that call, the meditator fulfills the devotional act which the lyric initiates.

All the lyrics which make use of the devotional form of the Complaints of Christ work in similar ways. They present a vivid image of Christ crucified, excite the imagination through detailed recreation of the marks of His suffering, and direct the emotion they thus arouse toward a demonstration of pity, love, or remorse. Some contain within them an ideal response articulated for the meditators. Christ says:

> O man unkynde / hafe in mynde
> My paynes smert!
> Beholde & see, / þat is for þe
> Percyd my hert;

and man replies:

> O lord, right dere, / Þi wordes I here
> with hert ful sore;
> Þerfore fro synne / I hope to blynne,
> And grefe no more.
> Bot in þis case / Now helpe, þi grace,
> My frelnes;
> Þat I may ever / Do þi pleser,
> With lastyngnes.[13]

The lyrics tend to be more explicit than the corresponding speeches in the Corpus Christi plays, and they can be more intense. They need to be both, for their devotional effectiveness relies upon an act of the imagination far greater than that called for by the drama. To the inherent power to move of Christ's words in the York Crucifixion play is added the force of their fully developed context in which Christ's wounds are freshly and violently inflicted, and of the immediacy of the dramatic situation in which Christ speaks actually and directly to the audience from the cross on which He has been newly raised. By situating the familiar devotional lyric form in such a carefully created context, the dramatist has activated all of that form's affective potential.

The meditative tradition to which the speeches of Christ from the cross belong is a substantial and varied one.[14] The monastic Fathers, most influentially St. Bernard and St. John of Bonaventura, had stressed the efficacy of meditation, an imaginative and pious dwelling upon the mysteries and truths of the Christian story, as a means of journeying from the corporeal to the ineffable, as a means of purifying the will and restoring the *imago Dei* at the heart of man's thoughts and actions. For the fourteenth-century mystic Walter Hilton, following in this monastic tradition but extending it to a wider audience, meditation is also a necessary form of devotion: its effects, he explains, "lieth principally in affection, without light of understanding of ghostly things."[15] The subject most likely to inspire the emotional response which is the basis of meditation is, Hilton and the monastic Fathers agree, the life of Christ, "For a man shall not come to ghostly delights in contemplation of Christ's Godhead, but he come first in imagination by bitterness and compassion, and by stedfast thinking of His manhood."[16]

While in the formalized writings on the spiritual life the efficacy of meditation is circumscribed (it is only one stage in a process that also calls for prayer, contemplation, and action), in the popular manifestations of devotional teaching the effects of meditation gain increasing sanction as worthy in themselves. The result—illustrated most noticeably in English works—is detailed recreations of scenes from the life of Christ, particularly the Nativity and Passion, in which no detail is spared in an attempt to stimulate the imaginations of a congregation:

> He was betun and buffetid, scorned and scourgid, that un-nethis was ther left ony hoole platte of his skyn, fro the top to the too, that a man myȝte have sette in the point of a nedil. But al his bodi ran out as a strem of blood. He was crowned with a crowne of thornes for dispite. And whanne the crowne, as clerkis seien, wolde not stik fast and iust doun on his heed for the longe thornes and stronge, thei toke staves and betun it down, til the thornes thrilliden the brayne panne. He was nayled hond and foot with scharp nailis and ruggid, for his peyne schulde be the more; and so at the last, he sufferid most peynful deeth, hanging ful schamefulli on the cros.[17]

Descriptions such as this have clearly influenced the scenes of the Passion in the Corpus Christi drama: in the York play of Christ's second trial before Pilate, for instance, the Soldiers torturing Christ do drive the crown of thorns into His head, grotesquely rejoicing that "it heldes to his hede, þat þe harnes out hales" and that "His brayne begynnes for to blede" (XXXIII, 400, 402). In the meditational works available to them, the dramatists would find the kind of narrative details, details of costume, of gesture, even of tone of voice, which could be readily transferred to dramatized versions of the scenes from the life of Christ. They would also find expressed there the reasoning behind even the most sensational representations—that they encourage the listener to "learn all the things that were said and done as though you were present,"[18] and that through the participation thus allowed they bring men closer to God in awareness of His love, and make them "buxom, supple, and ready for to fulfill all God's will."[19]

Just such a justification is, in fact, claimed for the Corpus Christi plays. The writer of the contemporary "Treytise Agenst Miraclis Pleying" mentions that one of the arguments put forward in support of the plays is that "ofte sithis by siche miraclis pleyinge, men and wymmen, seynge the passioun of Crist and of hise seyntis, ben movyd to compassion and devociun, wepynge bitere teris."[20] His criticism with respect to this argument, that these tears are "not principaly for theire oune synnes ne of theire gode feth withinne sorye, but more of theire siȝt withoute,"[21] no doubt had considerable basis; but it does not preclude the possibility that the dramatists did try to direct the emotional response of their audience to some efficacious devotional end. Such an attempt is, surely, the basis of those moments in the plays when the pervasive affective nature of the scenes of the Passion is focused, the narrative is suspended to allow an image to be dwelt upon, and Christ speaks directly to the audience:

> Þus for thy goode
> I schedde by bloode;
> Manne, mende thy moode,
>   For full bittir þi blisse mon I by.
>
> (XXXVI, 127–130)

Addressing both the "understanding" in their clarity and the "affection" in their immediacy, the words spoken by Christ from the cross bring the audience to as full a knowledge as possible of the saving truth they express.

Occasionally the dramatists imitate the ideal responses to Christ's suffering found in meditational lyrics for the dialogue of the plays. Thus, for example, Thomas appears at the start of one of the York plays recalling Christ's "bolnyng with betyng of brothellis full badde!" (XLVI, 7):

> Itt leres me full lely to love hym and lowte hyme.
> That comely to kenne,
> Goddis sone Jesus,
> He died for us,
> Þat makes me þus
> To mourne amange many men.
>
> (XLVI, 8–13)

Thomas is alone at this point so that his words act as much as an exhortation to the listening audience as an expression of his own state of mind. The effect is analogous to that noted in connection with the homiletic modes of the drama: the responses elicited from the audience by direct address are reflected within the action of the play, in this mode intensifying the affective potential of the appeal and at the same time confirming the involvement of the audience with the events dramatized. At some moments—as in the Crucifixion play—the reflection is a negative one capable of generating an intense irony; at others it positively affirms the instinctive responses of the audience.

The best known of the responses to Christ's Passion contained within the Corpus Christi plays are the laments of Mary for her Son.[22] Widely developed in Latin and the vernacular as monologues, they seem so clearly to demand a context that they have been seen as the root from which the full forms of the Passion play developed.[23] The Gospels say very little about the part played by the Virgin during the events of the Passion. They do, however, assign her a place at the foot of the Cross (a place she invariably occupies in pictorial representations of the Crucifixion), and as during the Middle Ages the devotional emphasis shifted from Christ triumphant to Christ suffering, the possibilities for exploiting what would be the natural grief of the mother for her son were widely seized upon and developed in some of the most beautiful devotional verse.[24] Especially in the English versions, the devotional purpose controls the poetic effects of these independent lyrics and of the analogous laments in the plays: as Rosemary Woolf has most recently commented, in both "It is clear that . . . the grief of the Virgin is expressed partly in order that the audience may identify themselves with her: they are to feel the same compassion for the sufferings of Christ as did she."[25] As with the appeals of Christ, the laments of Mary in the drama work most importantly not to characterize the speaker in any depth but to intensify the emotion expressed so that the audience might be compelled to share in it.

By far the finest of the laments of Mary in the York plays is that in the *Mortificacio Cristi* play (Play XXXVI). I will be examining this play in detail in a later section, and I leave until then a full discussion of the place of this lament in the action of that play; but at this point it can illustrate the subtle elaborateness of poetic effect which the *planctus* form and its devotional strategy can produce in the vernacular. Christ has just spoken from the cross, drawing attention to the agony He suffers and appealing for man's compassion. Mary is the first to respond:

> Allas! for my swete sonne I saie,
> Þat doulfully to dede þus is diȝt.
> Allas! for full lovely þou laye
> In my wombe, þis worthely wight.
> Allas! þat I schulde see þis sight
> Of my sone so semely to see.
> Allas! þat þis blossome so bright
> Untrewly is tugged to þis tree.
> Allas!
> My lorde, my leyffe,
> With full grete greffe,

Hyngis as a theffe.
Allas! he did never trespasse.
(XXXVI, 131–143)

The most obvious, and theatrically vivid, feature of this lament is the repeated exclamation "Allas!" which articulates the grief Mary instinctively feels in response to Christ's suffering. It gives to the expression of grief both a heightened emotional effect and a ritualistic quality which, reinforced by the balanced syntax of the first part of the stanza, shapes and formalizes it. The most complex effects are in the patterning of the sounds of the lines. The soft "s" sound of "Allas!" becomes the alliterating sound for the tender first line of the lament, only to be interrupted by the harder "d" sound of the second line, so expressive of the shock caused by the sight of Christ in His suffering. In the context of the monosyllabic words of the opening lines, the word "doulfully" stands out, focusing the initial sense of the Crucifixion for Mary. Its sounds, both vowels and consonants, suggest those for the following line where the alliterated "l" sound, melancholy and loving, also picks up the middle sound of the formulaic "Allas!" Similarly in the second quatrain the "s" sound of the opening "Allas!" lingers on, only here, in a surge of emotion to which the rhythmical enjambement also contributes, the sound is sustained over two lines; again, the sounds of the second line of this quatrain, specifically those of the phrase "sone so semely," are echoed in the "blossome" of the following line where the image, so seemingly inappropriate to the sight it refers to, is made vivid by the sudden "b" sound. This line also provides the alliterating sound for the following line as the "t" of "bright" is repeated to link the injustice of Christ's suffering and its violence. The tag line focuses Mary's grief; it is the pivot of the stanza's aural and rhythmical effects. In the shorter lines that follow the soft "f" sound of the rhyme words are the most noticeable, but there is also the contrast between the soft "l" sounds and the harder "gr" sounds which recapitulate the two main aspects of the lament, the compassion of Mary and the terrible suffering which elicits that compassion. The last line resonantly concludes the lament, its echoing internal rhyme concentrating the predominant sound of the stanza.

The language of the stanza also contributes to its poetic richness as it expresses the moving ironies of the Crucifixion. To Mary, Christ is both "swete sonne" and "my lorde, my leyffe." The suffering of her son's death is held in tension with Mary's recollection of the joy of His Nativity—behind this lament is the theme richly developed in meditational works and hinted at in the York Adoration play (XVII, 277–294), that while Mary miraculously felt no pain at the Nativity she feels excessive pain at His death. The thought of Christ in the womb suggests the discordant image of the "blossome" which sprung from her "tree": in origin the imagery is liturgical, although here it is twisted into new meaningfulness as, in the epitome of unnaturalness, *this* blossom is tied to the tree. In the last lines the suggestive, imagistic expression of Mary's grief and the wrongness of the Crucifixion give way to simpler but no less moving statements: the liturgical image is modulated through the formula of lament into the familiar image of Christ hanging like a thief from the scaffold which is the Cross.

Through such detailed poetic effects the lament delicately balances emotion and explanation, a personal grief simply revealed and a more public grief ceremonially expressed. It intensifies the affective potential of Christ's suffering by mirroring it, enacts Mary's exemplary response to the suffering she sees, and in its intensity compels the audience toward a similar response.

This is the most intense of the Marian laments in the York plays. Here Mary confronts most directly the sight of her son unjustly and cruelly put to death, and her response condenses the affective dwelling upon the humanity of Christ which is the basis of the drama's meditative address to its audience. If there is to this response a personalness which limits its resonance as a universally appropriate expression of grief, there are other laments which seem to speak more fully for the audience as well as for the character in the play. The lament of Mary Magdalene in the Resurrection play, for instance, is of this kind:

> Allas! what schall nowe worþe on me,
> Mi kaytiffe herte will breke in three
> Whenne I thynke on þat body free
>   How it was spilte!
> Both feete and handes nayled till a tre,
>   Withouten gilte.
>
> Withouten gilte þe trewe was tane,
> For trespas did he nevere none,
> Þe woundes he suffered many one
>   Was for my misse.
> It was my dede he was for-slayne
>   And nothyng his.
>
> How might I but I loved þat swete
> Þat for my love tholed woundes wete
> And sithen be graven undir þe grete
>   Such kyndnes kithe.
> Þer is nothing to þat we mete
>   May make me blithe.
>
> (XXXVIII, 270–287)

All the expressions and many of the formulaic phrases of this particular lament would be familiar to the audience from the private devotions offered to and for them in the vernacular lyric tradition. The compassionate grief, the sense of sinfulness, the love of Christ who showed such love for man that He died to redeem his sinfulness—these are the fruits of meditation on Christ's Passion.

We cannot isolate this lament from its dramatic context. That Mary Magdalene utters it is entirely appropriate to her treatment in the plays as a type of the repentant sinner. That she utters this lament after the audience has witnessed Christ's Resurrection generates an ironic discrepancy of awareness which serves to make her lament more poignant and the imminent resolution of her grief more urgent. Moreover, her readiness (and that of the other Marys in this play) to "thynke on" Christ's Passion and to respond with a love that moves her to repentance gains a considerable added force from its being such a complete and exemplary demonstration of an attitude which throughout the plays that dramatize Christ's Passion has been only fitfully articulated. The whole sequence of Passion plays is framed by the demand which Mary here fulfills. In the much earlier play of Christ's Agony and Betrayal, Christ's extended prayers had presented to His disciples and the audience a moving image of the human Christ anticipating His Passion and already suffering in His manhood:

> I pray þe interly þou take entent,
> Þou menske my manhed with mode.
> My flessh is full dredand for drede.
> For my jorneys of my manhed
> I swete now both watir and bloode.
>
> (XXVIII, 46–50)

Throughout His prayers, the words "manhed" and "flessh" echo insistently to stress the fact that Christ does suffer as a man. He prays that God might comfort Him and the disciples feel with Him in His suffering, but three times the disciples fail Him and He is forced to rebuke them:

> What! are ye fallen on-slepe
> Now ever-ilkone?
> And þe passioun of me in mynde hase no more?
> What! wille ȝe leve me þus lightly
> And latte me allone
> In sorowe and in sighyng
> Þat sattillis full sore?
> To whome may I meve me
> And make nowe my mone?
>
> (XXVIII, 66–70)

These questions haunt the long sequence of plays which follows. In them Christ finds only too few friends, only too few followers who are prepared to keep His Passion in mind and to listen to His words.

Presenting a Christ who is for the most part isolated and ignored, the plays that dramatize the Passion can be seen as providing an image of the world they address. The complaint that Christ in His suffering has been forgotten by mankind is a standard one in late medieval sermons:

> Þus God prechet and techeth, and ȝet þer byn but few þat wyll here hym, ne þat haven þes wordes sadde yn hor hertys. But all byn bysy to be rych and wylfull yn þys lyfe þat ys here, and recchyth lytyll of þe lyfe þat ys comyng, and takyth lytyll hede how sore Crist suffryd, to bryng us to blys þat ever schall last.[26]

To help remedy this situation, John Mirk follows his complaint with a long speech in which Christ is imagined to be addressing Mirk's congregation:

> "Thow man for vanyte syngyst and rowtes, and I for þe crye and wepe; þou hast on þy hed a garland of flowres, and I for þe on my hed suffyr a wreþe of stynkyng þornes; þou hast on þy hondys whyt gloves, and I for þy love have blody hondys; thow hast þyn armes sprad on brode ledyng carallys, and I for þy love have myn armes sprad on þe tre, and tachut wyth grete nayles; thow hast þy cloþe raggyd and pynchyt smale, and I have my body for thy love full of gret walus . . ."[27]

This particular version of the Reproaches of Christ is amongst the most popular—Mirk attributes it to St. Bernard—and is found in similar forms in many meditational treatises and lyric poems. Its specifically contemporary address and its satirical thrust provide a peculiarly ingenious and colorful way of bringing to life the suffering of Christ and of making His suffering a matter of immediate and local concern.

The York dramatists do not make direct use of this version of the Reproaches, but the ironies which are so starkly stated in it are precisely those which are given extended treatment in the plays that dramatize the events of Christ's Passion. From the image of the agonized Christ at the start of the Betrayal play, the drama moves into a sequence of plays which actualize the vanities, the worldly indulgence, the total disregard for Christ's suffering attacked in the sermon. In place of Christ, worldly princes present themselves to the audience demanding the kind of attention that Christ has asked for:

> Pees, bewshers, I bid no jangelyng ȝe make
> And sese sone of youre sawes & se what I saye,
> And trewe tente unto me þis tyme þat ȝe take,
> For I am a lorde lerned lelly in youre lay . . .
>
> (XXIX, 1–4)

This is Caiphas, and he proceeds to vaunt himself in language as glittering as his costume. The boasting prologues such as this in which the enemies of Christ present themselves have an exemplary aspect to them which replaces Christ's humility with their misplaced pride. But they are also to be recognized as parodies of the address to the audience that Christ makes from the Cross. J. W. Robinson has described the most obvious effect of these parodic meditations in the York plays: "since in place of supreme humility and physical sacrifice they put pride and luxury (and, in one case at least, all of the seven deadly sins), and instead of suffering from agonizing pain themselves, grotesquely threaten to inflict it on the audience, they receive not sympathy but derision."[28] The "one case" that Robinson refers to is Pilate, and at one point in particular Pilate draws attention to the details of his appearance in a way that is usually reserved for Christ on the Cross:

> For I ame þe luffeliest lappid and laide
> With feetour full faire in my face,
> My forhed both brente is and brade

And myne eyne þei glittir like þe gleme in þe glasse.
And þe hore þat hillis my heed
Is even lyke to þe golde wyre
My chekis are bothe ruddy and reede
And my coloure as cristall is cleere.
Ther is no prince prevyd undir palle
But I ame most myghty of all.

(XXXII, 17–26)

The inversion of the image of Christ offered for the audience's contemplation is reinforced by Pilate's misappropriation of the lyrical form of address.

The irony of Pilate's presentation of himself is obvious, but the derision with which it should meet is an ideal response, as ideal as the loving compassion which Christ in His suffering should elicit. There were doubtless those in the audience who would be impressed by Pilate, as they would be impressed by the display and pageantry of the Royal or Ecclesiastical Courts imaged in these plays—and there are certainly those in the plays who greet Pilate with awe and deference:

Caiphas: Hayle! prince þat is pereles in price!
Ye are leder of lawes in þis lande,
Youre helpe is full hendely at hande.
Annas: Hayle! Stronge in youre state for to stande,
Alle þis dome muste be dressed at youre dulye devyse.

(XXX, 265–269)

As Pilate's followers thus flatter him by celebrating his power and might, they bring forward Christ for judgment. Though bound and beaten, Christ is nevertheless for the audience at least the true Prince, the "leder of lawes" not of "þis lande" but of God's, who could be Pilate's help and surely will be his judge in ways that the followers of Pilate cannot understand. The stark juxtaposition of the images of

Pilate and Christ makes the irony explicit; and just as in Pilate's presentation of himself, the irony of what he presents is reinforced by his appropriation of a form of description which is Christ's, so here the ironic misapplication of the Priests' words is heightened by the fact that they appropriate a form of address which has already been established as that due to Christ.

It is a small point, but one indicative of the dramatists' sensitiveness to their material, that Christ in the York plays never asks to be greeted and worshipped as King; all He asks for is humility, compassion, and love, and it is left to the vain worldly princes to parade their power and demand obeisance. Yet Christ is the King, and His Divinity warrants praise as much as His humanity warrants compassion. Some of the most elevated moments in the drama occur as characters in the plays celebrate Christ:

i Burg: Hayll! prophette, preved withouten pere,
Hayll! prince of pees schall evere endure,
Hayll! kyng comely, curteyse and clere,
Hayll! soverayne semely to synfull sure,
To þe all bowes.
Hayll! lord lovely, oure cares may cure,
Hayll! kyng of Jewes.

ii Burg: Hayll! florisshand floure þat nevere shall
fade,
Hayll! vyolett vernand with swete odoure,
Hayll! marke of myrthe, oure medecyne
made,
Hayll! blossome bright, hayll! oure socoure.
Hayll! Kyng comely,
Hayll! menskfull man, [we] þe honnoure
With herte frely.

iii Burg: Hayll! david sone, doughty in dede,
Hayll! rose ruddy, hayll! birrall clere,
Hayll! welle of welthe may make us mede,
Hayll! salver of oure sores sere,

We wirschippe þe,
Hayll! hendfull, with solas sere,
Welcome þou be.
(XXV, 490–510)

These are the first of eight stanzas with which the citizens of Jerusalem welcome Christ to their city at the end of the play of Christ's Entry into Jerusalem. All eight stanzas are highly ornate, all eight follow the pattern established in these first three—the long lines of the stanza opening with the exclamation "Hayll!" followed by one or two epithets describing an aspect of Christ, the shorter lines more often than not expressing some communal attitude or gesture elicited by the appearance of Christ. The rich alliteration (it is strictly ornamental, although the number of alliterating words does seem to control the rhythm of the lines) is sustained throughout, as is the equally rich use of rhyme and assonance which plays musical patterns on the vowels and consonants. Throughout this litany of praise runs also the colorful imagery derived from liturgical hymns: for the fifth Burgess, Christ is "dyamaunde with drewry dight" and "jasper gentill of Jewry"; for the seventh He is the "sonne ay schynand with bright bemes," the "lampe of liffe," and the "lykand lanterne luffely lemes." The whole passage represents poetry of the most ceremonial kind in the York plays, ornate without being unduly aureate, public and spectacular.

Although the audience is not directly addressed in these verses of celebration, there is a rhetorical aspect to the poetry. It expresses, in ways analogous to the elevated laments over Christ's suffering, a response for the audience to which in its intensity and ritual it also encourages them. It compels the audience to associate themselves with the communal, public terms of the response to Christ as King. The pattern for this poetry of celebration is offered by the liturgy and by the many paraphrases and imitations of liturgical verses found in the vernacular lyric tradition, although the deliberate heightening of the stanzas probably owes much to classical prescriptions for panegyric verse.[29] Such hymns of praise are clearly devotional in impulse: they work as a kind of poetic *summa*, piling up epithet upon epithet to create an image of Christ who is wonderfully all things, and offering the rich image for joyful celebration.

Two customary uses of this and similar lyric forms (using, for example, a "Welcome" *anaphora*) reflect interestingly on its use in the Corpus Christi plays. Though the form is more usually used in hymns to Mary than to Christ (as it is at the end of the York cycle),[30] it appears consistently in "Prayers at the Elevation of the Sacrament" composed often for the congregation to rehearse at the appropriate moment in the Mass. The following stanza is from a poem by John Audelay composed *"De salutacione corporis Ihesu Christi"*:

> Hayle! ground ay of my goodness and my covernowre
> Hayle! sustenans to my soule and my saveour,
> Hayle! cumforder of þe sek and al here socoure,
>   In þe Lord hit is.
> Hayle! solans to hom þat beþ sory
> Hayle! help to hom þat beþ gulte,
> Hayle! hope of grace and of mercy
>   þou graunt us al þy blys.[31]

Perhaps recollections of prayers like this would add a poignancy to the celebration in the York Entry into Jerusalem play by reminding that though Christ enters as King, he comes to His sacrifice. To just such an end, there runs throughout the citizens' celebration a consistent thread of images which qualifies the brilliance of the verses: Christ is one who "oure cares may cure," He is "oure medecyne made," "oure socoure," "salver of oure sores sere," "boote of all oure bittir bales," "all oure mede," "rawnsoner of synfull all." That Christ is the Redeemer is cause for celebration of the most effusive kind, but to bring redemption He must first suffer death on the Cross. Implied by the very terms that praise Christ are the pain and humiliation of the

Passion, anticipated in the phrases celebrating His divinity are the events of the plays that follow which will focus on His humanity.

The other use of this lyric form plays much more directly into the citizens' welcome of Christ. Glynne Wickham has provided some samples of the kind of verses pronounced at a Royal Entry into an English city in the fifteenth century.[32] They sound similar to the verses sung by the "burgesses" of Jerusalem in the York play. With the pointed adjustment needed to accommodate a King who comes riding on a donkey, the moment at the end of the play would have been very familiar to the audience. They have no doubt cheered on previous occasions when one of their body sang to the King, "Hayll! and welcome of all abowte / To owre cete" (XXV, 544–545).

However uplifting this celebration is, in its dramatic context the image of a harmonious community praising Christ contains poignantly ironic anticipations. What lies in store for Christ and His followers in subsequent plays is isolation and abuse, and what lies in store for the audience that participates in the celebration is the insistent denial of the truth here asserted. The only community to be found in the plays of the Passion is that of Christ's enemies, the only words of celebration those with which the enemies of Christ greet each other or those in which they mock Christ:

i Mil: Ave, riall roy and rex judeorum!
Hayle! comely Kyng, þat no kyngdom has
kende,
Hayll! undughty duke, þi dedis ere dom,
Hayll! man unmyghty þi menȝe to mende.
iii Mil: Hayll! lord with-out lande for to lende,
Hayll! kyng, hayll! knave unconand.
iv Mil: Hayll! freyke without forse þe to fende.
Hayll! strang þat may not wele stand
To stryve.

(XXXIII, 409–417)

The irony here is intense. The Soldiers, following the

Scriptural account of the Passion, have mockingly dressed Christ in the "purpoure and pall" of a monarch, crowned Him with thorns and given Him a reed for His sceptre. But as they taunt Him by denying Him the qualities of a King, their words mock *them*, the very pattern of the verse asserting the might and royalty which they cannot perceive.

In general, the York dramatists show a surprising restraint and control in their use of the highly rhetorical "Hail!" *topos*—surprising because in other hands it can lead to verse which sacrifices all dramatic appropriateness to merely decorative effects. There is, of course, always some justification for the spectacular effects in the mood of celebratory joy they try to create, but in the York plays these effects always seem to be firmly anchored in the action of the drama. For example, these are the words with which the First King greets the Christ child in the play of the Adoration:

> Hayle! þe fairest of felde folk for to fynde!
> Fro þe fende and his feeres faithefully us fende.
> Hayll! þe best þat shall be borne to unbynde
> All þe barnes þat are borne & in bale [brende]!
> Hayll! þou marc us þi men and make us in mynde
> Sen þi myght is on molde misseis to amende.
> Hayle! clene þat is comen of a kynges kynde
> And shall be kyng of þis kyth, all clergy has kende.
> (XVII, 253–260)

The Adoration is the central moment of Epiphany and joy in the drama, and the poetry rises to the occasion; as in other versions of the "haill!" *topos*, the poetic elaboration is remarkable—here the two-line alliterative patterns and the assonance between the 'a' and 'b' rhyme sounds add to the effect of the anaphora to make the lines rich and impressive. Yet the language itself is simple and familiar, as if to acknowledge that the one the Magus greets as King is a child in a stable. Without undue explanation, the paradox of the Christ child is momentarily held while it is adored. In the parallel prayers of the Second and Third Kings, who doubtless repeat the gestures of worship as they repeat the verbal signs of celebration, the paradoxes continue unostentatiously to inform the language. The Second King's speech borrows images from the liturgy to praise Christ as "foode þat thy folke fully may fede" and "floure fairest þat never schall fade"—but these phrases, which seem so full of anticipation of the events of Christ's life, give way to the more somber image of Christ as judge to whom the King offers incense. The form of the stanza itself participates in this anchoring of the hymns of praise to both the immediate situation and to the complete action of salvation which Christ's birth redirects; in all three stanzas the octave—the elevated, elaborate part of the stanza—is balanced by the quatrain of shorter lines which accompanies each King's offering and explains the significance of the gift. The Third King's greeting makes most poignant use of the possibilities of the verse form: having acknowledged that however "mirthful" the moment of the Nativity is, Christ will be "bounden and bette—for oure boote," it ends:

> Hayll! duke þat dryves dede undir fete,
> But whan thy dedys ar done, to dye is þi dette,
> And sen thy body beryed shalbe,
> This mirre will I giffe to þi gravyng.
> The gifte is not grete of degree
> Ressayve it and se to our savyng.
>
> (XVII, 283–288)

The paradoxes generated by Christ at the moment of His birth are many, and they all seem to converge in that beautifully understated last phrase which, drawing on the contrasts imaged in the staging of the scene, invert the roles of King and child as this King makes offering to the child who will be—who is—King. In the verses of the Magi two responses to Christ are held in balance, inseparable and paradoxical, a tender and compassionate awareness of Christ's humanity and a joyful and awesome awareness of His divinity.

From Sorrow to Joy

The rhetorical effectiveness of the lyrical passages I have been describing lies most immediately in their ability to create in the audience a heightening of a devotional state by evoking deep feelings of grief and compassion or reverence and joy. Since much of their power derives from their immediate dramatic context, the effect of these passages as the drama unfolds is to a certain extent local and temporary. Narrative poets and preachers had, however, recognized the value of such temporary heightening of the emotions as part of a larger concern, and the dramatists' practice of punctuating an ongoing narrative with lyrical moments of stasis had been widely anticipated. Yet it is in the Corpus Christi plays that these lyrical moments and their affective potential find their most meaningful contexts, for the inclusive action of the cycle which they help to further has to it a well-defined emotional structure which is perhaps its most comprehensively persuasive aspect. When properly understood and, as it is in the Corpus Christi plays, fully represented, the form of Christian history is a comic one which embraces and transcends the "tragedies" of the fall of man and the death of Christ. The design of God for the salvation of mankind constitutes a movement from joy through sorrow to joy and from communion through isolation to communion, a movement allowed by and focused in the events of the Incarnation, a movement which is enacted in the process of history and which can be enacted in the life of the individual. In imitating the action of history, and in showing the design of God in it, the York dramatists prove to have been particularly sensitive to their emotional structure. Through insistent statement and varied enactment they realize this structure in the plays in such a way that it gives point to the expressions of lamentation and celebration within the plays and to the corresponding emotions which they seek to generate in the audience.

That the vernacular dramatists should have understood the action of their drama as comic in structure and sought ways so to represent it is thoroughly predictable. So, too, is their use of highly lyrical passages of verse to focus the movement from *tristia* to *gaudium* and to elicit the emotional participation of the audience in this movement. The liturgy of the Church, the ritual formulation of universal history and the life of man within this larger structure, realizes this pattern both in the Church year as a whole and in the individual Mass, with the lyrical hymns, antiphons and responses working to create a communion between congregation and celebrants in Christ and through Him in the action of God for man's salvation.[33] The liturgy for the Feast of Corpus Christi in particular aims at creating a communion in joy, an intention which the Papal bull first proposing the Feast clearly defines: "It is for this reason that on the same Thursday the devout crowds of the faithful should flock eagerly to the Churches—in order that clergy and congregation, joining one another in equal rejoicing, may rise in a song of praise, and then, from the hearts and desires, from the mouths and lips of all, there may sound forth hymns of joy at man's salvation."[34] In the dramatic representations of events from Christian history attached to the liturgy, the movement from sadness to joy provides a consistent structural and rhetorical principle, most clearly in the many Easter plays and the kernel drama of the *Visitatio Sepulchri:*

> The emotional action of the Visitatio . . . is a dramatic peripety, the turn from sorrow to joy, present in every one of the plays, even the simplest. The mourning women approach the tomb and receive the glad angelic announcement. In play after play they turn to the congregation with songs of joy, and the choir bursts into the *Te Deum.* The action may be extended, the witnesses may be multiplied, the risen Christ may or may not appear, but the essential peripety is always there.[35]

Through the hymns which are sung—through both their communal terms and their general emotional compellingness—the transformation which Christ brings to the Marys is extended to include the congregation as participants in the action of history which Christ's Resurrection redirects toward the joy of heaven.

The example of the liturgical plays, while showing how traditional the lyrical shaping of dramatic episodes is and how fundamental to the religious drama is the sense of emotional *peripeteia,* also enables us to see one of the most strikingly original aspects of the York playwrights' handling of this lyrical dimension of their drama. In the York plays, the representation of the Resurrection of Christ is not shaped according to the traditional pattern; it is, in fact, deliberately shaped to deny the audience the emotional release and satisfaction that the event more usually allows. The first part of the play deals with Pilate's determining to forestall the Resurrection of Christ which has been prophesied—in spite of the Centurion's very moving witness to the cosmic disruption caused by Christ's death—so that from the start of the play there is a compelling combination of irony and suspense caused by the audience's knowledge of the inevitability of the Resurrection. As the Soldiers position themselves around the tomb, the Resurrection does take place, resolving the irony and suspense. The moment is briefly celebrated as the Angels sing the Easter antiphon, *Christus resurgens,* but immediately, into this moment of triumphant confirmation come the three Marys still lamenting the death of Christ:

i Mar: Allas! to dede I wolde be dight
So woo in werke was nevere wight.
Mi sorowe is all for þat sight
    þat I gune see,
Howe Criste my maistir, moste of myght,
    Is dede fro me.

(XXXVIII, 187–192)

The discrepancy between the mood anticipated by the Resurrection and the mood here realized, between the audience's perspective and that of Mary, makes her lament all the more poignant; the response of the audience must have been delicately poised between sharing her grief and acknowledging its inappropriateness. The ambivalence is heightened as the lament continues with Mary praying to Christ as "medecyne" of "ilke a myscheve" and "bote of all"—something the Resurrection makes Him most profoundly. But the suggestions are not picked up. The Second Mary appears, seemingly in isolation from the first, not hearing her, repeating her lament:

> Allas! who schall my balis bete
> Whanne I thynke on his woundes wete;
> Jesu, þat was of love so swete,
> and nevere did ill,
> Es dede and graven under þe grete
> Withouten skill.
>
> (XXXVIII, 199–204)

Again, the question goes unanswered, though the answer is at hand and apparent to the audience; instead the Third Mary appears to confirm the Second's mood of sorrow and grief (205–210). The irony is very gentle here, as in the play of Joseph's trouble about Mary where sympathy and an urge to correct merge in the audience's response. That the audience has seen Christ emerge from the tomb casts an air of urgency over the situation—surely the three Marys will be brought to share the audience's joyful knowledge? But the laments continue as the Marys, convinced that "he is dede" (a phrase repeated in the stanza-linking that heightens the effect of this sequence) approach the tomb to anoint Christ's body. They find the stone rolled away and the grave empty. The Angels tell them that Christ has risen, in an exchange based on the liturgical *Quem quaeritis* trope:

> *Ang:* Ȝe mournand women in youre þought,
> Here in þis place whome have ȝe sought?
> *i Mar:* Jesu, þat to dede is brought,
> Oure lorde so free.
> *Ang:* Women, certayne here is he noght:
> Come nere and see.
>
> (XXXVIII, 235–240)

The quietness of this stanza, in which perhaps the most hallowed moment of Christian history is recreated, is as characteristic of the whole play as is the lucidity that Rosemary Woolf has noted.[36] Quietly, too, the Marys receive the news, and quietly the Second and Third Marys leave to take the news to Galilee.

They leave Mary Magdalene alone on the stage. I have already noted the extended lament she is given at this point. It is the loveliest of all the laments in the York plays, for while its use of devotional formulae establishes it as an exemplary response in which the audience can share, it also expresses a personal sense of the significance of Christ's death which the news of His Resurrection has not qualified. In her realization of the profound love that Christ has shown, Mary is brought to respond with love, her lament giving way to a quiet expression of penitence and compassion which is the goal of all meditation on Christ crucified. She does not celebrate the Resurrection; for that, as she tells the audience at the end of the speech, she must wait until she is rejoined with Christ. For the moment, the audience is left suspended between sorrow and joy, sorrow at the death of Christ encouraged by Mary's remembrance, and joy at the knowledge of His Resurrection which the play has confirmed. The ambivalence is apt. It is essential to the Christian response to the events of the Incarnation as, for example, the Papal bull proposing the Feast of Corpus Christi so beautifully acknowledges: "For surely we exult as we recall our deliverance and scarce contain our tears as we commemorate the passion of our Lord through which we were freed . . . we rejoice amid pious weeping and weep amid reverent rejoicing, joyful in our lamentation and woeful in our jubilation."[37] The central scene of the York Resurrection play leaves its audience with a strong sense of irresolution which the rest of the play capitalizes upon as it proceeds to situate the climactic event of Christian history not in the joy and celebration of a world that affirms the truth of Christ's triumph, but in the deceit and meanness of this world that tries to conceal or ignore it.

There is no peripety in the York Resurrection play in

spite of what must have been a vivid recreation of the moment of Christ's emergence from the grave. For the characters within the play nothing seems to have changed and, if we respond to the proverbial ring to Pilate's final comment that "Thus schall þe sothe be bought and solde, / And treasoune schall for trewthe be tolde" (229–450), perhaps nothing has changed for those outside the play. But while the dramatist thus turns the displacement of the expected peripety to homiletic advantage, what allows the displacement is that the kind of transformation associated with the Resurrection is realized, with different though reciprocal emphases, in the two plays that surround the Resurrection play, those of the Harrowing of Hell and the Appearance of Christ to Mary Magdalene. The Harrowing of Hell play had ended amidst the joyful celebration of the patriarchs rescued from hell by Christ after His climactic victory over Satan. Foremost amongst them is Adam:

We thanke his grete goodnesse
He fette us fro þis place:
Makes joie nowe more and lesse
Omnis we laude god of his grace,

Adam exclaims immediately prior to their being led from hell (XXXVII, 381–384), apparently inviting the audience to join him and the other characters in their rejoicing. And at the very end of the play it is Adam again who rejoices:

To þe lorde be lovyng
Þat us has wonne fro waa;
For solas will we syng
Laus tibi cum gloria.

(XXXVII, 405–409)

In the liturgical hymn the triumph of Christ is celebrated by all those whom Christ has "wonne fro waa"—the audience no less than the patriarchs.

Adam's last words look back in the cycle far beyond the

events of Christ's Passion. The last time the audience had seen him was when the Angel of God had driven Adam and Eve from Paradise. Then Adam had been lamenting his disobedience and its consequences:

Allas! for syte and sorowe sadde,
Mournynge makis me mased and madde
To thynke in herte what helpe y hadde
    and nowe has none.
On grounde mon I nevyr goo gladde,
    my gamys ere gane.
Gone ar my games with-owten glee,
Allas! in blisse kouthe we noȝt bee,
For putte we were to grete plente
    at prime of þe day
Be tyme of none alle lost had wee,
    sa welawaye.

(VI, 81–92)

In its mixture of mournfulness and self-reproach, this is a moving speech. While Adam is clearly the Adam who has just lost Paradise, one critic has found in this lament "the frailties of mankind down through the years since Adam first cried out in anguish to his God,"[38] another a "nostalgic sense of the brevity of happiness."[39] The contemporary audience might have recognized in it too echoes of the independent lyric versions of the lament of an old sinful man which would have given Adam's words a universal expressiveness.[40] The mood and style of lament which these stanzas introduce are sustained to the end of the play—by Eve as well as Adam—until at the very end, Adam leaves Paradise with the words:

On grounde mon I never gladde gange
    withowten glee.
Withowten glee I ga,
This sorowe wille me sla,
This tree unto me wille I ta

þat me is sende:
He þat us wrought wisse us fro wa
whare-some we wende.

(VI, 161–168)

The simple trust of these last two lines is a beautiful place to leave Adam, grieving, but hopeful, an eloquent representative of the audience with whom he associates himself in the last words of benediction. And when, much later in the cycle, Christ's victory does allow Adam to praise the one "þat us has wonne fro waa," his hope is justified and the pledge made to him is fulfilled. The celebration in which Adam urges the audience to join at the end of the Harrowing of Hell play is for the universal redemption that Christ's victory has made available, imaged in the Adam who is all men. With its basic conflict between Christ and Satan and its essential moment of release and peripety, both of which can vividly be acted out on the stage, the Harrowing of Hell lends itself far more readily to dramatic representation than does the Resurrection.[41] The York dramatists, recognizing this, have not tried to duplicate the effect of the Harrowing in the Resurrection play; they avoid a potentially distracting anticlimax by giving to the two plays completely different emotional structures and emphases.

The play that follows the Resurrection play is again completely different from the preceding two—the very variety at the heart of the York cycle carries its own dramatic interest. Only in York is a whole play devoted to the appearance of Christ to Mary Magdalene. Out of this episode, the dramatist has created a full and rich scene of sustained lyricism. Essential as it is to the cycle's realization of the emotional structure of the action of the drama as a whole, it allows us an important examination of the dramatic use of lyric structures and themes and of the ways in which, in its lyrical address, the drama works to assure the knowing participation of the audience in that action.

At the heart of this play is a long speech by Christ which has recently been criticized as "a little jarring in its transplantation of a traditional theme to an unsuitable context."[42]

Mary has recognized Christ and prayed to Him for mercy. Christ responds:

> Marie, in thyne harte þou write
> Myne armoure riche and goode:
> Myne actone covered all with white
> Als cors of man be-hewede
> With stuffe goode and parfite
> Of maydenes flessh and bloode.
> Whan thei ganne thirle and smyte
> Mi heede for hawberke stoode.
> Mi plates wer spredde all on-brede,
> Þat was my body uppon a tree;
> Myne helme covered all with manhede,
> Þe strengh þer-of may no man see;
> Þe croune of thorne þat garte me blede
> Itt bemenes my dignite.
> Mi diademe sais, withouten drede,
> Þat dede schall I nevere be.
>
> (XXXIX, 94–109)

The speech begins with the form of devotion found in the most popular of all Middle English devotional lyrics, that in which the meditator asks Christ to write His Passion on his stony heart,[43] a form here made fresh and urgent by its transformation into a commandment from Christ. This form is then merged with the more esoteric, but nonetheless popular, allegory of the wounds of Christ as the armor in which He fought for man and overcame the devil.[44] The allegory seems crude to a modern reader, and there is in this speech an awkwardness in its handling and an imprecision to the statement of the paradox it images which it shares with almost every other contemporary lyric treatment of the *topos*. Yet the very statement that Christ's suffering *is* His victory represents a crucial turning point in the emotional sequence this play enacts, and the strikingness and liturgical authority of the imagery have their own rhetorical effectiveness in objectifying Christ's suffering. The point of the speech is to turn suffering into triumph and death into life, and by so doing, to qualify grief at Christ's suffering by an awareness of its redemptive aspects. Just such an awareness is expressed by Mary in response to Christ's words:

A, blessid body þat bale wolde beete,
Dere haste þou bought mankynne;
Thy woundes hath made þi body wete
With bloode þat was þe with-inne.
Nayled þou was thurgh hande and feete,
And all was for oure synne.
Full grissely muste we caitiffis grete,
Of bale howe schulde I blynne?
To see þis ferly foode
Þus ruffully dight,
Rugged and rente on a roode—
Þis is a rewfull sight.
And all is for oure goode
And nothyng for his plight,
Spilte þus is his bloode
For ilke a synful wight.

(XXXIX, 110–125)

In strict dramatic terms, this speech might seem inappropriate: Mary's words seem to place her much more immediately before an image of the crucified Christ "Rugged and rente on roode" than before an image of the risen Christ. But this surely is the point—that the two images are inseparable (a paradox frequently asserted in pictorial representations)—a point which the speech seems deliberately and carefully fashioned to express. The first two lines compactly assert the mystery of the Passion which the rest of the speech works to clarify by merging evocations of Christ's suffering with statements of the universal redemptive significance of that suffering. Mary provides the answer to the question she asks: to overcome her grief she has only to realize that "Spilte þus is his bloode / For ilke a synful wight." The communal terms of her statements are also strictly inappropriate, for Mary is alone with Christ on the stage; but they, too, are justified by their rhetorical function, for they economically serve to incorporate the audience into the awareness that Mary so beautifully expresses, softening even as she clarifies the harsher imagery of Christ's words to her.

The last quatrain of Mary's speech summarizes the expository aspects of this play: the audience learns that "all is for oure goode." But the play also works to support and enrich its exposition by showing how this truth can transform man as it transforms history. The play consists of a series of lyrical speeches which in their expression of moods of sorrow, recognition, and joy, realize a movement from isolated grief to communal joy—the same movement that more extendedly had shaped Adam's story. In the opening speeches of the play, Mary's grief at Christ's death is fully imaged:

> Allas, in þis worlde was nevere no wight
> Walkand with so mekill woo,
> Thou dredfull dede, drawen hythir and dight
> And marre me, as þou haste done moo.
> In lame is it loken all my light,
> For-thy on grounde on-glad I goo;
> Jesus of Nazareth he hight,
> The false Jewes slewe hym me froo . . .
> My doulfull herte is evere in drede
> To grounde nowe gone is all my glee.
> I sporne þer I was wonte to spede:
> Now helpe me, God in persones three.
>
> (XXXIX, 1–8, 13–16)

Her complaint borrows from the familiar lyric form of lament found elsewhere in the York plays, here used to generalize Mary's expression of grief at Christ's death. Yet however compelling Mary's grief may be, for the audience it is qualified by the fact that they, and Mary, know of Christ's Resurrection from the dead. There is a gentle irony to the discrepancy between what the audience knows and what Mary seems to know which is increased as Jesus now appears in response to Mary's prayer, and she fails to recognize Him. She asks for information about Christ that might help her to "mende" her "chere" as "the gardner" urges her to do. In response Jesus tells her that although she would not be able to comfort Christ in His suffering,

> . . . he schall cover mankynde of care:
> Þat clowded was, he schall make clere,
> And þe folke wele for to fare
> Þat fyled were all in feere.
>
> (XXXIX, 54–57)

In their careful alliterative patterning, these words serve both to assert the universal dimension of Christ's redemptive act and to establish Mary, dramatically, as an exemplar in whom the promise Christ makes can be seen to be fulfilled: she has expressed the "care" which will be cured and she, unable to recognize Christ, has shown herself "clowded." Now Jesus addresses her by name:

> Marie! of mournyng amende thy moode,
> And be-holde my woundes wyde.
> Þus for mannys synnes I schedde my bloode
> And all þis bittir bale gonne bide.
> Þus was I rased on þe roode
> With spere and nayles that were unrude:
> Trowe it wele, it turnes to goode,
> Whanne men in erthe þer flessh schall hyde.
>
> (XXXIX, 62–69)

Behind the exchange between Christ and Mary Magdalene lies a traditional form of devotion widely used in contemporary vernacular lyrics, a dialogue between Christ and His mother in which her expression of natural grief is set against His assertions of the redemptive aspect of His suffering in a kind of dialectic which works toward an expository end by eliciting the meditative participation of the audience in the scene and the dialogue.[45] But where in the lyric forms the dialectic frequently remains unresolved, leaving the meditators in a delicate tension of sorrow and joy, in this play it is finally resolved. The movement toward resolution begins as Mary recognizes Christ in an elaborate and moving prayer:

> A! mercy, comely conquerour,
> Thurgh þi myght þou haste overcome dede.
> Mercy, Jesu, man and saveour,
> Thi love is swetter þanne þe mede.
> Mercy, myghty confortour,
> For are I was full wille of rede;
> Welcome, lorde, all myn honnoure,
> Mi joie, mi luffe, in ilke a stede.
>
> (XXXIX, 86–93)

The combination of liturgical language and a more intimate language of love (the poetry here approaches that of the contemporary mystics) is dramatically important in that it sustains Mary as the exemplar in whom Christ's act as "mighty confortour" is seen to be fulfilled. That Christ is both "man and saveour" is the paradox that the Passion plays have exploited for their affective appeal to the audience; here the focus shifts from the man and His suffering to the Savior and the joy He brings, though the dependence of the one upon the other is affirmed by the very sequence of the play's action.

In this context, the "obtrusive" allegory of Christ's wounds as His armor is seen to be an integral development of the play's action. Sustaining the heightened language of Mary's prayer, Christ's words confirm the public and victorious nature of His death and Resurrection, which are then fully extended to the audience in the communal terms of Mary's lyrical clarification of the redemptive significance of His suffering. The dramatist leaves little doubt about what the cumulative effect of his presentation of the meeting between Mary and the risen Christ is meant to be. Christ tells Mary that He will soon ascend to heaven having fulfilled God's will on earth, and then He turns to speak directly to the audience:

And therefore loke þat ilke man lere
Howe þat in erthe þer liffe may mende.
All þat me loves I schall drawe nere
Mi Fadirs blisse þat nevere schall ende.
(XXXIX, 130–133)

The Redemption Christ has brought, which has been so fully enacted in the figure of Mary Magdalene, now is offered to all those who believe in Christ. To confirm this extension, Mary's final song of joy speaks for herself and for all men:

Alle for joie me likes to synge,
Myne herte is gladder þanne þe glee,
And all for joie of thy risyng
That suffered dede uppone a tree.
Of luffe nowe is þou crouned Kyng,
Is none so trewe levand more free.
Thy love passis all erthely thyng,
Lorde, blissed motte þou evere bee!
(XXXIX, 134–141)

In its presentation of the first appearance of Christ after the Resurrection, this beautiful play makes full use of the emotional emphases and affective potential of the vernacular lyric meditations, working them together into a pattern which both dramatically and rhetorically enacts a movement from isolated grief to communal joy. All the action in this still play is in the poetry; the only movements called for by the play's dialogue are Christ's displaying His wounds to Mary and her gestures of affection and reverence. The displacement of the emotional peripety of the Resurrection into this play allows both a conclusive demonstration of the divine truth of Christ's Passion in personal terms and an extended yet focused development of the emotional responses to that demonstration. At the end of the play, Mary and the audience are brought together in the presence of the risen Christ as the action of the drama as a whole begins to move toward its resolution in the bliss of God, a resolution anticipated in the benediction on which the play ends as Christ offers His "blissing" to Mary and to "all þat we leffe here" (XXXIX, 148–149).

Two essentially complementary aspects of the comic structure of the York cycle's action are focused in the plays of the Harrowing of Hell and Appearance of Christ to Mary. The first is the universal, "objective" aspect in which history itself is recognized as being redirected toward the bliss of heaven by Christ's victory over Satan and death, and the second is the individual, "subjective" aspect in which each man is restored and regenerated by the coming of Christ into his life, so that the life of the individual is reformulated according to the pattern of history. Together, these plays work to demonstrate for the audience the significance of the Resurrection and to make them participants in the *comoedia* which is the Christian story.

In both its aspects, the comic structure is constantly held out to the audience as an encouragement to them to reformulate their lives according to the examples they see in the plays. The conduct of events in individual plays is often shaped to realize a movement from sorrow to joy—the plays of Noah's salvation from the Flood, of Abraham and Isaac, of the Exodus all anticipate the transformation brought by Christ in the plays of His Nativity and Resurrection, and the bliss to which they lead is even more frequently extended to the audience in the blessings with which so many of the plays end. Individual examples of personal restoration are also to be discovered in many of the plays: Noah as he comes to obey God, Joseph as he is brought to understand the nature of the birth of Christ, Simeon as he is allowed to welcome Christ to the temple, and, as we will see in a moment, the disciples as they are granted a sight of the risen Christ. These enactments in plots and characterizations within the plays are consistently marked by brief lyrical exclamations of sorrow and then of joy which also serve to sustain the patterns of language and verse upon which the more extended lyrical passages of lamentation or celebration are founded. And everywhere we look in the plays, the terms in which the comic structure of the plot of the drama is articulated are to be found. In large part it is through insistent statement that the emotional poles of the action are imaged for the audience within the plays—the words "blisse" and "bale" and their synonyms echo throughout the plays. Sometimes they are found in unexpected places, as when the Counselors of Herod, having devised their plan to kill all children under two years of age, convince Herod that as far as the Christ child is concerned, "belyve his bliss schall blynne / With bale when he schall blede" (XIX, 158–159). These phrases not only comment ironically on the immediate action of this play in which Herod will fail in his attempt to kill Christ, but also look ahead to the Passion of Christ when He will bleed, and even beyond to the moment when the "bale" of Christ and all men will be turned to bliss through the Resurrection. Even in the following play of Christ with the Doctors in the temple, a play whose primary mode is not lyrical and whose primary emphasis is not the transformation accomplished in Christ, the terms still inform the play. At the start, Mary and Joseph appear joyful, their hearts filled with "mirth" (XX, 1, 6), only to be brought to "bale" (17) when they realize Christ is missing. Mary briefly laments, "Of sorowes sere schal be my sang, / My semely sone tille I hym see" (43–44). But Christ brings "mirthis" (74) to the Doctors, presents Himself to them as one "anoynted . . . as leche" (102), is recognized by the Doctors as the child sent "to salve oure sare" (135–136), and, though Mary and Joseph appear still lamenting that "mournyng may not mende" (214), brings joy to His parents. Joseph is overjoyed that the sight of his son "hath salved us of all oure sore" (265–266), and Mary, at the very end of the play reflects back on the action not just of this play but of the Incarnation as a whole as she exclaims, "Full wele is us þis tyde / Nowe may we make goode chere" (285–286).

At this same level of verbal repetition, the plays are likewise full of formulaic phrases which affirm God and Christ as the ones who can save man from sorrow, bring man from distress, turn sorrow into joy, resolve all strife, provide comfort in misery. The sheer repetition of these formulae, far from being unimaginative as has often been claimed, has a cumulative impact which is essential to the audience's discovery of the meaning of the drama. The formulae serve constantly to focus and define an important aspect of the action. So constant are they that they can be used with immediate ironic effect. When Christ is led before Herod for judgment, Herod's son, as blind as his father to the true nature of Christ, urges Him to pay due respect to the King: "Look uppe, ladde, lightly, and loute to my lorde here / For fro bale unto blisse he may nowe þe borowe" (XXXI, 307–308). As well as keeping the emotional and spiritual action of the drama in the audience's mind, the verbal details of the plays frequently image the transformation from sorrow to joy or joy to sorrow. In the opening play of the cycle, as we have noted, Lucifer's speeches in particular make strategic use of the rhetorical devices of *contentio* and chiasmus, and from this moment on, whenever they are used (which is frequently) they become brief enactments themselves of the central action of the drama.

Through verbal details such as these, as well as details of plot and characterization, the structure of the action involving a movement between sorrow and joy is constantly defined and enacted for the audience. The expository emphasis placed upon this pattern at crucial moments means that the audience understands it; but that they come to *participate* in it is the result of the dramatists' handling of the lyrical aspects of the dialogue. It is not coincidence that nearly all the predominantly lyrical plays in the cycle come after the representation of the Resurrection of Christ. From that moment on, the action of the drama, like the action of history, is redirected toward its resolution in the blessing of God on which the cycle ends. The play of Christ's Appearance to Mary Magdalene establishes the pattern for the action and the poetry of the final plays of the cycle. Centered upon Christ who, though risen, still displays the wounds which reproach man with his sinfulness, they all enact the movement from isolation and grief to communion in joy, celebrating finally the restoration which Christ has made available to man. In the play of Christ's appearance to the Travellers on the Road to Emmaus, for example, an elaborate and extended recital of the events of the Passion by the pilgrims serves to express their sense of loss and grief at the start of the play. Formalized by the use of the stanza-linking and made vivid by the effects of heavy alliteration, their recital has a considerable emotional appeal which is further heightened for the audience by the ironic discrepancy that tries to deny the knowledge the audience has gained from the immediately preceding plays. For the audience, the appropriateness of the First Pilgrim's interpretative comment, "Me thynkith myn herte is boune for to breke / Of his pitefull paynes when we here speke" (XL, 46–47) is qualified by their awareness that those "paynes" are also the sign of Christ's triumph and the cause of great joy. Only after Christ has appeared and made Himself known to them is their grief resolved. In the litany-like sequence with which the play ends, the suffering of Christ, again described in detail, becomes the premise of the Resurrection to the truth of which the Pilgrims, like the audience, prepare to give joyful witness. To the expository, "evidentiary" effect of these plays is thus added their effect as emotional confirmation of the truth which is preached.

The opening plays of the cycle had twice enacted a movement from bliss and joy to sorrow and lamentation—in the Fall of Lucifer and in the Fall of man. At the end of the cycle, not twice but many times, the movement back from sorrow to joy is enacted, nowhere more completely or elaborately than in the three plays which deal with the Death, Assumption and Coronation of the Virgin Mary. All of the lyric forms and modes discussed in this section—and more—are found in these plays, and all the dramatic uses of their expressive and affective potential elsewhere dispersed are focused in these dazzling plays.[46] The first of the three plays is more interesting for its narrative than for its lyrical aspects (though these are themselves impressive, the play containing a rich "Hail" lyric, brief but poignant laments, and quiet prayers), for it reaches back to recapitulate the events of the Incarnation, the Annunciation and Nativity, and the death of Christ. The play ends with Christ and the Angels preparing to receive Mary "to þe highest of hevene /

With mirthe and with melody hir mode for to mende" (XLV, 177–178)—and the mirth and the melody begin as the Angels celebrate Mary's defeat of the devil (which recapitulates the Harrowing of Hell) by singing the liturgical hymn, *Ave regina celorum.* The middle of the three plays, the Weavers' play of the Appearance of Mary to Thomas, is the most elaborately lyrical play in the whole of the cycle. In the York Register, the play is accompanied by the music for the three hymns which are sung in the course of the play.[47] On its own, the music—which seems to have been composed specifically for this play—would be enough to create and sustain the various moods which mark the play's action. But as well as creating moments of ceremonial spectacle, it serves mainly to highlight what is more extensively developed in the elaborate speeches of the play—and although there are definite signs of the linguistic and prosodic display which marks the encroachment of the "aureate" style, in these speeches there is nonetheless a careful controlling of poetic effects to a coherent dramatic end. In structure, the play is very simple, yet from this structure emerges a sequence of richly developed emotional states. Thomas appears at the start of the play:

In waylyng and weping, in woo am I wapped,
In site and in sorowe, in sighing full sadde:
Mi lorde and my luffe, loo, full lowe is he lapped
Þat makes me to mourne nowe full mate and
 full madde.
What harling and what hurlyng þat hedesman he
 hadde!
What breking of braunches ware brosten aboute hym,
What bolnyng with betyng of brothellis full badde!
Itt leres me full lely to love hym and lowte hym.
That comely to kenne,
Goddis sone Jesus,
He died for us,
þat makes me þus
To mourne amange many men.

(XLVI, 1–13)

The predominant feature of the unusual stanza form is the contrast between the two parts, the *frons* consisting of the heavily alliterated long lines, the *cauda* of the quieter, shorter lines where alliteration is an ornamental option, with the slightly longer last line giving to the stanza an essential balance and form. The rhyme scheme of the stanza is complicated, and its effects are constantly enhanced by assonance both within the lines and between the rhyme words. And to add further to the musical effects of the stanza form itself, there are sustained passages in which the stanzas are linked in sequence by the repetition of a key phrase from the last line of one stanza in the first line of the next.

Not the least of the play's achievements is the skill with which such a demanding verse form is maintained and its rich variety of effects is ordered to dramatic ends. In the opening stanza, for example, the lines of the octave voicing Thomas' grief and describing the cruel death of his lord which causes his grief are vigorous and colorful, summoning up for the audience a vivid picture for their contemplation; the lines of the last part of the stanza are quieter, more intimate, with the last line lingering on its extra syllable with the melancholic "m" alliteration leaving a moving image of Thomas. The presentation of Thomas' mourning is so compelling and his account of Christ's Passion so fast moving that there is no time to question the appropriateness of the feelings expressed. Some of the lines are overwhelming, if obvious—"Þei dusshed hym, þei dasshed hym, / þei lusshed hym, þei lasshed hym, / Þei pusshed hym, þei passhed hym" (XLVI, 36–38); others are tellingly precise—"Þei toke hym with treasoune, þat turtill of treuthe" (XLVI, 32); and still others, notably those in which Thomas recalls the doubts he had about the truth of Christ's Resurrection, are very moving. Most of the effects of this speech can be paralleled in independent lyric and narrative meditations; what the play adds most crucially to them is the anticipation, based on the experience of previous plays and on the movement of the action of the cycle as a whole, of joyful things to come.

As Thomas, finding himself miraculously in "þe Vale of

Josophat" (97), lies down to rest, wearied by grief, the Angels sing the first of the Latin hymns, *Surge proxima mea columba mea.* Its heightened ceremonial effect is continued when the Angels call upon Mary in the first of a series of vernacular hymns which will mark the action of this play. Twelve Angels sing one line of the hymn each, the first eight addressing Mary in highly liturgical epithets, bidding her arise, and the rest, in simpler language but with the quickening pace of the short lines of the stanza, urging her to come to them:

vii Ang: Rise, semely in sight, of þi sone to be semande!
viii Ang: Rise, grathed full goodely in grace for to grewe!
ix Ang: Rise uppe þis stounde.
x Ang: Come, chosen childe!
xi Ang: Come, Marie milde!
xii Ang: Come, floure unfiled!
viii Ang: Comme uppe to þe kyng to be crouned!
(XLVI, 111–117)

Now another hymn is sung, the beautiful hymn based on the Song of Solomon, *Veni de libano sponsa.* Again, the heightened effect of the liturgical Latin is imitated and sustained in the following dialogue as Mary appears to Thomas as if in a vision, eliciting from him a lengthy "Hail" lyric. The appropriateness of this speech is that it expresses not only the praise due to Mary on which her Coronation is founded but a newfound vitality and confidence which Mary has inspired in Thomas. In some of the epithets, the two effects combine. Thomas praises Mary as "salve þat is sure . . . lettir of langure . . . bote of oure bale in obeyesaunce" (XLVI, 141, 142, 143). The solemn mood is relieved slightly as, with the stanza form now deftly fitted to the needs of dialogue, Mary urges Thomas to tell the other disciples what he has seen and gives him a girdle to attest to the truth of his report. The dialogue gives way to yet another series of elaborate lyrical stanzas in which Thomas' hymns are contrasted with the quieter prayer for help that Mary offers. Thomas' first song is particularly fine:

> I thanke þe as reverent rote of oure reste,
> I thanke þe as stedfast stokke for to stande,
> I thanke þe as tristy tre for to treste,
> I thanke þe as buxsom bough to þe bande,
> I thanke þe as leeffe þe lustiest in lande,
> I thanke þe as bewteuous braunche for to bere,
> I thanke þe as floure þat nevere is fadande,
> I thanke þe as frewte þat has fedde us in fere—
> I thanke þe for evere!
> If they repreve me,
> Now schall þei leve me!
> Þi blissinge giffe me
> And douteles I schall do my devere.
>
> (XLVI, 170–182)

The elaborateness of the stanza has forced the poet into some redundancies and awkwardness (which I doubt would be at all bothersome when the stanza was recited), but the handling of the image of the hymn, the use of the stanza to imitate the growing of the tree from root to fruit climaxing in the almost mystical ecstasy of the first of the shorter lines, the contrast in styles here used not to undercut but to balance the ecstasy and to tie it down to the dramatic situation—these aspects of the stanza are remarkable. Moreover the image itself seems to lead from Mary to Christ—the image of tree and blossom is as widely used of Christ as it is of Mary, and the last phrase of the sequence, "as frewte þat has fedde us," has resonances of the Eucharist—and in her response to this hymn Mary makes explicit what is implicit in the image, that she is the intercessor with Christ for man.

The balance achieved between the sublime and the humble in the stanza form is realized too in the structure of the play as the highly ornate scenes now give way to the much simpler scene in which Thomas carries the news to the other disciples. Just as impressive as the elaborate poetic effects of the first scene is the handling of the verse to image the surliness of the disciples as they reproach Thomas for not being present at Mary's burial and the scepticism with which they greet his explanation. But these attitudes, too, are changed, to the gratitude to Mary and the joy in which the play appropriately ends. In this last scene, the unearthliness of the earlier scene is qualified, made appreciable to the audience which witnesses the miraculous events of the play. Encouraged by the hymns of Thomas to the attitude of devout and joyful prayer which is Mary's due, confirmed in their knowledge of the divinity of Mary by the demonstration of the first scene and the explanation of the second, they are implicitly addressed in the play's final moments as the Apostles leave "þe trewthe for to teche . . . þe pepull to preche / To lede þame and lere þame þe lawe of oure lorde" (XLVI, 300, 303–304) and as Thomas finally offers a blessing on the audience.

The third play of this sequence in part repeats the events of the second, though the perspective from which they are viewed is not now that of Thomas, of "doubting" man, but of Christ and the angels. The audience is transported along with the action to heaven. It is a quieter play which instead of sustained rhetorical passages works primarily through patterned repetitions of the key words "joie," "mirthe" and "blisse" which together focus and describe the mood and the rhetorical goal of this play—in statistical terms, these three words are used 34 times in 160 lines. In accordance with these themes, the highlight of the play is the speech with which Christ and the Angels welcome Mary to heaven, not in elaborate liturgical terms (though these do find a place) but in the simpler language of the vernacular devotional form of the Five Joys of Mary.[48] Here the life of the Virgin and that of her Son, from the Annunciation to this present moment, are retold from the divine perspective which sees all the grievous events of those lives as necessary preliminaries to the joy which awaits all who put their faith in Christ and pray to Mary for her intercession with her son. Reminding the audience that lamentation and suffering are the premises of the joy they now witness, the speech takes the play onto a solemn, reflective level which makes Christ's final assurances as He crowns Mary that all her prayers for those who call on her will be granted, all the more effective.

I have hardly communicated the richness of these plays; they have to be heard, with their liturgical hymns and aurally elaborate lyric verse, for such richness to be appreciated. At least the first two of the plays seem to have been written at the very latest stages of revision of the collection, but care has been taken to fit them into the style of the cycle as a whole and to the shaping of its action. Their place in the unfolding plot of the cycle is clear: they not only provide a satisfying narrative conclusion to the life of the Virgin who is, after Christ, the most important figure in the drama for the audience, but they also mediate between the historical time of the Ascension and Pentecost and the indefinite future time of the Last Judgment. They stress, in accordance with the devotional emphases of the late Middle Ages, the role of Mary as mediator between Christ and man. Explicitly acknowledged in Mary's prayers that Christ be merciful to "all þat are in newe or in nede" (XLV, 144) and in Christ's assurances that to Mary is given "bothe grace and might / In hevene and erþe to sende socoure" (XLVII, 146–47), the role of Mary becomes the basis of the rhetorical design of these plays. As Mary herself moves from earth to heaven, the lyrical passages that mark the structure of these plays reach out to the audience to urge them to share in the joy which replaces sorrow and which Christ through His mother offers to all men. They are spectacular plays, involving miracles, comings and goings between "earth" and "heaven" on the stage, extensive singing, and some very elaborate verse. In their predominantly joyful, celebratory mood they provide at the end of the cycle what the final play of the Last Judgment cannot provide, the sense of triumphant, joyful resolution to the scheme of salvation. The dramatists of the York plays acknowledge and even stress that the fulfillment of the will of God demands that there are those who, at the end, will "sing of sorowes sere"; but all the lyrical resources of their verse and of their drama are directed toward encouraging the audience to be among those who at the Last Judgment will celebrate with the Angels in the joy and mirth of God's blessing.

The Play of the Death and Burial of Christ (Play XXXVI)

Of the extant cycles only York devotes a whole play to the subject of the Death of Christ. In the other cycles, the moment comes as the climax of the Crucifixion.[49] Yet the York play nonetheless contains a large cast of characters and a variety of episodes. The list of Corpus Christi pageants at York compiled in 1415 by the town clerk Roger Burton gives an accurate summary of the contents of the dramatic play of the Death of Christ:

> Crux, duo latrones crucifixi, Jesus suspensus in cruce inter eos, Maria mater Jesu, Johannes, Maria, Jacobus, et Salome *(sic)*, Longeus cum lancea, servus cum spongea, Pilatus, Anna, Cayphas, Centurio, Josep *(sic)* et Nichodemus deponentes eum in sepulcro.[50]

In spite of this variety, however, the play is perhaps the most carefully unified of all the York plays. Burton's description points to the reason—the "crux" to which it gives such prominence. From the start of the play, the figure of the crucified Christ hanging on the Cross dominates both the stage and the dramatic action.[51] It is the focus of all the words and movements of the characters as the episodes of the play demonstrate their varying responses to Christ. That figure is clearly also the focus of the audience's attention throughout the play, so that the responses of the characters become the means of eliciting, testing, and directing the responses of the people in the audience. The impressive unity of the York Death of Christ play comes as much from its consistent rhetorical design as from the coherence of its dramatic action.

In both aspects, the play draws richly from the meditative tradition I have described in this chapter. Here the audience is confronted with the icon of the Crucifix made vivid visually and verbally—and the basis of the play's effectiveness lies in the directness of this confrontation. But just as the Baptism play created dramatic interest by internalizing the rhetorical modes of instruction that inform the York plays, so here does the dramatist internalize the action of responding to the image of the crucified Christ to make it the primary concern of the play's internal action. There is an exemplary edge to the dramatization of the episode—the characters serve to instruct the audience in how to respond to Christ. For the most part, however, it is to the handling of the lyrical elements of this moving play that we must pay attention. We will find some of the most accomplished poetry of the York cycle in this play, poetry that enhances the power of the visual image to bring the audience to a full and active awareness of the meaning of the Crucifixion for them. But it is more than a play of set pieces. The lyrical verse of this play combines with other styles and tones to image the variety of the play's episodic action but also to concentrate that action on the image of Christ which the play offers for the audience's contemplation.

At the start of the play, Pilate, having announced himself in characteristically bombastic terms, points to the area of the stage where Christ and the two thieves can be seen hanging on the crosses, and says, as much to the audience as to those who accompany him: "Who þat to ȝone hill wille take heede / May se þer þe soth in his sight" (16–17). Pilate knows, or thinks he knows, the true significance of Christ's Passion and Crucifixion, and he asserts it with a defiant and self-vindicating assuredness:

> To dye schall I deme þame to dede
> Þo rebelles þat rewles þame un-right.
> Who þat to ȝone hill wille take heede
> May se þer þe soth in his sight,
> Howe doulful to dede þei are dight
> That liste noȝt owre lawes for to lere;
> Lo, þus be my mayne and my myght
> Tho churles schalle I chasteise and cheere
>   Be lawe.

Ilke feloune false,
Shall hynge be þe halse,
Transgressours als
    On the crosse schalle be knytte for to knawe.

(14–26)

There is perhaps something imposing about Pilate in his verbal and costumed splendor—the trilled "rebelles" and "transgressours" sound particularly threatening, and "knytte" has a convincingly contemptuous ring to it—but his blindness and unwarranted self-satisfaction should be obvious. At this point Pilate makes no distinction between Christ and the two thieves, and while the thieves might well deserve the punishment they endure and the epithets Pilate disdainfully uses, Christ is a rebel, a churl, a "feloune fals," and a lawbreaker only when He is judged according to the law of men that Pilate (and the verse form) insist on. As he attempts to vindicate his law and his actions, Pilate unwittingly judges and condemns himself.

That the audience would be responsive to the ironies of this stanza has been assured by the dramatist in the opening stanza of the play. Pilate's pompous self-introduction aligns him unmistakably with the enemies of Christ whom the audience has heard adopting similar verbal postures in the sequence of plays immediately preceding this:

Sees, Seniours, and see what I saie,
Takis tente to my talkyng enteere;
Devoyde all þis dynne here þis day
And fallis to my frenschippe in feere.
Sir Pilate, a Prince with-owten pere,
My name is full nevenly to neven,
And domisman full derworth in dere,
Of gentillest Jewry full even
    Am I.
Who makis oppressioun
Or dose transgressioun,
Be my discressioun
    Shall be demed dewly to dye.

(1–13)

In an earlier play, too, the audience has seen Pilate condemn Christ to the brutal treatment they have just seen inflicted upon Him, and as a powerful reminder of Pilate's responsibility for Christ's suffering, the figure of the crucified Christ is now clearly visible as a judgment on Pilate's every word and gesture. Even as Pilate parades himself, the true "Prince with-owten pere," the true "domisman" can be seen nailed to the cross, and in his demand for the audience's attention, Pilate tries to appropriate for himself what at this point should be given to Christ. The irony is reinforced by the sounds and rhythms of the stanza as they characterize Pilate: the forceful tag, "Am I," that interrupts the flow of the verse focuses the repeated sounds of "I . . . my . . . my . . . my . . ." in his words. In the context created by the preceding plays and the staging of this play, Pilate's self-concern is recognized as the antithesis of the humility that has received its most moving demonstration in the Crucifixion. From the start of the play, Pilate's posturing is undercut in ways that make him ridiculous and even frightening, though not for the reasons he claims.[52]

As Pilate turns to Annas and Caiphas, however, his words reveal a slight change of attitude:

> Of Jesu I holde it unhappe
> Þat he on yone hill hyng so hye
> For gilte.
> His bloode to spille
> Toke ye you till
> Þus was youre wille
> Full spitously to spede he were spilte.
> (33–39)

The presentation of Pilate in this and other plays of the York cycle is not completely one dimensional; in the York plays he most closely resembles the complicated, almost sympathetic Pilate of the Gospels. Here his expression of regret over Christ's suffering—the "gilte" of the tag line seems more his than Christ's—provides a dramatically important qualification of his initial arrogance. It suggests that for Pilate at least there is a chance that he might be brought to discover for himself the real truth about the Crucifixion.

This suggestion controls the following movement in the play. In the face of Pilate's misgivings, Annas and Caiphas become more adamant, more vehement in their accusations. In their words the ironies of the opening of the play are intensified, for the attitude they display is one of unqualified presumption and blindness, and the colloquial coarseness of the terms in which they abuse Christ works dramatically both to characterize and to judge them:

> *Cay:* He called hym kyng,
> Ille joie hym wring,
> Ia, late hym hyng
> Full madly on þe mone for to mowe.
> *Ann:* To mowe on þe moone has he mente.
> We! fye on þe, faitour in faye.
> Who trowes þou, to þi tales toke tente?
>
> (75–81)

The sustained insistence of Annas and Caiphas on their own will, their own law, and their own version of the truth, serves as a kind of dramatic challenge to the audience to assert *their* understanding of the truth. They are helped in this by verbal resonances that counter the increasingly violent taunts. Thus, as Annas mocks Christ with His prophecy that at His death the temple would be destroyed and on the third day rebuilt, his words carry a timely anticipation of the Resurrection which Christ has promised and which, as the audience well knows, will miraculously assert the power His enemies try to deny Him. Similarly Caiphas' scornful demands that Christ prove that He is the Son of God by descending from the cross anticipate later events which will prove unambiguously, though not in Caiphas' terms and not to his satisfaction, what the audience already knows, that Christ is indeed the Son of God.

The differences in attitude between Pilate and Annas and Caiphas, and the suggestions and ironies to which they give rise, are focused—though not resolved—as Pilate's refusal to let any change be made in the inscription over the cross seems to verify the identification of Christ as the King of the Jews:

> *Quod scripci, scripci,*
> Ȝone same wrotte I,
> I bide þer-by,
> What gedlyng will grucche there agayne.
> (114–117)

With this assertion the opening movement of the play comes to an end, the dialogue and gestures, we can be sure, directing attention to the figure of Christ on the cross. The predominantly ironic mode of this movement serves an essential function not just in characterizing the figures involved but by creating a discrepancy between what these figures acknowledge and what the audience, however imprecisely, knows to be the true meaning of the Crucifixion, a discrepancy through which they are drawn into the action of the play.

At this point in the play, Christ speaks from the cross. He addresses both those on the stage and the audience:

> Þou man þat of mys here has mente,
> To me tente enteerly þou take.
> On roode am I ragged and rente
> Þou synfull sawle, for thy sake.
> For thy misse amendis wille I make.
> My bakke for to bende here I bide,
> Þis teene for thi trespase I take.
> Who couthe þe more kyndynes have kydde
> than I?
> Þus for thy goode
> I schedde my bloode.
> Manne, mende thy moode,
> For full bittir þi blisse mon I by.
> (118–130)

Pilate, Annas, and Caiphas have all appealed to the audience for its attention, but Christ's appeal is both more familiar to the audience and more urgent. Poetic and staging effects combine to compel those whom Christ addresses to contemplate and feel for themselves the agony of His suffering. The visual icon which has reproachfully dominated the stage from the start of the play is now animated. Christ's words are imposing and moving. The apostrophe of the first line of the stanza reinforced by the consecutive stresses, the echoing sounds of the first two lines, the imperative of the second line with the inverted syntax emphasizing the words "to me . . .," the forceful monosyllables that allow weight to be given to every word and highlight the polysyllabic "enteerly"—all these effects serve to draw attention fully and immediately to the speaker. The elaborate patterning of sounds and rhythms is sustained throughout the stanzas—rhyme words are anticipated and echoed internally, alliteration sets up associations among the lines, the few strategic polysyllabic words stand out—to encourage the audience to feel the reality of Christ's suffering on the cross and to lead beyond this emotional response to an awareness of the essential, mysterious, disturbing connection between man's sinfulness and Christ's redemptive suffering. All the resources of the stanza are directed to making Christ's appeal to man as compelling as possible. The tag line (perhaps for the observant listener echoing the tag from Pilate's opening stanza) gains added force from the rhythmical enjambement to make Christ's direct question uncomfortably unavoidable; then the shorter lines and forceful rhymes of the "wheel" state clearly the true significance of the Crucifixion—which seems to be summed up in the juxtaposition of "bittir" and "blisse" in the last line.

This is the most impressive of the speeches from the cross in the York plays—even in isolation it rivals the best of the independent lyric *improperia.* But the speech cannot be taken in isolation. It gains added force and significance from its place in the developing action of the play. In its movement from a recreation of Christ's suffering to its unambiguous assertion that Christ submitted Himself to death on the cross that man's sinfulness might be redeemed, the speech reveals the truth that has been denied in the opening scene of the play. The unwarranted demands for attention and the mistaken interpretations of Christ's suffering in the opening scene have provided a fresh context in which Christ's appeal can be made with a new urgency; to the force of His words is added their effect as the resolution of the ironic discrepancies on which the play has so far depended. In Christ's words a new and more satisfying direction is given to Pilate's earlier statement, "Who þat to ȝone hill wille take heede / May se þer þe soth in his sight."

Besides Christ and the two thieves, and Pilate and his followers, there has been another group on the stage from the start of the play, that of John and the three Marys grouped at the foot of the cross. As the mother of Christ now speaks, attention is drawn to this group: they, too, have been contemplating the figure of the crucified Christ and listening to His words, and Mary's lyrical lament expresses her response to Christ's appeal:

> Allas, for my swete sonne I saie,
> Þat doulfully to dede þus is diȝt.
> Allas, for full lovely þou laye
> In my wombe, þis worthely wight.
> Allas, þat I schulde see þis sight
> Of my sone so semely to see,
> Allas, þat þis blossome so bright
> Untrewly is tugged to þis tree,
>   Allas!
> My lorde, my leyffe,
> With full grete greffe
> Hyngis as a theffe.
>   Allas, he did never trespasse.
>
> (131–143)

The meaning of the Crucifixion that Mary's contemplation of Christ's suffering has led her to is an intimate and very human one, that her "swete sonne" suffers undeservedly; and in its intensity her lament does express a genuinely felt grief which reaches its climax in the sudden, telling image of the blossom tied to the tree "untrewly." Yet at the same time the ritualistic anaphora, the balanced syntax of the long lines, and the stanza form itself shape and formalize the expression of grief. There is a theological (and dramatic) point to this shaping in that uncontrolled grief would be inappropriate to the Virgin;[53] but there is an important rhetorical point to it as well, in that her lament accommodates the response of the audience to Christ's appeal and directs it toward the awareness expressed in the more generalized statements of the last lines of the stanza. In the opening scene of the play Christ's enemies had insisted on His guilt; now Mary asserts His innocence which is as much a part of the truth of the Crucifixion as the suffering it entails and the redemption it accomplishes.

In the movement of the play which Mary's lament introduces, the dramatist seeks further to direct the involved response of the audience to the scene they witness. In this movement, Mary's sustained lamentations alternate with the words of comfort offered to her by Christ, John, and Mary Cleophas. Christ's words from the cross to Mary are gentler than His earlier address:

> Þou woman, do way of thy wepyng,
> For me may þou no thyng amende;
> My fadirs wille to be wirkyng
> For mankynde my body I bende.
>
> (144–147)

The consolation that Christ offers points again to the truth that transcends grief at His suffering, that His Passion is the fulfillment of God's will for the salvation of mankind. His words also reveal an attitude which is an example for all those who suffer with Him: through the faith and humility which are here voiced, Christ has reconciled Himself to the pain that He endures. Mary's intense grief, however, prevents her from seeing the consoling truth which Christ both states and enacts, and her expression of sorrow at the imminent separation from her son calls forth another demonstration of compassion from Christ as He offers her John as her son and urges John to accept Mary as his mother. When John speaks, it is clear that he has learned from Christ's example. He too has been contemplating the figure of Christ throughout the play, but he has heeded Christ's words, and as he tenderly offers himself to Mary he both obeys and imitates Christ. Mary, however, is still reluctant to be consoled, and Mary Cleophas joins John in trying to comfort her by assuring her that Christ will send help and consolation to them. Their words finally have some effect upon Mary. Her grief subsides, and an attitude of patient resignation takes the place of her sorrow and despair: "To he be paste / Wille I buske here baynly to bide" (181–182).

The effect of this delicate movement in the play is analogous to that of the lyric dialogues between Mary and Christ. The alternation of words of lament with words of comfort does more than highlight the different responses to Christ's suffering which the characters demonstrate. It articulates in emotional terms the paradox which Christ's words had stated to be at the heart of the Passion, that the suffering He endures and which man is asked to share is the basis of His victory and the "blisse" which that victory makes available to man. The change that comes over Mary dramatically initiates a development crucial for the action of the play and the audience's participation in it, and encourages those in the play and those who watch to discover a poignant ambiguity to Christ's words, "Mann, mende thy moode, / For full bittir þi blisse mon I by."

These words are, in fact, recalled as Christ now speaks again from the cross in a general address to the audience:

> With bittirfull bale have I bought
> Þus, man, all þi misse for to mende.
> On me for to looke lette þou noȝt
> Howe baynly my body I bende.
> No wighte in þis worlde wolde have wende
> What sorowe I suffre for thy sake.
> Manne, kaste þe thy kyndynesse be kende
> Trewe tente un-to me þat þou take
>   And treste.
> For foxis þer dennys have þei,
> Birdis hase ther nestis to paye,

But þe sone of man this daye
Hase noȝt on his heed for to reste.
(183–195)

This second appeal is very similar to the first, insisting still on the pain Christ suffers; but it is not as intense in its effect, and its emphasis is different. Participation in the suffering of Christ is no longer the primary aim of Christ's words. The display of grief evoked by the earlier address has been qualified in the movement of the play that separates the two speeches, and this second address seems to build upon the immediately preceding promises of comfort to urge the audience explicitly to return Christ's demonstration of love for man in kind (the pun is present in Christ's words) and to have faith in Christ's power to save. Again the rhythmical resources of the stanza form are carefully ordered to highlight the tag line, where the rhetorical address of the play reaches its climax in Christ's appeal to men that they trust in Him. The last lines of Christ's address may seem to be out of place: they are not among the "Seven Words" which devotional tradition had established as being spoken by Christ from the cross,[54] and the version of the *Northern Passion* which the dramatist might have been using here saves them for Christ's last words before He dies.[55] In part the effect of the dramatist's having Christ speak these words at the end of His second address to the audience is that they stress, as they do in the *Northern Passion*, Christ's isolation. But there is another suggestion to these lines which, though it is not made explicit, makes them more intimately a part of the developing action of the play. The words are taken from Luke ix, 58, where they are spoken by Christ in answer to one who promises to become a disciple of Christ, as if to warn him that being a disciple will necessitate his sharing in the isolation that Christ has met with. This resonance to the lines gives added point to Christ's appeal that man have faith in Him—participation in the redemptive action of the Incarnation necessitates sharing in its agony, something which the affective thrust of the play so far has also tried to impress upon the audience.

The exchange between Christ and the two thieves following this second address from the cross (the dramatist's displacement of this scene is deliberate) presents an immediate enactment of the appeal that has just been made—and of its implications. Based closely on the scriptural account in Luke xxiv, 39–42, in its context the exchange is integrated with the action of the play as the manifestation of antithetical responses to Christ's words:

Lat. a sin: If þou be Goddis sone so free
Why hyng þou þus onþis hille?
To saffe nowe þi selffe late us see
And us now, þat spedis for to spille.
Lat. a dex: Manne, stynte of thy steven and be stille,
For douteles thy God dredis þou noȝt.
Full wele are we worthy ther-till
Unwisely wrange have we wrought
i-wisse.
Noon ille did hee,
Þus for to dye,
Lord, have mynde of me
Whan þou art come to þi blisse.
(196–208)

The taunts of the first thief echo at every point phrases used earlier by Annas and Caiphas, and the scornful, skeptical attitude they reveal shows that he at least has learned nothing from what he has seen and heard. In particular, he does not understand that the salvation Christ offers involves suffering for both Christ and for those whom He suffers to save. But the thief on the right hand of Christ has become convinced of Christ's divinity and of His innocence, and his prayer that Christ remember him in the bliss of heaven reveals that attitude of penitent and loving faith which Christ has urged upon all men. For his faith, the second thief receives the blessing of Christ:

For sothe, sonne, to þe schall I saie
Sen þou fro thy foly will falle
With me schall dwelle nowe þis daye
In paradise place principall.

(209–212)

This paradigmatic scene at the heart of the *Mortificacio Cristi* play makes an obvious homiletic point about the necessity of repentance for salvation, but it also formalizes what has emerged as the primary focus of the play's action: by sharing the agony of Christ and believing in his power to save, the second thief shares too in the glory and triumph of Christ.

Suddenly Christ cries out in His agony:

Heloy, heloy,
My God, my God full free,
Lamaȝabatanye,
Whar-to for-soke þou me
    In care?
And I did nevere ille
Þis dede for to go tille,
But be it at þi wille.
    A! me thristis sare.

(213–221)

The suffering, the sense of isolation and injustice so vividly expressed in the language and rhythms of Christ's cry are once more resolved in His complete acceptance of the will of God which He fulfills. The example that Christ enacts is, as earlier, one of humble and patient obedience even in the face of death. But His death does not come straight away. What follows instead are the reactions of Garcio, Pilate, Annas, and Caiphas to Christ's cries, shattering the mood of the moment as completely as they distort the appeals that Christ has made. Garcio's comment as he starts to fetch a drink for Christ, "I hope I schall holde þat I have hight"

(225) is the most pathetic indication of their complete ignorance of the promise of salvation which Christ has made and has just fulfilled; similarly their complete failure to understand the example Christ presents to them is made unmistakable as Garcio, offering the drink of "aysel and galle" to Christ, mockingly adopts a posture of social humility and selflessness toward the example of true humility and supreme selflessness:

> Nowe, swete sir, youre wille yf it ware,
> A draughte here of drinke have I dreste
> To spede for no spence þat ȝe spare.
>
> (239–241)

Recalling the opening scene of the play where the truth of the Crucifixion had similarly been inverted, this brief episode serves to make more urgent and memorable the lessons the play has so far presented to its audience. It also, with a dramatic sureness that has too often been denied the Corpus Christi dramatists, allows for a lessening of the emotional pitch of the play so that the moment of Christ's death can achieve its full power to move the audience.

The moment of Christ's death is delicately handled by the York dramatist. The Gospel accounts all describe Christ crying to God in a loud voice, but here His words are quiet and awesome:

> Nowe, fadir þat formed alle in fere,
> To thy moste myght make I my mone.
> Þi wille have I wroughte in þis wone;
> Þus ragged and rente on þis roode;
> Þus doulfully to dede have þei done.
> Forgiffe þame be grace þat is goode:
> Þai ne wote noȝt what it was.
> My fadir, here my bone,
> For nowe all thyng is done.

My spirite to þee right sone
Comende I in manus tuas.

(248–260)

The displacement of the prayer of forgiveness is particularly effective, coming as is does after the audience has witnessed anew the taunting of Christ by His enemies. Moreover, the words of the prayer themselves seem to be significant: the *Northern Passion* follows the Vulgate—"Bot, fader, forgif þam þaire gilt . . . ffor whi þai wate noght what þai do"[56]—but in the play Christ prays for those who "ne wote noȝt what it was." The variation is doubtless in part due to the exigency of the stanza's rhyme scheme, but it does precisely focus that inability to see and understand the significance of the Crucifixion which has just been demonstrated. As a whole, the prayer looks even further back, to Christ's earlier address from the cross and to Mary's laments which are verbally echoed, even to the moment of Creation at which the design which Christ here fulfills was first willed by God.

The Latin of Christ's last words adds to the somberness of the moment of His death—but the audience is not allowed to dwell on the moment. In a daring touch, Mary at first fails to recognize that these words were Christ's last:

Now dere sone, Jesus so iente,
Sen my harte is hevy as leede,
O worde wolde I witte or þou wente.
Allas! nowe my dere sone is dede,
Full rewfully refte is my rede,
Allas! for my darlyng so dere.

(261–266)

As Mary approaches the cross only to find her son dead, the naturalness of her words to Christ (emphasized by the homely simile) and of her response to His death seem to accommodate the unearthly moment of Christ's death to the experience of the audience.

John and Mary Cleophas gently lead the Virgin away from

the cross, and the play seems to come to an end. But with a sudden shift of mood, those left on the stage rudely reassert themselves. For Caiphas, now Christ is dead there remain only a few technical details to be taken care of so that they can celebrate their sabbath day, and Pilate summarily sends his "knights" off to take care of "ȝone harlottis" (286). Whatever suggestions there may have been earlier in the play that Pilate might come to learn the true significance of Christ's Passion are here crushed as the threat to his authority seems to have been removed. He hands Longeus a spear and dispatches him with explicit instructions: "In Jesu side / Schoffe it þis tyde" (296–297). Longeus' physical blindness is imaged in his silent cooperation with Pilate, but as he pierces Christ's side his blindness is cured and Pilate's blindness is exposed. He greets the restoration of his sight with an exultant prayer of praise:

> O! maker unmade, full of myght,
> O! Jesu so jentile and jente
> Þat sodenly has lente me my sight,
> Lorde, lovyng to þe be it lente.
> On rode arte þou ragged and rente
> Mankynde for to mende of his mys,
> Full spitously spilte is and spente
> Thi bloode, lorde, to bring us to blis
>   full free.
> A! mercy my socoure,
> Mercy my treasoure,
> Mercy my savioure,
>   Þi mercy be markid in me.
>
> (300–312)

In the figure of Longeus the play presents the most compact and compelling enactment of its controlling action as through Christ's mercy he is brought to "se þer þe soth in his sight."[57] He is, as the last line of his prayer makes clear, both a witness to and an enactment of the redemptive nature of Christ's Passion which his words so fully encompass and so richly celebrate. His plea for mercy is also the fulfillment within the play of the devotional impulse behind the representation of Christ's suffering.

The heightened tone of celebration is sustained in the words of the Centurion that follow the healing of Longeus:

> O! wondirfull werkar, i-wis,
> Þis weedir is waxen full wan,
> Trewe token I trowe þat it is
> Þat mercy is mente unto man.
> Full clerly consayve þus I can
> No cause in this corse couthe þei knowe,
> Ȝitt doulfully þei demyd hym þan
> To lose þus his liffe be þer lawe
>   No riȝte.
> Trewly I saie
> Goddis sone verraye
> Was he þis daye
>   Þat doulfully to dede þus is diȝt.
>
> (313–325)

Like Longeus before him, the Centurion here bears joyful witness to the truth of the Crucifixion, which he comes to see, paradoxically and miraculously, only in the darkness which he describes descending upon the scene. The cosmic manifestation of the effects of Christ's death generalizes what has been seen in more personal ways in the healing of Longeus—"þat mercy is mente unto man"—but in the Centurion's assertion of the truth which he discovers there is a similar balance between personal testimony and public statement. Together these prayers through explicit reference and verbal echoings seem to recall all aspects of the play's action as it has so far developed, restating them in the mood of prayerful rejoicing to which they have inevitably led and resolving them in the quiet statement of the simplest but most profound truth of all, that "Goddis sone verray / Was he þis day / þat doulfully to dede þus is diȝt." Holding together in a single perception an awareness of Christ's divinity and His humanity, His triumph and His suffering, the Centurion's words articulate for all men the truth to which contemplation of Christ leads.

What follows this climactic moment might seem to be a disappointing rounding off of the narrative accounts of the death of Christ, as Joseph and Nichodemus, with Pilate's ungrudging but self-serving permission, remove Christ's body from the cross and prepare it for burial. But in concluding the plot of the play, this episode provides one further enactment of the play's central action, one that is crucial to the play's final effectiveness. As they remove the body from the cross, Joseph and Nichodemus rehearse what the play has presented to its audience:

Jos: All mankynde may marke in his mynde
To see here þis sorowfull sight;
No falsnesse in hym couthe þei fynde
Þat doulfully to dede þus is dight.
Nicho: He was a full worthy wight
Nowe blemysght and bolned with bloode.
Jos: Ȝa, for þat he maistered his myght,
Full falsely þei fellid þat foode
I wene,
Bothe bakke and side,
His woundes wide;
For-þi þis tyde
Take we hym doune us betwene.
(365–377)

While dialogue of some kind is needed to accompany the possibly awkward stage business, the dramatist takes full advantage of the necessity to impress upon the audience once again the full significance of what they have seen. The lyrical emphasis of the play's action is also sustained as Joseph and Nichodemus, preparing Christ's body for burial, intimately and compassionately detail the marks of Christ's suffering. As they do so they themselves are brought to an understanding of the significance of that suffering which controls their grief. Their awareness is dramatically voiced in their prayers of humble faith in Christ:

Nicho: Nowe saviour of me and of moo,
Þou kepe us in clennesse ilkone.
Jos: To thy mercy nowe make I my moone
As saviour be see and be sande.
Þou gyde me þat my griffe be al gone
With lele liffe to lenge in þis lande
And esse.
(393–399)

But even as these prayers work dramatically to characterize Joseph and Nichodemus, they also work rhetorically to direct the involvement of the audience in the action of the play to the same attitude. The highly rhetorical style and complex appeals of the earlier movements of the play now give way to the simplicity of these prayers and the very human recollection of Nichodemus' which is in some ways the play's most moving, certainly its most accessible, statement:

Nicho: He highte me full hendely to be his
A nyght whan I neghed hym full nere:
Have mynde, lorde, and mende me of mys
For done is oure dedis full dere
Þis tyde.
(408–412)

At the very end of the play, Joseph turns to the audience whom the play has most importantly been leading to an understanding of the truth demonstrated in Christ's Crucifixion. Now Joseph's benediction offers a final clarification of that significance and urges upon them the penitent faith which he has exemplified and to which the play as a whole has encouraged them:

Þis lorde so goode
Þat schedde his bloode,
He mende youre moode,
    And buske on þis blis for to bide.

(413–416)

The blessing which Joseph offers the audience is a figure of that which Christ through His death offers them.

IV

Poetry and Fulfillment

The Narrative Modes

For more than one hundred years the Corpus Christi plays were presented every year at York. There would be little variation from one year to the next. A speech might be added or a scene reworked. Every now and again there would be a new play—more probably a reworking of an old play than a new play dealing with a new episode. Sometimes a new guild might present one of the plays. And occasionally a play might be dropped, like the play of the Burial of Mary which the linen weavers were relieved of presenting because it had been drawing some unseemly laughter from the audience.[1] Like the pageant-wagons, the plays were brought out every year, touched up perhaps, but never markedly altered. The audiences that came to the plays year after year were not looking for originality or surprises. They came no doubt partly because the plays had the familiarity of ritual, but they also came because the story the plays told was such a good story, varied in incident and mood, entertaining as well as uplifting. This story showed them heaven and hell, God and devils. It also showed them their own place in this magnificent scheme. Even much more skeptical modern audiences have found the plays worth going back to.

The story told by the plays was the most familiar of all. Versions of it could be found everywhere—in the services of the church, in sermons, in poems and treatises for those who could read, in painted murals and stained glass windows for those who could not. Probably no aspect of the Corpus Christi plays has been more thoroughly investigated than the relationship between its version of the Christian story and the versions found in earlier and contemporary analogues. Scholars have been looking for a long time if not for direct sources of the plays at least for related versions that might have determined the principles of selection and arrangement of episodes that have produced the plot, the narrative structure of the plays.[2] In the distance, we know, was the liturgy of the church in which the understanding of the Christian story had been formed, and the liturgical plays whose influence can still be seen in the structure of some of the episodes and in some of the details of representation. Closer to the plays are pictorial cycles which seem to have exercised both a general and a local influence, and vernacular poems like the *Northern Passion* which may well have been used directly by the playwrights as they composed or revised their plays. But whatever analogues have been tested, none have proved substantially or coherently close enough to the English plays to be considered as definitive sources or even determining influences. As in most respects, the Corpus Christi playwrights were not slavish in their handling of the narrative but eclectic and independent. Even the familiarity of the story they dramatized, once felt to be an obstacle, can be seen as a resource.

My purpose in turning to examine the narrative aspects of the York plays is not to rehearse these theories about narrative principles, and certainly not to offer any new potential sources. I am not concerned with precedents; I am concerned with how the narrative is handled in the plays as we have them. The emphasis on sources in previous studies has tended to emphasize the structural aspects of the narrative—that is, the ways in which the story is told within the plays. My starting point is with the narrative as a rhetorical aspect of the drama—that is, the ways in which the audience is included within the story the plays tell. The beginning, middle, and end of the plot of the plays are the beginning, middle, and end of time itself; the audience and their present moment are necessarily conceived of as part of the process articulated in the plot, and my interest is in how the audience is made aware of its involvement, and to what end. One way has already been suggested: in bringing out the exemplary significance of the episodes dramatized, the playwrights try to make the audience aware of the immediate relevance of the biblical stories. This is the kind of appeal the Chester Expositor refers to when he explains that

> This storye all if we shold fong
> to playe this moneth it were to longe;
> Wherfore most frutefull there amonge
> we taken, as shall be sene.[3]

But the rhetorical appeal of the narrative is more varied and thoroughgoing than this direct homiletic thrust; we will have to look for it in the details of presentation as well as in the ordering of the cycle as a whole.

My focus in this chapter is more inclusive than that of previous chapters. In examining the homiletic and lyric aspects of the York plays, I could pay attention initially to moments when the action seems to pause to allow moments of exposition or celebration. Here our concern will be the dynamic movement of the plot, a movement which incorporates those static moments to direct them and give them their effectiveness. This combination of static and dynamic modes is not unique to the Corpus Christi plays; it could be paralleled, for instance, in the narrative poems that lie closely behind the drama. But in one crucial respect, the plays are different: they take place in time before an audience that experiences the passing of time as they watch the plays. Tom Driver has usefully stressed this dimension of drama:

> Narrative, taken alone, is certainly not a peculiar attribute of drama. It belongs equally to the romance, to

> the novel, or to narrative poetry. Drama, however, is distinguished from these literary forms by its special, complex relationship to the reality we call time. As a *narrative* art, along with the others just mentioned, it addresses itself to the telling of events which take place in the past, present, or future; and by its use of language it may refer consciously to the phenomenon of passing time. But as a *performing* art, along with music and the dance, it has its very existence in time. The fully realized drama is itself a temporal act.[4]

As Driver goes on to explain, the fact that the drama does use time "as a constituent factor in its performance" means that we must conceive of plays in the theater. In this respect, my examination of the narrative of the York plays is limited: my concern is not primarily with the staging of the plays and, more crucially, we know so very little about how the plays were staged. Were the plays all presented in any given year? Were they presented sequentially? Did the audience experience the plays as an unbroken and coherent process taking place in time? We do not know the answers to these questions, and that uncertainty should be borne in mind. However, the plays do present a narrative that allows us to see how the playwrights thought of the connections among the episodes, and the sense of time and process embodied in that narrative can be recognized in almost every moment of the plays. Moreover, the texts of the plays allow us clearly to imagine the ways in which the historical time of the plays relates to the actual time of the audience. In examining those ways I am pointing to a potential of the drama which performance could make real.

Although we can no longer be certain that the York plays were ever performed processionally, the processional origins of the plays are still readily apparent. The cycle consists of a large number of independent scenes, marked off from each other usually by devices such as a prologue and a benediction, and following one after another. What is the connection among these scenes? What is the point of the sequence? What relationship do the scenes and the sequence have to the audience? I have asked these questions from the audience's point of view rather than approaching them from a theoretical point of view in order to draw attention to the ways in which the dramatists' understanding of the significance of the events they present has been communicated. The answers, however, will be familiar: the events of the plays are relevant to the audience since the will of God that so clearly informs them informs all moments in time, most urgently the present time; and the events of the plays are part of a process which, incorporating the present, is ordained by God and moves toward its fulfillment in the Last Judgment when the world will cease to be and all men will be brought before God. The first part of the chapter deals with aspects of the narrative that remain for the most part implicit. As the plot unfolds, the audience is encouraged to discover analogies among the discrete scenes and between those scenes and its own present moment. The events of the plays are not just isolated events from the past, nor are they simply events from the past. In the ways they are presented, in their closeness to the audience's experience, and in patterns that link episodes, the audience recognizes that the time of Noah, the time of Christ, and its own time are somehow all related. The second part of the chapter examines how the plays make that "somehow" explicit. In part this is a matter of straightforward announcement. More pervasively—and persuasively—it is also a matter of the audience's experience as they watch. Events anticipated come to pass as the cycle progresses, thus offering experiential proof of the inexorable process of the working out of God's will, reassuring proof that the promises God makes to men will be fulfilled, and constant encouragement to believe in and place themselves in accordance with the will of God that directs all history toward the fulfillment of His will.

Examination of how the poetry works to further the narrative design of the York plays also calls for a different and more inclusive focus than that of the preceding two chapters. For the expository and lyric poetry of the plays there were distinct traditions available to the dramatists from which they could borrow forms and strategies. To be sure, vernacular narrative poems were also available to the dramatists, some, like the *Cursor Mundi,* with a scope larger than that of the plays, others, like the *Northern Passion* or the *Stanzaic Life of Christ*, with a smaller scope which they covered in greater detail. There is evidence that the playwrights were familiar with these poems,[5] and it seems plausible that they could find principles of structuring narrative in these poems. But the rhetorical strategies of the poems are for the most part those I have already discussed in looking at the homiletic and devotional modes of the drama; only the anachronisms of the descriptions and the interruptions of the narrative to address the listener (effects which are, as we shall see, paralleled in the plays) suggest any deliberate use of the narrative form for rhetorical purposes. Mainly because of the difference in form that makes time so present in the drama, we do not find in the narrative poems that constant interaction between the temporal aspects of the world of the poem and the world of the audience which characterizes the drama. That interaction is a matter of the language of the poetry rather than of styles and forms, and therein lies a further difference between the drama and the narrative poems. Where the language of the poems has to describe action (when it can), the language of the plays is freer to comment on the action which the audience sees. That freedom, however, could lead to emptiness and redundancy, to a weakening of the effects of the staged action rather than a heightening of them. That it all too rarely does in the York plays has been suggested by my examination of the moments in the plays where the action is most obtrusively interrupted for expository or devotional effects, and that sense can be confirmed by hearing how the language works to support the representation of events and create the connections among them and between them and the audience that watches and listens.

The Congruence of Events

The Travellers to Emmaus, convinced by Christ's appearance to them that His Passion has ended miraculously in His triumphant Resurrection, prepare to announce their great news:

ii Peregrinus: On every ilke side prestely prech it we:
Go we to Jerusaleme þes tydingis to telle;
Oure felawes fro fandyng nowe fraste we.
More of þis mater her may we not melle.
i Peregrinus: Here may we notte melle more at þis tyde
For prossesse of plaies þat precis in plight.
He bringe to his blisse on every ilke side
Þat sofferayne lorde þat moste is of myght.
(XL, 187–194)

Ostensibly, they leave to join their companions in Jerusalem—yet they rush off not because their news is so astounding or urgent but because there are still more plays to be presented before the day ends! No matter how smoothly the stanza-linking accomplishes the merging of the historical event with the actuality of performance, this is still a startling moment. For modern readers, used to self-enclosed and internally consistent fictions, it may well seem slightly comical. But we should see in it an economical and vivid way of pressing home the point of the play. The truth, the reality, of Christ's Resurrection is timeless. The audience has been allowed excitedly to exclaim with the Travellers, "We saugh hym in sight" (XL, 178–179); this shared experience justifies the unembarrassed coalescence of times in the benediction, and also is confirmed by it—that Christ *has* been seen risen from the dead is proof that He is "þat sofferayne lorde þat moste is of myght" who can bring all men to His bliss, specifically those "on every ilke side" of the stage.

Almost two-thirds of the York plays end with some such explicit acknowledgment of the audience from the stage. Seeing the plays, we would be more aware of the device than we are reading them, for only once or twice does it draw attention to itself quite as deliberately as at the end of the Peregrini play. Cain, marked by the Angel of God with the curse of exile, exits spitting the same curse on the people in the audience (VII, 136–138), and, more remarkably, as Pilate's soldiers lead Christ, stripped and bound, off to His Crucifixion, one of them approaches the audience—"If anye aske aftir us," he says to them, "Kenne þame to

Calvarie" (XXXIV, 349–350). Usually, however, one of the characters quietly turns to the audience to offer a prayer or a blessing for them, to urge them to join him in singing, or simply to bid them farewell. The effect of such moments is clearly analogous to that of the other direct appeals we have examined. By transcending the boundary between the stage and the audience they breach also the illusion that the events of the drama are *only* set in the past. They bring the "then" of historical time directly into the "now" of the time in which the audience watches the plays.

These brief addresses to the audience at the end of the plays are, however, more exclusively tied in to the narrative aspects of the drama than the expository or lyrical appeals. Their most obvious purpose is to bring an episode to its close (in almost every case they are immediately preceded by a speech that sets the actors moving off the stage). Yet they are not merely a functional device; by resolving the individual play in its predominant mood or focusing some basic significance of that play's action, their formulaic phrases are usually informed with a specific appropriateness. Moreover, they acquire also a more general significance from the action of the whole cycle by serving to image the ends of that action as they have been announced in the Creation play and will be fulfilled in the Last Judgment play—chaos or harmony, damnation or salvation. If, for example, the audience responds to the Israelite's exhortation, "*Cantemus domino*, to god a sange synge wee" (XI, 406), they share briefly in the joy that awaits all those saved by God. Or when Christ, having raised Lazarus from the dead, pauses to say "ȝe þat have sene þis sight / My blissyng with ȝo be" (XXIV, 208–209), the people in the audience who *have* just seen the miracle enjoy for a moment the blessing of Christ that will be granted for eternity to those who believe truly in Him (cf. XXIV, 190–193).

As an aspect of the narrative of the drama, the endings of the plays work together with the addresses to the audience that begin so many of the plays not just to frame the episode but to confirm the present relevance of the historical scene. In the prologues, too, there is variety of effect. In some, a character speaks directly to the audience—notoriously the Herods and Pilates who threaten the audience in their noisy demands for silence, more subtly, as we have seen, John the Baptist who recreates his historical role as precursor of God in announcing to the audience the coming of Christ to Baptism. In other plays the opening speech is not directed at the audience but is spoken generally: the speeches of God are of this kind—He, with a notable consistency, never speaks directly to the audience, as if to confirm His essential sublimity. Although this device is an obvious way of beginning a play, we should not miss its potential for mediating between the world of the audience and the world of the play. At the start of the play in which Christ is led to Calvary, a soldier from Pilate's army appears leading the wounded Christ with His cross. The soldier's cries for order and room suggest that he is in the midst of the audience, and his complaint that his colleagues have let him down by not appearing to help him suggests that he is on his own (XXXIV, 29–31). His noisy opening speech, then, comes directly to the audience, which is briefly cast in the role of the crowd on the way to Calvary:

> Therfore I comaunde you on every ilke a side
> Uppon payne of enprisonment þat noman appere
> To suppowle þis traytoure, be tyme ne be tyde—
> Noght one of þis prees;
> Nor noght ones so hardy for to enquere.
> But helpe me holly, all þat are here
> Þis kaitiffe care to encrees.
>
> (XXXIV, 9–15)

The two demands should arouse the same response from the audience—to defy the soldier. Yet defiance of the first demand draws them into the play to go to the aid of Christ, defiance of the second makes them withdraw from helping the soldier. The presence of the audience and their involvement on the one hand, and on the other their actual separation from the stage and the play are both drawn upon to invest the historical moment with a present reality.

Direct acknowledgment of the audience, whether within the play or in the speeches which begin and end it, is only one of the ways in which the dramatists bring the scenes from biblical history within the audience's experience. J. W. Robinson has nicely described such direct address of the audience as "the supreme anachronism of a kind of drama that is regularly anachronistic,"[6] acknowledging that throughout the cycles, scenes from the past are presented as if they were contemporary. Consistently, the fifteenth-century audience is encouraged to recognize itself and its world in the scenes they see acted out. Early critics of the drama saw such anachronism as a sign of the naivete of the dramatists and their audience; now we recognize it as a frequently purposeful and often imaginatively handled feature of the drama's narrative.

It is easy to make too much of the fact that in the York plays, for example, Moses tends "the bisshoppe Jetro schepe" (XI, 95), that Pilate speaks "in Parlament playne" (XXXII, 33) or tries to bribe his soldiers to keep the news of the Resurrection to themselves by offering them "a thousande pounde" (XXXVIII, 427–428). V. A. Kolve's comment is well taken: "Much of the anachronism and anglicisation requires little explanation: it furnished convenient ways of talking, it saved the trouble of long, complicated expositions of foreign terms and institutions, and it filled some very considerable gaps in knowledge."[7] This kind of casual anachronism is found in narrative poems and pictorial representations as well. Yet the anachronism of the Corpus Christi plays does seem peculiarly strategic. In part it furthers the expository impulse by aiding the understanding and application of the lessons of the biblical stories; in part, too, it is fostered by the meditative function of the plays which seeks to make the scenes as vivid as possible. But so pervasive is it that it is most appropriately discussed as an aspect of the narrative, as indicating a sense of the nature of history and of time that sees history and the present as inseparable.

To some extent, the drama's way of making past events contemporary is a matter of staging. Costumes, for example, as Glynne Wickham has documented,[8] were frequently contemporary: the Doctors in the York play of Christ before the

Doctors intimidate Joseph because of their "furres fyne" (XX, 232). But supporting such effects and giving them their point is the anachronism of the language. I have mentioned already the general effect of the use of the vernacular. When Herod rants in the liturgical plays it is in scholarly Latin; in the York plays he curses in broad Yorkshire colloquialisms or postures in what to a northerner would be the effete French of the court. In the popular drama, even God and the Angels speak to the audience in its own language.

Often in these plays it takes no more than a quick touch to allow the audience to recognize the biblical scenes as familiar and current. We have seen the stable at the Nativity as a bad example of the Tile-thatchers' craft, Cain and Abel as men called upon to pay tithes, Joseph as the fifteenth-century *mal marié*. To these we could add the effect of substituting pestilence—so devastatingly common in the audience's time—for the Biblical death of the first-born as the tenth plague visited upon the Egyptians (XI, 345–348); or the delightful moment when the Travellers to Emmaus invite the risen Christ to enter the "castell" with fifteenth-century courtesies (XL, 141, 151).

There are other scenes in the plays, however, some extended, when the dramatic action and the staging and poetry are particularly noticeable for their contemporaneity. The Trial scenes, it has often been pointed out, take place in a setting that thoroughly imitates the life of the castles and courts of late medieval England; the language of these plays is full of popular oaths and local terms, its rhythms are those of prosaic speech, the images it helps create are of scheming "bishops," powerful "Dukes" and sadistic "chevaliers."[9]

The primary objects of the satire in these plays are the figures of worldly power, Pilate, who "busses" his wife with ridiculous ostentation, Annas and Caiphas made vicious by their allegiance to their own ecclesiastical law, and Herod. This is how Herod appears:

> Pes, ye brothellis and browlys in þis broydenesse in
> brased,
> And frekis þat are frendely your freykenesse to frayne,

Youre tounges fro tretyng of trifillis be trased,
Or þis brande þat is bright schall breste in youre brayne.
(XXXI, 1–4)

Herod tries to be the mighty lord, but everything in his speech undercuts him. In its vigorous alliteration and syllabic excess his speech aligns him unmistakably with Pilate and Caiphas of the preceding plays and, through the persistent stylistic paradigm I have elsewhere described, with Satan. This irony is given point—almost an "objective correlative"—in the sword Herod brandishes, which recalls his earlier role in the drama as the ruler responsible for the slaughter of the Innocents, setting up a telling analogy between that cruel but ultimately futile act and the one he now prepares to perform as judge of Christ. But Herod is not just the enemy of Christ. To the audience he is more familiar:

Dragons þat are dredfull schall derke in þer denne
In wrathe when we writhe, or in wrathenesse ar wapped,
Agaynste jeauntis on-gentill have we joined with ingendis,
And swannys þat are swymmyng to oure swetnes schall
 be suapped,
And joged doune þer jolynes oure gentries engenderand;
Who so repreve oure estate we schall choppe þam
 in cheynes.
All renkkis þat are renand to us schall be reverande.
(XXXI, 11–17)

For all his claims to be a giant-killer and dragon-slayer, Herod betrays himself as an effete and tyrannical overlord who cares more for his swans than his tenants. The blustering and parading are allowed to go on just long enough to backfire and set Herod up as a contemporary focus of antipathy guaranteed to elicit from the audience the angry derision which his Scriptural actions and his role in this drama demand and justify.

Elsewhere, the audience's recognition of Biblical characters and events is directed to more positive ends. In the first of the Noah plays, for example, God brings to Noah His warning that the world will be destroyed by the flood and His instructions on how Noah is to build the ark in which he will be saved. Rosemary Woolf has wondered why these instructions are given in such detail in the play and has suggested that it is because "the measurements and structure of the ark were replete with symbolic meaning"[10] since the ark was considered a type of the cross, of the church, or of man. But the real effect of these instructions seems more available and more enjoyable. They are difficult, overly technical instructions, even no doubt to a member of the Shipwrights' guild responsible for staging this play. And while the actor playing Noah probably was a member of this guild, Noah himself is not—he knows nothing about "shippe-craft" (VIII, 67). It is his ignorance which forces God into becoming an instant expert shipbuilder. The relationship between God and Noah on which the salvation of the world depends is briefly remade as the relationship between the master and his apprentice, with the only unfamiliar element being that this five-hundred-year-old apprentice learns with astonishing—miraculous—speed:

> To hewe þis burde I will be-gynne
> But firste I wille lygge on my lyne;
> Now bud it be alle in like thynne
> So put it nowthyr twynne or twyne.
> Þus sall I iune it with a gynn
> And sadly sette it with symonde fyne.
> Þus sall y wyrke it both more and myne
> Thurgh techyng of god maister myne.
>
> (VIII, 97–104)

Using the most unlikely material for his poetry, the dramatist, no doubt to the delight of his audience, has here created a perfect fusion between the sublime event of salvation history and fifteenth-century labor relations: the servant of God is the sharp apprentice, being saved a matter of learning a craft well. "He þat to me þis crafte has kende / He wysshe us with his worthy wille," Noah aptly prays at the end of the play (VIII, 150–151).

Less precisely, but no less pointedly, the interpenetration

of historical and contemporary time is sustained in the following play where the flood and the salvation of Noah and his family are staged. There Noah has trouble with his wife. She refuses to go into the ark; they fight, the dialogue keeping pace with the physical action. "You might have told me where you were going when you kept leaving me sitting at home," she complains:

> *Noah:* Dame, þou holde me excused of itt—
> It was goddis wille with-owten doutte.
> *Uxor:* What? wenys þou so for to go qwitte?
> Nay, be my trouthe, þou getis a clowte.
> *Noah:* I pray þe, dame, be stille.
> Thus god wolde have it wrought.
> *Uxor:* Thow shulde have witte my wille . . .
> (IX, 117–123)

The whole exchange is lively and funny—but not without point. What the audience is asked to witness is a very familiar scene in which the wife has the upper hand. Antediluvian history is seen as a chaotic (and sinful) upsetting of prescribed (if not normal) relationships in a fifteenth-century English family.[11] The "synne . . . reynand so ryffe" that causes God to regret having made "outhir man or wiffe" (VIII, 14, 16) is as timeless as the teaching and the "craft" that save the world.

The contemporary coloring of the Noah plays has an obvious homiletic impulse behind it, in that it makes the examples offered by the play more directly available to the audience. But that it is not just homiletic, that it involves a more basic conception of the nature of the event as event, is suggested by the fact that at the same time as resonances to the poetry enable the audience to associate the action of the Flood play with their own experience, other resonances encourage them to associate it with other events staged in the cycle. Just three plays earlier, husband and wife had quarreled—the most vivid sign of the complete disruption brought about by Adam and Eve's disobedience. "Allas! what womans witte was light!" Adam had complained (VI,

133). Eve had granted him this, but countered: "Mans maistrie shulde have bene more / agayns þe gilte" (VI, 137–138). "But you would never have listened to me," Adam had insisted:

> Thurgh ille counsaille þus casten ar we / in bittir bale.
> Nowe god late never man aftir me / triste woman tale.
> For certis me rewes fulle sare
> That evere I shulde lerne at þi lare.
> Thy counsaille has casten me in care / þat þou me kende.
> *Eve:* Be stille, Adam, and nemen it na mare / it may not mende.
>
> (VI, 147–156)

In Noah and his family, things *have* begun to mend: Noah asserts his "maistrie" and now it is Noah's wife, not Adam, who complains "Allas! þat I þis lare shuld lere" (IX, 105) as she is taken forcibly into the Ark. It will take another marriage, with the wife, Mary, showing an exemplary obedience, to mend things completely.

By the end of the play of the Flood, when familial concord has been re-established and the ark has firmly settled on "þe hillis of hermonye" (IX, 264), correspondences between this and other plays have become paramount. Urging his family to begin "Gud lewyn . . . so þat we greve oure god nomore" (IX, 273–274), Noah recalls the words in which God had at the start of the previous play announced His intention to destroy the world:

> He was greved in degre
> And gretely moved in mynde
> For synne, as men may see:
> *Dum dixit penitet me.*
> Full sore for-thynkyng was he
> That evere he made mankynde.
>
> (IX, 275–280)

Now, Noah explains, God has given them His covenant that the world will never again be destroyed by water—the rainbow—though he quickly adds that this covenant does not mean that the "worldis empire" (IX, 297) will endure for ever: "For it sall ones be waste with fyre / And never worþe to worlde agayne" (IX, 301–302). Both this explanation (though it is given to Noah, it is based on the second Epistle of Peter, 3:3–7) and the echo of God's words look forward to the play of the Last Judgment, the one explicitly, the other indirectly. As God prepares to destroy the world for the second time, He will again repent the Creation because man has proved so sinful, and His words then will be recognized as a recapitulation of those with which He had announced the first destruction of the world (cf. XLVIII, 1–8, 57–64; VIII, 1–4, 13–24).

Furthermore, God's words at the start of the Noah play had themselves looked backwards, beyond the creation of Adam and Eve whom He recalls having instructed to "waxe and multiplye / To fulfille þis worlde withowtyn striffe" (VIII, 11–12), to the original Creation. What God has in mind as He prepares to send the flood is a recapitulation of His first Creation: "wirke þis werke I will al newe" (VIII, 24). Through Noah's obedience, he and his family come to participate in this re-Creation as Adam and Eve had participated in the first. At the end of the play of the Flood, Noah's sons ask how they are to live since they are the only ones left alive on the earth, and Noah tells them:

Sones, with youre wiffes ȝe salle be stedde
And multyplye youre seede salle ȝe.
Ȝoure barnes sall ilkon othir wedde
And worshippe god in gud degre;
Beestes and foules sall forthe be bredde
And so a worlde begynne to bee.

(IX, 311–316)

Noah, as *imitator Dei,* gives the same instructions to his family that God had given to Adam and Eve (cf. III, 16, 24, 66; IV, 50–52, 60–65, VIII, 9–12). But the effects of man's fall are not yet to be repaired completely. For their failure to do God's will, Adam and Eve had been told that they would "swete and swynke / And travayle for . . . fode" (V, 161–162), and the descendants of Noah inherit this painful duty:

> Nowe travaylle salle ȝe taste
> To wynne you brede & wyne,
> For alle þis worlde is waste.
>
> (IX, 317–319)

In one sense, the most obvious, Noah means only that since the world has been devastated by the flood his sons will have to cultivate the earth for physical sustenance. However, the phrase "brede and wyne" reaches beyond this meaning and this moment in the play to the sacrament of the Eucharist, the body and blood of Christ which *will* repair the effects of the Fall, the sacrament which will provide spiritual sustenance for all men, most meaningfully at this point to the people in the audience who are celebrating Corpus Christi by their attendance at the plays. In their constant movement backwards and forwards, the final words of the play transcend the play's narrative discreteness to link it to other events in the cycle's plot, to the audience's present moment, and to the action of God for the salvation of man inherent in them all, the action which will end as this play ends, "in goddis blissyng" (IX, 322).

This examination of the language of the York Noah plays has brought us to an issue familiar to students of the Corpus Christi drama, the sense of time to which the plays bear witness. To modern readers, it is a strangely fluid sense of time that allows the kind of resonances which, as in the Noah plays, transcend the narrative and fictive autonomy of the representation of an event from the past. It is, we now well know, the medieval Christian understanding of time which sees time as an artifact of God through which He, in whom there is no distinction of times, makes Himself known to man. As the manifestation of the eternal will of God, events are not self-sufficient moments in a linear process. They are multivocal. They do have a historical actuality (the Flood did take place) and they are part of a process moving forward in time (in history, the Flood did take place after the fall of man and before the Incarnation), though chronology does not imply causality since the cause of events lies outside time, in God. But earthly events are most importantly recognized as being connected "vertically" with God and His eternal order which encompasses and informs them all. And since every moment expresses the eternal, unchanging will of God, every moment is connected analogically with every other moment. Specifically, the past is not just past: it contains the future and is thus eternally present, imbued with a timeless significance.[12]

Precisely how this understanding of the past and of temporal reality has influenced the Corpus Christi drama and is manifested in the plays is a matter of some debate among critics. In the rest of this section I will be examining some of the ways in which the structure of the drama reflects it, the ways in which the interpenetration of all moments is manifested in correspondences established among events in the cycle. But we cannot separate this internal aspect of the drama from those aspects of the narrative that make the events dramatized familiar and contemporary. Both are prompted by the dramatists' understanding of the narrative and of time. The anachronism that extends the situations in the drama to the audience is the rhetorical aspect of those resonances which associate events within the cycle. The York Noah plays, for example, fully support V. A. Kolve's claim that in the Corpus Christi drama, "Every moment is charged with memories of the past and expectations of the future, thereby we discover unity in a drama that tells several stories, each separate and apparently discontinuous, which span all human time."[13] But they also encourage us to see that the audience and their present moment are themselves brought into the patterns and connections that link those moments from the past which the drama recreates in its perpetual present. The "unity" is not just aesthetic; it involves the audience as also encompassed by the will of God which orders human time.[14]

In order to account for the connections between the various episodes of the Corpus Christi cycles, Kolve, like many other commentators, adduces the long tradition of typological exegesis of the Scriptures. Following the example of Christ who had Himself claimed that the events of the Old Testament history were signs of the Incarnation which were now fulfilled, learned commentary on the Bible had developed a comprehensive set of detailed correspondences between characters and events recorded in the Old Testament, and those recorded in the New. These correspondences are the stuff of typology: a "type" is "a person, thing, or an action, having its own independent and absolute existence, but at the same time intended by God to prefigure a person, thing, or action."[15] Thus an elaborate system of echoes and anticipations, of prefigurations and fulfillments links the events of Biblical history, focused on the figure of Christ who is the fulfillment of all types.

There is no need to rehearse here the history of typological interpretation of the Scriptures or to examine its details. At issue is the influence of the tradition on the Corpus Christi drama's representation of Biblical events and on the poetry of the plays. Some large claims have been made for the extent of this influence. Elizabeth Salter, for example, noting that recent studies of the drama have made extensive use of typology, has said: "The plays demand such attention since their very principles of selection are typological. The basic structure of the cycles is dictated by the fulfillment of the events, characters, and words of the Old Testament in those of the New, and the promise of ultimate fulfillment beyond Judgment Day."[16] But had typology been the controlling concern that this comment suggests, the cycles would probably have looked very different in structure. Typologically determined models existed in pictorial art, in Latin and vernacular treatises, and even, it seems, in pageant processions.[17] They are constructed to juxtapose the New Testament episode against its Old Testament type—and we nowhere find this patterning in the popular drama. To be sure, the dramatists show themselves aware of the terms of typological exegesis, and occasionally force typological connections on the audience's attention, as when the Chester Expositor explains Melchisedech's offering of the bread and wine to Abraham as a "signification" of the Eucharist.[18] But especially in the York plays, there is very little trace of typological significance. If it at any point influenced the selection of episodes, it does not seem to be part of the meaning of the narrative that the dramatists communicate to their audience. As the next section of this chapter will show, the York dramatists are primarily concerned with the process of events rather than their patterns, and consistently organize events to take advantage of their sequentiality rather than their typological significance. That time and history are ordained by God is shown through the motif of prophecy and fulfillment rather than that of figures and their fulfillment.[19]

While we do not find a rigid insistence on typological meaning in the York plays, there are nonetheless resonances to the representations (they are no more systematic than that) which, perhaps reflecting traditional—even inevitable—typological interpretation, work to allow the audience to discover reconciling analogies among the various scenes. Noah is first of all Noah the patriarch who is saved because he fulfills God's will. But as one through whom mankind is saved, Noah does anticipate Christ, and in his words the audience is alerted to the connection. In a digression unique to the York plays, Noah recounts how Lamech his father prayed to God that "he to hym a sone shulde sende," and how "at þe laste þer come from heven / Slyke hettyng þat hym mekill amende" (IX, 20–22); how Noah was born in answer to his prayer and how Lamech rejoiced—"Loo, he saide, þis ilke is he / That shalle be comforte to mankynne." (IX, 31–32). We think perhaps first of Abraham and Isaac; but phrases such as "mekill amende" and "comforte to mankynde" are used so frequently with reference to Christ that the anticipation of Christ in Noah would seem to be deliberate.

The most extensive reflection of typology in the York plays is in the Abraham and Isaac play. Again, the primary concern is *not* typological: having tested Abraham's obedience, God promises that from the seed of his son will come the Savior, and the play ends with Abraham arranging the marriage of Isaac through which the promise is to be accomplished. But the types found in this event were particularly familiar. John Mirk, for instance, confidently explains that "by Abraham ȝe schull undyrstonde þe Fadyr of Heven, and by Isaac his sonne Ihesu Christ. Þe whech he sparyd not for no love þat he had to hym."[20] And in the York plays, correspondences between the sacrifice of Isaac and the Passion of Christ are undeniable. Some of them are conveyed by the staging: an ass is used to carry the wood as Abraham and Isaac journey to the place of sacrifice, as an ass will later be used to carry Christ into Jerusalem; Isaac, like Christ after him, discards the ass and carries the wood on his back as Christ will later carry His cross; and Isaac lies down on the altar of his own sacrifice as Christ will lie down on the cross. Moreover, Isaac would be *seen* to be a young man "Thyrty ȝere and more sum dele" (X, 82). There are also precise correspondences in the language of the plays. Isaac learns that he is to be sacrificed, and immediately pledges his compliance with the will of God and his father: "And I sall noght grouche þer agayne / To wirke his wille I am wele payed / Sen it is his desire" (X, 191–193); in His agony, Christ will likewise say to His Father, "Be it worthely wrought / Even at thyne awne will / Evermore both myldely and still" (XXVIII, 60–62), and "Be it worthly wroght even at thyne awne will, / For, fadir, att þi bidding am I buxum and bayne" (XXVIII, 94–95). Isaac prays: "In worde, in werke, or any waye / That I have trespassed or oght mysdone / For-giffe me fadir" (X, 255–257); so Christ prays, "But Fadir, as þou wate wele / I mente nevere a-mys / In worde nor in werk / I never worthy was" (XXVIII, 53–54). Isaac trembles at the thought of his death: "My flessche for dede will be dredande . . . My flesshe waxis faynte for ferde" (X, 210, 270); and so does Christ: "My flessh is full dredand for drede . . . My flesshe is full ferde and fayne wolde defende" (XXVIII, 48, 105; cf. 123, 130).

At the climax of the Abraham and Isaac play, language and staging coincide to offer perhaps the most meaningful correspondence between the sacrifice of Isaac and the Crucifixion, one that emphasizes the difference between the events that is, paradoxically, so crucial to their relatedness. Isaac is spared; Christ is not. As the Angel of God stays Abraham's hand, he says:

> Sla noght thy sone, do hym no mysse;
> Take here a schepe thy offerand tyll
> Is sente þe fro the kyng of blisse.
>
> (X, 303–305)

The "ram" of Genesis has become a sheep. Abraham celebrates God's sending the sheep for sacrifice: "A, sone, thy bloode wolde he noght spill / Forthy this shepe thus has he sente" (X, 327–328; cf. 311–312, 315–320). Again, nothing insists on the type; but the moment is poignantly enriched by its reference to the iconographic symbol and verbal metaphor of Christ as the Lamb of God.

Between the two moments here brought together, other plays develop the motif of sacrifice focused in the image of the lamb. The play of the Purification of Mary and the Presentation of Christ begins with the Prisbeter rehearsing the Law of Moses that requires a woman who has given birth to offer a lamb and two doves for sacrifice. He explains: "The lame is offeryd for Goddes honour / In sacrefyes all onely dight" (XLI, 45–46). If the woman is poor, he continues, then the Law asks only that she bring two doves. A few moments later, Mary and Joseph appear bringing their offering. Mary recalls the Law: "Both beest and fewll hus muste neydes have / As a lambe and ij dove byrdes also" (XLI, 236–237). But, she says, they have no lamb—what shall they do? Joseph tries to comfort her. The Law, he gently explains, makes exceptions for poor people like themselves. They need only two doves, and he has them "in a panyer, loo, / Reddy at hand" (XLI, 252–253). And then, in one of the most beautiful moments in all of the York plays, Joseph says:

> And yf we have not both in feer,
> The lame, the burd, as ryche men have,

Thynke that us muste present here
Oure babb Jesus, as we voutsave
    before Godes sight.
He is our lame, Mary, kare the not,
For riche and power none better soght;
Full well thowe have hym hither broght
    this our offerand dight.
He is the lame of God, I say,
That all our syns shall take away
    of this worlde here.
He is the lame of God verray
That muste hus fend frome all our fray,
Borne of thy womb all for our pay
    and for our chere.

(XLI, 254–269)

Reversing the substitution of the Isaac play, here the lamb is replaced by the human sacrifice. The metaphor and the reality momentarily fuse. The Crucifixion figuratively inheres in the moment of Christ's presentation.[21] Simeon's prophecy to Mary that "the sworde of sorro thy hart shal thyrll / Whan thowe shall se sothly thy son soffer yll" (XLI, 440–441) is thus well prepared for.

Before this prophecy and the type offered by the event are fulfilled, Christ, like Mary, will appear to fulfill the Law of Moses: "Of Moyses lawes here make I an ende / In som party, but noght in all" (XXVII, 25–26). These words are spoken at the Last Supper where, before Christ establishes the Sacrament which will perpetuate the redemptive action of His death, He also announces:

But þe lambe of Pasc þat here is spende,
Whilke Jewes uses grete and small,
Evere forward nowe I itt deffende
Fro cristis folke, what so befall.

(XXVII, 29–32)

The actual institution of the Eucharist is missing from York. In the *Ludus Coventriae* play, a lengthy exposition of Christ as the true Paschal lamb which His followers will thereafter eat precedes Christ's offering communion to the disciples.[22] In the Chester play, more simply, Christ explains that "the tyme is come / that signes and shadows be all done" and says:

> and here in presence of you all
> and other sacrifice beginne I shall,
> to bring mankynd out of his thrall,
> for helpe him nede I muste.[23]

At York the Bakers responsible for the Last Supper play owned a model of a lamb which was no doubt prominently displayed as Christ spoke.[24]

The parallels of language and staging that link the independent events of the Sacrifice of Isaac, the Presentation of Christ, the Last Supper, and the Crucifixion, suggest that for the dramatists the correspondences between the events were important as a way of encouraging the audience to look for continuity and coherence in what they saw. The associations created are not at all esoteric—the audience would be familiar with them from pictorial representations and from sermons. Moreover, for the most part verbal correspondences are made theatrically viable by visual correspondences established by stage properties and by the movements and gestures of the actors.[25] But the main reason for claiming correspondences such as those I have described as a relevant aspect of the narrative is that behind them lies a feature of the drama which is prominent and pervasive—the patterns to be discovered in the characterizations and language of the plays, and in the shaping of the various episodes.[26] We have discovered many of these patterns in the homiletic and lyric modes of the drama. In the exemplary mode, for example, repeated gestures and patterns of speech organize the characters of the drama into *imitatores Christi* or *imitatores diaboli.* While each of the characters takes part in a distinctive episode, Noah, Abraham, Isaac, Moses, and Christ are all linked analogically because the response they articulate to the commandment of God is one of obedience. Likewise, though Satan, Pharaoh, Herod, and Pilate all appear in different plays, they too are to be associated by the general similarities of their speech and actions. These general analogies provide a basis on which the dramatist can (it *is* an option) construct more precise and extensive parallels. Thus, as Rosemary Woolf has pointed out, when Pharaoh appears at the start of the Exodus play, a precise connection is established between him and the Satan of the later Harrowing of Hell play, "not merely by the extraordinary frequency with which he swears by the devil, but also by a small nexus of vocabulary which is conspicuously used in both plays: 'lads,' 'lurdans,' 'boyes' (as terms of contempt), 'gaudis' (to refer to the supposed trickery of the good), and 'maistris' (as a derogatory term for God's power)."[27] These verbal parallels are reinforced by the fact that general correspondences between the plays are established at every point. Woolf has pointed to "larger stylistic resemblances": the jeering tone Pharaoh adopts toward Moses is precisely that which Satan adopts toward Christ, and the speeches of Moses and later of Christ are alike in their "calm asseverations of power."[28] There are other connections: God's message to the Egyptians is to "lette my pepull passe" (XI, 124) as Christ's to Satan is to "lette my pepull passe" (XXXVII, 194). In both plays there are opposing parties, no doubt making similar use of the stage—the Egyptians and the Israelites, the Devils and the servants of God; in both, one character moves between them—Moses, then Christ; in both, one group is led safely from one area of the stage to another while the other group is sent tumbling to the floor. Both end in rejoicing as the people of God are saved. The connection between the Exodus and the Harrowing of Hell is, again, a traditional one; in the plays it will be recalled when the Shepherd at the birth of Christ recalls the prophecy that "The children of Israel shulde be made free / The force of the feende to felle in sighte." (XV, 30–31), and it will be fulfilled when Moses is led from Hell by Christ at the Harrowing.

We have similarly seen patterns of action established by the lyrical modes of the drama. Moments of epiphany are linked by exalted celebration: thus the Adoration at Christ's birth is, poignantly, linked to the Entry into Jerusalem. Lamentation, too, produces connections which are not casual. The central lament for the suffering of Christ is that of Mary before the cross in the play of the Death of Christ. On its own, it is moving. In context, it is more so, for it comes as the climax to a long series of laments which it recalls and focuses—the lament of Mary at the flight into Egypt (XVIII, 134–147), the laments of the mothers of the Innocents as their children are put to death (XIX, 210–233), and the laments of Mary and Martha over the death of their brother Lazarus (XXIV, 147–168). All those laments, though justified, had proved to be premature—Christ had been saved from Herod, Lazarus had been raised from the dead—and this cumulative experience comes to inform Mary's lament with a sense of expectation that increases its poignancy. This pattern culminates in the beautiful conversion of Mary's grief at her death and Assumption into heaven. As she dies, surrounded by the disciples who have been miraculously brought to her side, her handmaidens lament her death as she had lamented her son's:

> Allas for my lady þat lemed so light,
> That evere I leved in þis lede þus longe for to lende,
> That I on þis semely schulde se such a sight.
> (XLV, 96–98)

Finally, when she gives up her spirit to Christ as He had done His to God (XLV, 170–174), Christ sends His Angels to bring her to bliss, "with mirthe and with melody hir mode for to mende" (XLV, 178).

Although such patternings tell us as much about habits of dramatizing as about habits of mind, what lies behind them is the dramatists' inherited sense that the events of Scriptural history are both history and prophecy. However, the future these events contain is not only the future of the dramatic action; it is the present of the audience. And while the cumulative effect of the congruences and correspondences that link the events of the plays is to lend coherence to the variety of episodes, that coherence is not just aesthetic. It is the reflection of the coherence given to all temporal moments by the unchanging will of God—including the audience's moment to which the drama so clearly addresses itself.

From Promise to Fulfillment

Such analogical correspondences between events and between time past and time present as those I have pointed to in the York plays must have been more readily available for the original audience than they are for us, and a source of great richness in the experience of the plays. Yet even for that audience they remain a secondary consideration of the narrative. What is only suggested by the figural resonances of the events as they are dramatized is also openly stated; and what is openly stated is most immediately reinforced by the very "prossesse of plaies" which the audience watches passing before them. Everything the audience sees taking place is willed by God. Everything that is willed by God is seen to take place. In simple terms, these are the controlling aspects of the plot of the plays—and as such they come also to give the most comprehensive point to the interaction between audience and plays that this study has been concerned with. From the moment God announces Himself as "*Alpha et O*" at the start of the Creation play, the action He initiates is seen to move forward under His guidance until it culminates in the Last Judgment play with the announcement "Nowe is fulfillid all my for-þoght." The plot of the cycle, as an analogue of history itself, unfolds in time to reveal and fulfill the will of God. Drawing upon the audience's familiarity with the stories and upon the actualities of performance, it demonstrates that the process in which the audience (as the plays have reconfirmed) is involved, will end as God promises, in damnation or salvation. This is both the warning and the assurance the York plays extend to their audience.

To the extent that the definition of these aspects of the narrative is a matter of direct announcement, we have to consider again poetry in the expository style of the York plays. But clear and plain as they are, the passages of exposition that articulate the movement of the plot differ from those discussed earlier in their dynamic quality: they imitate the movement they summarize. The opening stanza of the Doctor's prologue to the Annunciation play provides a good example:

> Lord God, grete mervell es to mene
> Howe man was made with-outen mysse,
> And sette whare he sulde ever have bene
> With-outen bale, bidand in blisse;
> And howe he lost þat comforth clene
> And was putte oute fro paradys,
> And sithen what sorouse sor warre sene
> Sente un-to hym and to al his;
> And howe they lay lange space
>   In helle lokyn fro lyght,
> Tille god graunted þam grace
>   Of helpe, als he hadde hyght.
>
> (XII, 1–12)

This summary comes at a strategic moment in the plot to link Old and New Testament history. Yet as the verb tenses of the *cauda* tell us, the Redemption still to be acted out is seen as already accomplished. The summary thus includes a prophecy fulfilled.

What is important in this stanza, as it is in the cumulative experience of the cycle, is the process that lies behind the details of history. The stanza defines that process. It begins in God, and ends in the fulfillment of His promise to men. The divisions of the stanza mark off the stages of history—Creation, Fall, Redemption—all linked through the repeated "howe . . ." to the "mervell" of God here being celebrated. The parataxis that gives them equal prominence is countered first by the rhyme scheme of the *frons* which links the Creation and the Fall, then, although the change in rhythm and rhyme in the *cauda* announces the change the Redemption will bring, by the temporal conjunctions "sithen" and "tille" which link the Redemption with the Fall through the "grace" of God. Reaching back to the start of the cycle, and forward through the Incarnation to the Harrowing of Hell, the stanza offers an image of the action of the drama as a cumulative process initiated by God and moving toward its fulfillment. The stanza as a whole, like the scheme it describes, shapes and gives significance to the parts it contains.

In subsequent stanzas, as we have seen, the Doctor proceeds to recite and explain the most familiar Old Testament prophecies of the birth of Christ. One thing his words insist on is that "god þe fadir in heven / Ordand in erthe man kynde to mende" (XII, 17–18), that the Redemption of mankind announced through the prophets is ordained by God. Amos, Abraham, Isaac, and Isaiah, Hosea, Jacob—all are cited to witness to the mystery of the Incarnation as being the will of God. The last prophecy is not so much a prophecy as an announcement of the event the following play is to present, so that as the Doctor's words summarize the account of the Annunciation in Luke, they lead back into the events of the play:

To god his grace þan grayd
    To man in þis manere,
And how þe Aungell saide
Takes hede all þat will here.

(XII, 141–144)

Immediately Gabriel appears with his message for Mary. The event so precisely predicted is seen to come to pass. The validity of prophecy is theatrically confirmed and along with it, implicitly, God's ordination of events.

This prologue to the Annunciation play offers the audience two perspectives on the plot of the cycle. The opening stanza allows them an overview from which they can see the process that lies behind events; the rest of the speech brings them back into the time of the play and places them in the position of the people of God eagerly awaiting the Messiah. The first of these perspectives is the one the audience has enjoyed throughout the Old Testament sequence of plays. The second will be dramatically developed as the New Testament plays proceed. Since this latter aspect of the plot is more extensively and imaginatively developed, it will be my main concern in this section. But for its rhetorical coherence it depends upon patterns established in the Old Testament plays.

In trying to explain the selection of Old Testament events dramatized in the Corpus Christi cycles, V. A. Kolve refers to the *Reule of Crysten Religioun* by Reginald Pecock. Pecock defines three ways in which God revealed His Advent in the flesh: first, through direct announcement to the Fathers; second, by announcements through the prophets to the people at large; third, by signs and figures. Kolve comments: "It is chiefly this third form of announcement that is selected by the dramatists from the Old Testament material. The basic stuff of drama is action rather than words; the Corpus Christi cycles played announcements made in 'figures.' "[29] Kolve has ignored some important dramatic effects in the Old Testament plays in his search for a single principle to explain their presence. In the York plays at least, a variety of effects prepares the way for the central event of the Incarnation. One, to be sure, is the figural resonances that have been discussed which work primarily to set up Noah, Isaac, and Moses as agents of God's will in anticipation of Christ. But there is also direct announcement. To Adam and Eve, the Angel brings not only God's judgment but also His promise: they will, the Angel tells them, "lyff ay in sorowe, / Abide and be in bittir bale / tille he þe borowe" (VI, 38–40). The rainbow accompanying the salvation of Noah from the Flood is the sign of God's vigilance over men. At the end of the Abraham and Isaac play, an Angel brings to Abraham God's promise that from Isaac's seed will spring the Savior. The Old Testament plays at York also contain explicit assertions of God's control over events—and not just the Creation plays. Once the Fall of Man has been confirmed by Cain's sinfulness, God intervenes to direct events toward the salvation of His chosen people. He appears directly to Noah, asserting His control as He prepares to destroy and recreate the world, as He had at the first Creation. Although in the Abraham and Isaac play, God works through His Angel (the York dramatist rather delicately avoids associating God directly with the problematical test of Abraham's faith), in the Exodus play He again openly appears. After Moses has celebrated his escape from Pharaoh's slaughter of the Hebrew children by exclaiming "Thus has god shewed his myght in me" (XI, 92), God appears to him in the burning bush that is not consumed. He recalls the promise He made to Abraham and Isaac that their seed should be blessed. Now, He explains, He will prevent Pharaoh from frustrating His will by forcing him to let the Israelites pass from Egypt. One obvious way in which these plays prepare for the Incarnation is, then, that they show the readiness of God to intervene to assert His control over events.[30] With the Annunciation begins His most complete and decisive intervention in history.

There is still one further emphasis established in the opening sequence of plays of the cycle which the developing action will frequently refer to. What God says will come to pass, comes to pass. God tells the Angels they will remain in heven "To-whils ȝhe ar stabill in thoghte" (I, 30), and they do. God promises to make man to restore the bliss of heaven (I, 140–141), and He does (Play III). He tells Adam and Eve that they will remain in the bliss of Paradise as long as they are obedient to His commandment, and they do. And so in the plays of Noah, Abraham, and Moses: to all of them God makes a pledge which the events of the plays show Him to keep. However disjunctive the Old Testament scenes are in their narrative organization, they come to be associated as analogous enactments of those attributes of God announced at the very opening of the cycle:

> I am gracyus and grete, god withoutyn begynnyng,
> I am maker unmade, all mighte es in me,
> I am lyfe and way unto welth wynnyng,
> I am formaste and fyrste, als I byd sall it be.
>
> (I, 1–4)

The effect is simple, but theatrically sure. Just by watching and listening to these opening plays of the cycle, the audience comes to learn that God is almighty and yet gracious, that He orders all things, yet orders them for man to share His "wealth." This experience provides an essential premise of the audience's understanding of the events of the Incarnation and its participation in them.

Although with the salvation of the children of Israel God the Father passes from the stage, His ordination of events and their participation in His controlling plan for the salvation of mankind continue to be manifested in the plot of the plays. Now, however, they are differently asserted—through prophecy rather than figures or direct announcement:

> He sais þus, god þe fadir in heven
> Ordand in erthe man kynde to mende;
> And to grayth it with godhede even
> His sone he saide þat he suld sende
> To take kynde of man-kyn
>   In a mayden full mylde.
> So was many saved of syn
>   And the foule fende begyled.
>
> (XII, 17–24)

The prophecy of Amos which the Doctor here paraphrases and explains at the start of his speech looks briefly over the whole central sequence of the cycle to establish the scheme which will define it. Christ's Incarnation is the fulfillment of the will of God, and as such the fulfillment of prophecies like this, and of all prophecies. The theme will emerge in different ways and different contexts in the plays of Christ's life. Its importance to the drama is not just that it informs the variety of episodes with a sense of coherence and singleness of purpose; it also precisely defines and significantly extends the audience's repeated experience during these plays. That expectations created by the plays are consistently fulfilled is itself a sign of God's working and His will.[31]

Unlike the prophecies rehearsed in the Chester plays which, as the Expositor carefully explains, anticipate in order the Incarnation, Passion, Resurrection, Ascension, and Pentecost,[32] those of the York Annunciation play direct attention almost exclusively to the Incarnation, to Mary's receiving the Holy Ghost. If they lose anything in the narrowness of their scope, they gain in intensity: the quiet scene of the Annunciation is suffused by the emotional richness that comes from its being the fulfillment of expectations so fully aroused.

All the plays surrounding the Nativity make use of the motif of Christ's birth as the fulfillment of prophecy established by the Annunciation play, though with different effects. The play of Joseph's Troubles, as we have seen, draws upon it ironically. The Nativity play joyously confirms the motif as first Mary and then Joseph celebrate Christ's birth as the fulfillment of Baalam's and Habbakuk's prophecies. Even the Shepherds in the York plays appear, not complaining about the weather like their more famous counterparts in the Towneley plays, but reciting prophecies they have heard. This is the Second Shepherd:

> Or he be borne in burgh hereby
> Balaham, brothir, me have herde say
> A sterne shulde schyne and signifie
> With lightfull lemes like any day.
> And als þe texte it tellis clerly
> By witty lerned men of oure lay,
> With his blissed bloode he shulde us by
> He shulde take here al of a maye.
> I herde my syre say
>   When he of hir was borne
> She shulde be als clene may
>   As ever she was by-forne.
>
> (XV, 13–24)

In similar stanzas the First Shepherd has elaborated upon the prophecies of Hosea and Isaiah concerning the Redeemer, and the Third Shepherd will pray that they might see the child who, he has heard, will overcome "the force of the feende" and set the children of Israel free. These clerkly Shepherds are probably derived from liturgical drama;[33] here, however, the dramatist has tried to merge their expository role with their nature as simple shepherds. All that the Second Shepherd knows about prophecy he has picked up from "witty lerned men" or from his master, and the Third Shepherd, in a marvelously bumbling nonsequitur, sees in his erudite typological association of the Exodus and the Harrowing of Hell a reason for them to "Flitte faste overe thees felles / To frayste to fynde oure fee / And talke of sumwhat ellis" (XV, 34–36). Perhaps their secondhand knowledge of prophecy is meant to reflect the audience's—at least the confirmation of their expectations coincides with that of the audience in the tender conclusion to the play. The Magi play more aptly and surely continues the motif of Christ's birth as the fulfillment of prophecy. As the Magi recite the prophecies of Balaam, Isaiah, and Hosea before a skeptical Herod, the recital focuses the predominant concern of the play—the Christ child's claim to Kingship and authority as against that of Herod. The strength of prophecy is sufficient even to convince Herod:

> *ii Rex:* Þat fadirs has talde beforne
> Has noman myght to marre.
> *Herod:* Allas! þan am I lorne—
> Þis waxith ay werre and werre.
> (XVII, 177–180)

He soon recovers: convinced by his Counselors that the Magi might be wrong, he sends them away to find out the truth about the Christ child. Prophecy is once again validated as the audience watches the Kings arrive at the stable where they find the one who is both "sone and saveour" announced by Hosea. Yet this moment is more than one of the prophecy fulfilled. The hymns the Magi offer to the child themselves contain the prophecy that Christ will judge men at the Last Judgment, that He will be "bounden and bett," that while He will drive "dede undir fete" He will Himself die and be buried.

In various ways, then, the scenes of Christ's Nativity in the York cycle all establish the event as the fulfillment of Old Testament prophecies. There is little didactic insistence on this basic tenet of the Christian faith, but it is there as a focus that lends coherence to the episodic sequence and clarifies the essential place of the Nativity in God's scheme for the salvation of mankind.

For the fullest and richest treatment of the motif of these plays we must look to the play that follows the Magi play, that of the Purification of Mary and the Presentation of Christ in the Temple.[34] In this play an expository emphasis becomes the very basis of the dramatic action. Here prophesier and prophesied come together, here Christ comes to those who have long awaited Him. Moreover the theme of fulfillment is extended: Christ not only fulfills prophecy in this play, He also fulfills the Old Law of Moses. In this play, the whole temporal scope of the action of the cycle is concentrated in a single moment, a moment which is extended to the audience for them to share in and celebrate. Although the play may well have been written later than most of the plays in the cycle, and might even have been at one time an independent play, in its place in the developing action of the cycle it serves to focus the movement of the plot of the whole cycle as it is transformed by the Incarnation. It reiterates and heightens the effects of the plays that have gone before—and in no feature more noticeably or imaginatively than in its poetry. In both the Shepherds' play and the Magi play, as expository statements had given away to the songs and hymns to the Christ child, the poetry had reflected the emotional and theological richness of the Nativity. In the Purification play, such a transformation is at the heart of the play's achievement.

The opening speech of the play is a sermon, spoken as we find out at the end of it, by the Prisbeter at the Temple. With an opening prayer to God, "The maker of all heven and erth," he announces his theme:

> In nomber, weight, and mesure fyne
> God creat here althyng, I say:

His lawes he bad men shulde not tyne
But kepe his commandmentes all way.

(XLI, 5–8)

Obedience to the Law of God—this is the lesson this preacher brings. In the sober quatrains so appropriate to the sermonic mode of the speech, he recalls how God had given to Moses commandments by which the children of Israel should "lerne thame lely to knawe Goddes wylle" (14). The punishment for disobedience to these Laws was, he explains, to be stoned to death—and to make the most of this striking point he warns his present congregation:

Therefore kepe well Goddes commandement
And leyd your lyf after his lawes;
Or elles surely ye mon be shent
Bothe lesse and more, ylkone on rawes.

(XLI, 21–24)

Now he proceeds to the specific point of his sermon. Explaining the demands made by the Law of Moses that sacrifices must be offered for purification after sickness or, for a woman, after giving birth, he insists on the absoluteness of the Law—"There shulde no man to this say nay" (44). The Prisbeter is an embodiment of the Old Law. So is his speech: in its expository style it establishes the Old Law as a set of precepts, in its terms it unyieldingly stresses obedience to the Law through fear of punishment. Only at the very end is there any qualification of its harshness, as the priest announces that he serves to receive offerings brought to the temple and to pray that God grant "helth and lyfe" to His people (56).

With the end of the Prisbeter's speech, an old woman comes forward. She speaks softly as she announces her intention to remain in the temple to serve God "With prayer and fastyng in ever ylk a tyde" (60) and explains that she has long been waiting "For the redempcyon of Israell" (64). Her "holy conversacion" (65) has not gone unrewarded, for in His grace, God has granted her the power "To tell by profecy for mans redempcion / What shall befall by Goddes entent" (67–68):

> I tell you all here in this place,
> By Goddes vertue in prophecy,
> That one is borne to oure solace
> Here to be present securely
> within short space,
> Of his owen mother a madyn free,
> Of all vyrgens moost chaist suthly
> The well of mekenes, blyssed myght she be
> moost full of grace.
>
> (XLI, 69–77)

The prophecy which attests to the power Anna has received through the grace of God is also an announcement of the event the play is to present—it draws the audience's expectations into the action of the play. It also marks a change from the tone and style of the opening speech as the stanza form becomes more lyrical and the language replaces fear and punishment with "solace" and "grace." Anna has a further prediction, that Simeon, "that senyour / That is so semely in Godes sight" (78–79) will receive the Savior and take strength from the Holy Ghost.

In the context of Anna's prophecy, the lament with which Simeon comes forward becomes gently ironic. The audience expects that his feebleness will soon be transformed by the granting of his prayer that he might see the one born to save mankind. As the double quatrains of his complaint are replaced by the lyrical stanza form Anna had used, Simeon adopts his traditional role of prophet. He surveys the familiar Old Testament prophecies that foretell the appearance of Christ and His mission: like a giant, this "blyssed babb" (116) will harrow hell to redeem Israel:

> Thus say they all
> There patryarkes and ther prophettes clere:

'A babb is borne to be oure fere,
Knytt in oure kynde for all our chere
to grete and small.'
(XLI, 127–131)

With growing excitement and a tender lovingness, Simeon prays again that he might see the baby whose coming has been prophesied: "Lorde, len me grace yf that thowe pleas / and make me light" (151–152). Immediately, God's Angel appears to grant Simeon his prayer, and as Simeon rejoices at the grace he has received, the child and his mother are named for the first time, Mary, and "Jesu, my joy and savyour ay" (181).

Law-giver, prophet, patriarch—all three of these characters belong to the Old Testament world; yet all three look forward to the event that will transform that world, arousing increasing expectations in the audience that hears their soliloquies. As Mary and Jesus are named, the play begins to move toward the fulfillment of these expectations. Now Mary and Joseph appear, bringing the Christ child and their offering to the temple. I have already described many of the effects of this beautiful central scene. Recalling the Prisbeter's opening speech, Mary comes to fulfill a Law that does not apply to her, not out of fear, but "with goode chere" (198), and not just to obey the law but to establish an example of meekness. In her, precept is fulfilled in example, commandment is superseded by willing action, obedience becomes one with humility. For the lamb which they are too poor to buy, they substitute their son, "the lame of God verray" (266) and offer it to the Prisbeter. The Old Law is fulfilled; the New Law of humility is established.

From this moment on, the silent Christ child is the focus of the action as the "blyssed babb" is celebrated in the sustained, exultant hymns and prayers of the Prisbeter, Anna, and Simeon. The Prisbeter accepts the offering, and where before his words had stressed the rigorousness of the Law, now they joyfully acknowledge the grace of God through which this "specyall gyft / Gevyn to mankynde" is freely offered (309–310). "Grace" informs his language and the plain style of his earlier sermon gives way to lyrical celebration:

> Welcome! oure wytt and our wysdome.
> Welcome! our joy all and somme.
> Welcome! redemptour omnium
> tyll hus hartely.
>
> (XLI, 320–323)

The liturgical phrase triumphantly expands Anna's and Simeon's earlier anticipation of "the redempcyon of Israell" (64, 126, 184) as the hymn ceremonially brings the audience into the moment of joy. Anna's hymn of celebration is just as joyful:

> Welcome! blyssed Mary and madyn ay.
> Welcome! mooste meke in thyne array.
> Welcome! bright starne that shyneth bright as day,
> all for our blys . . .
> Welcome! thowe blyssed babb so free,
> Welcome! our welfayre wyelly,
> And welcome all our seall, suthly,
> to grete and small.
>
> (XLI, 324–327; 332–335)

For her devotion and steadfastness, Anna has been allowed to see her prophecy fulfilled. So too has the audience, and the communal terms of her ritualistic lyric of welcome confirm the audience's presence at the scene.

Only Simeon remains outside this joyful community worshipping Christ—briefly. As the Angel of God instructs him to go to the temple to receive Mary and her son, Simeon, now dancing where before he had stumbled, joins the other characters to join his praise for the "blyssed babb that Mary bare" (353) with theirs. The moment when Simeon takes the Christ child has been anticipated almost since the beginning of the play; now the anticipation is fulfilled, the promise made to him by God is fulfilled, and, as Simeon himself emphasizes, the prophecy is fulfilled. But it is not just for Simeon that Christ comes. Simeon's regeneration is an example that Christ comes to heal all men, and the moment of fulfillment dramatized in the play stands as confirmation that God fulfills His promise to save all mankind.

The play does not, however, end with this climatic moment. Simeon continues to speak. In the context created for it in this play, Simeon's familiar song, *Nunc dimittis,* becomes a significant comment on the action of the whole play. This is the very fine vernacular paraphrase of the song:

> In peace, lorde, nowe leyf thy servand,
> For myne eys haith seyne that is ordand,
> The helth for all men that be levand
>   here for ay.
> That helth lorde hais thowe ordand, I say,
> Here before the face of thy people.
> And thy light hais thowe shynyd this day,
> To be knowe of thy folke that was febyll
>   for evermore,
> And thy glory for the chylder of Israell
> That with the in thy Kyngdome shall dwell
> Whan the damnyd shall be dreven to hell
>   than with great care.
>
> (XLI, 415–426)

Simeon's repeated claim that God has "ordand" the salvation of men has behind it the dramatic force not just of the demonstration this play has offered that prophecy is fulfilled, but also of the witness Simeon himself bears that the coming of Christ restores "the helth" of men. Looking back to the Old Testament in its reference to the "chylder of Israell" and forward to the Last Judgment, his prayer illuminates the significance of the moment he celebrates by placing it in the scheme of history that directs all moments.

On this note of suspension between things fulfilled and things awaiting fulfillment, the play draws to its close. The Old Law and its precepts, the patriarchs and their prophecies have been transformed by the appearance of Christ.

Yet this appearance contains its own anticipation of the future: in his role as prophet Simeon now looks ahead to warn Mary that "the sworde of sorro thy hart shal thyrll / Whan thowe shall se sothly thy son soffer yll" (440–441) and also to reassure her that her sorrow will be turned to joy when her son "as a gyant," as "the myghtiest mayster," will fight victoriously on behalf of all men (448, 449). The play ends with Simeon bidding a rich farewell to the "former of all," praying that He might "grant us thy blyssyng / to fynd our dystresse" (458–459).

The late fourteenth-century *A Stanzaic Life of Christ* summarizes the significance of Christ's Presentation thus:

> ffor purificacioune fulle werray
> came when Christ light in oure kynde
> thenne figuratif moste passe awaye
> and skilfully be putte behynde
> ffor he purifiet us on right
> with waray fait at his comyng
> and hevy hartes made hem light
> that long havden been in mislykyng.[35]

Some such understanding of the event clearly lies behind the effects of the York Purification play. Ranging back even to the Creation and forward to the Last Judgment, the play draws into itself the whole movement of history, focusing it in the action of "putting behind," in the fulfillment and transformation Christ's Incarnation represent. Coinciding with this narrative effect is the play's rich lyrical aspect through which the "lightening of hearts" is dramatically realized and rhetorically extended to incorporate the audience as joyful celebrants of the one who comes "In redemption of many and recover also" (438). That redemption will, however, involve the suffering and death of Christ: the Purification play also contains anticipations of future events in the cycle, and, as the Nativity sequence proceeds from this play with the Flight into Egypt and the Slaughter of the Innocents, the joy of this play gives way to ominous lamentation.

Earlier critics of the Corpus Christi drama used to claim that the familiarity of both dramatists and audience with the stories dramatized precluded any imaginative handling of the subject matter—there could be no surprises and little conflict when the outcome of the action was so well known, and the dramatists "found themselves cramped by the necessity of sticking essentially to the biblical episodes."[36] The York Purification play is by no means the only play that forces a rejection of these claims. Not only does the dramatist carefully and independently structure the episodes of the scriptural story; he does so to take advantage of the familiarity of the story, even to the extent of offering his audience precise predictions of what will happen. The familiarity of the story here and elsewhere becomes a resource. By creating expectations and then fulfilling them, the drama brings the audience into the very process that the cycle enacts, that of an ordained sequence of events moving towards its fulfillment. At times, as in the Purification play, the audience's experience can be the source of great communal affirmation and joy. But the joy is rarely unqualified. Just as Christ's birth is the fulfillment of prophecy, so is His Passion and Death; and just as the salvation of the faithful is ordained by God, so is the damnation of those who will not follow His way.

There are two other plays in the York sequence dealing with the life of Christ which, like the Purification play, derive much of their effectiveness from their crucial place in the plot of the cycle. The play of Christ's Entry into Jerusalem and the play of the Harrowing of Hell both mark a new stage in the movement of the action, a stage which has been anticipated and is presented as the fulfillment of the will of God revealed through prophecy. Neither of these plays makes as remarkable use of the poetry to define and image the action of the play. Yet in both, the language draws into the action of the particular play the scope of the action of the whole cycle; and in both, the significance of the action is reflected and extended as the plays move toward their climax in celebration.

With Christ's Entry into Jerusalem begins His Passion.

Though he comes as King, He comes to be sacrificed—this paradox is at the heart of the emotional effect of this lengthy and very skillful play. And at the moment before His Passion, this play acts much like the extended hymns of praise which end it to offer a dramatic and poetic *summa* of Christ in all His aspects: He is King, He is the son of man, He is the healer, the redeemer, the conqueror, the Judge, the teacher, the sacrifice. He is also the prophet and the fulfillment of prophecy:

> From heven to erth whan I dyssende
> Rawnsom to make I made promys;
> The prophicie nowe drawes to ende,
> My fadirs wille forsoth it is
> Þat sente me hedyr.
>
> (XXV, 8–12)

Fulfilling God's will, Christ enters the city of prophets to fulfill His own promise to man and the prophecies through which God's will has been revealed. The motif frames the action of this play. Christ announces His intention to enter Jerusalem on an ass,

> So þe prophicy clere menyng
> May be fulfilled here in þis place:
> 'Doghtyr Syon,
> Loo! þi lorde comys rydand on an asse
> Þe to opon.'
>
> (XXV, 24–28)

Philip and Peter obediently leave to fetch the ass—"For prophycye / Us bus it do to hym by skyll / To do dewly" (47–49)—and tell the Janitor who guards the ass that it is needed by the prophet of Nazareth (81). In his turn, the Janitor announces to the burgesses of Jerusalem that there is "Att hande þe prophete called Jesu" (123), and they, recalling how Christ Himself explained that "What þe prophettis saide in þer sawe / All longis to hym" (153–154), briefly recite prophecies of Isaiah and David as "gud ensampelys" that Christ is indeed their King. Only a few moments later, the burgesses again assert the sovereignty of Christ:

> Oure kyng is he, þat is no lesse,
> Oure awne lawe to it cordis well,
> Þe prophettis all bare full witnesse
> Qwilke full of hym secrete gone telle:
>   And þus wolde say,
> 'Emang youre selff schall come grete seele
>   Thurgh god verray.'
>
> (XXV, 225–231)

Moses, Jesse, David, Solomon, and "þe Genolagye"—all are brought forward to prove Christ's claims to be King and to persuade the citizens to prepare to greet Him as King.

Coherent and cumulatively powerful as it is, this motif of prophecy is much more than an expository emphasis introduced on the verbal level. As in the Nativity plays or the Purification play, it serves to focus and define what is the audience's actual experience as the action of the play proceeds. For from the very start of the play, what is to take place has been precisely anticipated. Christ's first words to the disciples are, "I schalle ȝou telle þat shalbe in dede" (3): He tells them that the time at which He is to save men's souls draws near. He proceeds to instruct them to go to "ȝone castell" (15) where they will find an ass which they are to bring to Him; he even anticipates that they will be challenged. The disciples eagerly obey His will, and "als he saide" (51), they find the ass. They are also challenged as Christ has predicted, the Janitor's questions eliciting from the disciples the further anticipation that Christ "comes at hande" (87). Encouraged by the disciples, the Janitor leaves to announce to the citizens that "Her comes of kynde of Israell / Att hande þe prophete called Jesu / Lo! þis same day / Rydand on an asse" (122–125), and they, after a delay in which they confirm Christ's claims to be King, prepare to greet Him as a King:

> Go we þan with processioune
> To mete þat comely as us awe,

With braunches, floures, and unysonne,
With myghtfull songes her on a rawe.
  Our childir schall
Go synge before, þat men may knawe
  To þis graunte we all.

(XXV, 260–266)

Clearly the dramatist does not want the audience to be surprised by the Entry of Christ. On the contrary, he has deliberately created and fostered the expectation that they are very soon to see Christ enter the city: there is even, perhaps, in the Burgess's words an exhoration to the audience to join him in celebrating this Royal Entry. The very ordering of events in the action of the play thus provides an analogue to the motif of prophecy. The audience's perhaps impatient expectation is that of the world waiting for the Redeemer. Finally, Christ comes—after a long delay in which He acts out His rule as healer and forgiver of sins. But before He enters, He also demonstrates His power as prophet:

My dere discipulis, beholde and see,
Un-to Jerusalem we schall assende,
Man sone schall þer be-trayed be
And gevyn in-to his enmys hande
  With grete dispitte.
Ther spitting on hym þer schall þei spende
  And smertly smyte.

(XXV, 462–468)

The audience knows that this prophecy, too, will come to pass, so that there is a poignant ominousness to the First Burgess's opening verse of praise for Christ—"Hayll! prophette preved withouten pere" (490).

All that has been said about prophecy at the start of the play comes to bear on Christ's climactic Entry, and all the carefully created anticipations of this theatrical moment. Fulfilling prophecy and resolving the audience's expectations, the Entry thus brings the historical action of the plays and the audience together. In their hymns of praise, the Burgesses of Jerusalem speak too for the citizens of York who welcome Christ to their city. Their joyful praise serves also to locate this specific moment in the action of the whole cycle: Christ is "david sone," "blissfull babe in Bedleme borne," "sege þat schoppe boþe even and morne," "conquerour," and "domysman dredful þat all schall deme" (504, 511, 513, 525, 539).

In the plays that follow, Christ's prophecy concerning His Passion and Death is relentlessly fulfilled. The will of God demands Christ's sacrifice and He is obedient to that will: "My fadir saide it schall be soo, / His bidding will I noȝt for-berẹ," Christ tells the disciples at the Last Supper as they prepare to meet His enemies—enemies who are themselves "ordand" (XXVII, 182–183, 181). Only after the death of Christ is there time for the audience to pause to contemplate what they have seen inexorably taking place before them. At the start of the Harrowing of Hell play Christ speaks, His words reaching out to the audience:

> Manne on molde, be meke to me,
> And have thy maker in þi mynde,
> And thynke howe I have tholid for þe
> With pereles paynes for to be pyned.
> The forward of my Fadir free
> Have I fulfillid, as folke may fynde.
> Þer-fore a-boute nowe woll I bee
> Þat I have bought for to unbynde.
> Þe feende þame wanne with trayne
> Thurgh frewte of erthely foode,
> I have þame getyn agayne
> Thurgh bying with my bloode.
>
> And so I schall þat steede restore
> Fro whilke þe feende fell for synne;
> Þare schalle mankynde wonne evermore
> In blisse þat schall nevere blynne.
> All þat in werke my werkemen were
> Owte of thare woo I wol þame wynne,
> And some signe schall I sende be-fore

Of grace to garre þer gamys be-gynne.
A light I woll þei have
To schewe þame I schall come sone,
My bodie bidis in grave
Tille alle these dedis be done.

My Fadir ordand on þis wise
Aftir his will þat I schulde wende
For to fulfille þe prophicye
And, als I spake, my solace to spende.
My frendis þat in me faith affies
Nowe fro their fois I schall þame fende,
And on the thirde day ryght uprise
And so tille heven I schall assende.
Sithen schall I come agayne
To deme bothe good and ill
Tille endles joie or payne:
Þus is my Fadirs will.

(XXXVII, 1–36)

Beginning with a reference to the Creation, ending with a reference to the Last Judgment, this dignified prologue surveys the whole scheme of Redemption. Especially after the loudness, harshness, and devotional intensity of the Passion sequence, after one play has followed another without respite to bring Christ to His death on the cross, Christ's own words serve as much through emotional relief and reassurance as through explicit statement to assert God's order.

The Harrowing of Hell plays have properly been described as the climax of the Corpus Christi cycles.[37] Inherently more dramatic than the Resurrection scene, the episode is developed to provide the structural and thematic center of the dramatic action, most carefully and impressively in the York version, which was borrowed for the Towneley cycle. I have already discussed the play as the focus of important aspects of the homiletic and lyric modes of the drama. Its centrality, too, to the narrative aspects is at every point communicated to the audience through the motifs and devices I have been pointing to in this section.

In fulfillment of the promise made to the audience in the prologue to the play, Christ sends His light before Him into hell. There the patriarchs and prophets, Christ's "werkemen," joyfully welcome it as a sign of their imminent release: Adam, waiting for this moment for "Foure thousande and sex hundereth ȝere," now sees that "oure helpe is nere / And sone schall sesse oure sorowes sadde" (39, 43–44); for Eve, the light that now shines is that which shone on them when they were still in Paradise; Isaiah welcomes the light as the fulfillment of his prophecy that for the "folke in mirke walkand . . . a light schulde on þame lende" (53–54); to Simeon too the light is the fulfillment of the prophecy he had made that Christ would come to heal His people—"Þe same þat I þame saide / I see fulfillid in dede" (71–72); John the Baptist celebrates the coming of Christ to hell as confirmation of God's announcement at Christ's Baptism that Christ is the Son of God; and finally Moses—for him the light is the one that shone wonderfully at Christ's Transfiguration, one that holds the promise that they "schalle sone passe fro payne" (96). The audience has seen most of these figures before in the plays, heard their prophecies and witnessed the events they refer to. Sensing that all that has gone before has been a preparation for this moment, they readily share the excitement of the characters in the play.

In all this celebration, however, the devils in hell hear only a "harrowe" (98)—the irony is superbly comic—and an "uggely noyse" (101). They too help to build the audience's expectations as they frantically prepare their attempt to prevent Christ from entering hell. Predictably, their efforts fail. With irresistible verbal force, Christ breaks down the gates of hell:

> *Principes, portas tollite:*
> Undo youre ȝatis, ȝe princis of pryde,
> *Et introibit rex glorie:*
> Þe kyng of blisse comes in þis tyde.
> (XXXVII, 181–184)

Satan is stunned, and David appears to confirm his imminent defeat:

Þat may þou in my sawter see
For þat poynte of prophicie:
I saide þat he schuld breke
Youre barres and bandis by name
And on youre werkis take wreke.
Nowe schalle ȝe see þe same.

(XXXVII, 187–192)

David's last words seem to speak as much to the audience as to Satan.

And of course Satan is destroyed. He cannot resist the ordained course of events which, Christ tells him, brings Him to free His people (225–228). Nor can his attempt to overcome Christ by argument resist the overwhelming power of prophecy:

I wirke noght wrang, þat schal þow witte,
If I my men fro woo will wynne:
Mi prophetis playnly prechid it
All þis note þat nowe be-gynne.
Þai saide þat I schulde be obitte,
To hell þat I schulde entre in,
And save my servauntis fro þat pitte
Wher dampned saulis schall sitte for synne.
And ilke trewe prophettis tale
Muste be fulfillid in mee:
I have þame broughte with bale,
And in blisse schal þei be.

(XXXVII, 265–276)

As always in these plays, the prophecy is fulfilled: Satan is cast down to the pit of hell and, in the spectacular climax of the play which theatrically resolves all the audience's anticipations and fulfills all the promises that have been made, Michael leads the patriarchs and prophets out of hell toward Paradise. At the head of the procession goes Adam, who long ago in the cycle had been promised that he would be redeemed from the bitter sorrow to which his disobedience had condemned him, and who now leads both characters and audience in rejoicing.

While the three plays that I have examined present different scenes from the life of Christ, they have this in common: each presents an event which is explicitly defined as the fulfillment of the will of God revealed through prophecy, and each realizes this expository motif in the structure of the play's action so that the audience following the play comes to share in the fulfillment dramatized and celebrated within the play. The effect achieved is that sought also in the homiletic and lyric modes of the drama—a complete merging of the world of the play with the world of the audience. To the extent that the action of these plays—especially the Harrowing of Hell play—involves understanding and celebration, they incorporate aspects of the expository and lyric modes of action and poetry. But what makes them distinctive is that the language of the plays ranges over the whole of historical time, concentrating it into a single moment shared by the audience, to demonstrate that the will of God informs all moments and ordains time itself to be its revelation and fulfillment. In so doing, these plays also serve to focus the movement of the plot of the whole cycle, and its significance.

Prophecies and predictions do not end with the Harrowing of Hell play, nor is the motif of the fulfillment of prophecy forgotten. On the contrary, as events continue to unfold in their ordained sequence, the motif is expanded to include an even more direct involvement of the audience than it has so far produced—one in which prophetic promises are made expressly to them. At the end of the Harrowing of Hell play, Christ first announces:

> Mi grave I woll go till
> Redy to rise uppe-right
> And so I schall fulfille
> That I be-fore have highte.
>
> (XXXVII, 393–395)

Then He promises:

Mi blissing have ȝe all on rawe,
I schall be with youe where ȝe wende,
And all þat lelly luffes my lawe
Þai schall be blissid with-owten ende.
(XXXVII, 401–404)

This second promise involves more than the figures being led to heaven on the stage—it is spoken to no one as much as to the audience. Reinforcing the exhortation is the audience's sure knowledge that Christ will keep the first of these promises just as He has kept every promise made by God. Similarly after He *has* risen from the dead, His announcement to Mary Magdalene that He will next ascend to heaven, having completed the work of His Father, is accompanied by the words:

And therfore loke þat ilke man lere
Howe þat in erthe þer liffe may mende:
All þat me loves I schall drawe nere
Mi Fadirs blisse þat nevere schall ende.
(XXXIX, 130–133)

Shortly hereafter Christ does ascend into heaven, and the speech in which He describes how He has fulfilled His Father's will contains this promise:

Right als I wende als wele will seme
So schall I come in flessh and fell
Atte þe day of dome, whan I schal deme
Þe goode in endles blisse to dwell
Mi fomen fro me for to fleme
With-outen ende in woo to well.
Ilke levand man, here to take yeme.
(XLIII, 122–128)

Now the prophecy is of an event which, unlike all those of the preceding plays, has not yet taken place in historical time, of one which in the audience's time as in the time of the drama is yet to be accomplished. As Christ's words insist, this prophecy has a peculiar urgency for the audience, and it is this prophecy which He leaves as the Gospel that His disciples are to preach in "þe ȝere of grace" (XLIV, 129):

> He badde us preche and bere wittenesse
> That he schulde deme bothe quike and dede.
> To hym all prophettis prevys expresse
> All þo þat trowis in his godhede
> Off synnes þei schall have forgiffenesse.
>
> (XLIV, 15–19)

This is one prophecy which the audience of the plays can—and must—themselves help to fulfill. For Christ will keep His promise to return to earth to judge all men.

The Play of the Last Judgment (Play XLVIII)

All the Corpus Christi cycles stage the Last Judgment, and that they do is one of their most distinctive features.[38] The contemporary Cornish plays end with the Ascension; the French Passion plays end with the Resurrection, the Ascension, or the descent of the Holy Spirit to the disciples. But the Corpus Christi cycles continue the action of salvation history to its consummation when God destroys the world He creates in the opening plays of the cycle and Christ returns to heaven having exiled the damned and set the saved in His bliss. The most obvious and impressive effect acquired by staging the Judgment scene is the sense of formal completeness the cycles acquire: all four cycles begin with God announcing He is *Alpha et Omega,* and they all present that beginning and ending. In none of the cycles, however, is this sense more noticeable than in the York plays. Consistent with the strategic use made of the sequential plot throughout the York cycle, the Judgment play draws together previous events in the plot to focus them in this final moment. And as God comes to destroy the world as He had prophesied, and Christ comes to judge men as He had promised, the motif of the fulfillment of prophecy and promise which has provided the basis of the narrative throughout the cycle is itself fulfilled. It is from this sense of resolution and fulfillment that much of the impact, both homiletic and aesthetic, of this highly formal play derives.

Nevertheless, there were difficulties as well as advantages to staging the Judgment scene.[39] The event is unknown and still to come, one which, coming at the end of time, sums up all of history and all the actions of men. The York dramatist solves this problem in much the same way as the writer of the Creation play. He anthropomorphizes and literalizes the action, drawing upon the poetry and the staging to establish the event's vast dimensions and significance. A further problem is one of the tone of the play. Where the Ascension of Christ brings the Cornish plays to an end on a note of joyful triumph, by dramatizing the Judgment the Corpus Christi plays necessarily end on a more ambivalent note. For the Christ of the play is the divine Judge who, with mercy set aside, judges with justice the trembling dead. Accompanying the joy of the saved—inseparable from it—are the lamentations of the damned. As countless sermons and didactic poems had shown, the scene most readily served as a call to repentance by arousing fear at the fate of the damned. But in the context of the cycle drama, it had to be capable, too, of arousing joy and celebration as the will of God for the salvation of mankind was shown to be fulfilled. Although the York play, like the other Judgment plays, stresses the homiletic aspects of the scene, they are never allowed to become overwhelming. In the structure of the play and, most beautifully, in its poetry, gladness and sorrow, love and fear, reconciliation and separation are held in balance to be finally resolved in the singing of the Angels in which the play ends.

These two difficulties in representing the scene can be expressed in other terms. How is the play to address its audience?[40] The representation of the time when time and the world will cease to be has to address itself to those for whom time and the world still are, and the representation of the time of justice must address itself to those alive in the time of mercy and of grace. And how, having assured the participation of the audience in the action of the drama, is the drama to leave its audience when it brings that action to a close? What we have discovered so far about the ways in which the York plays address the audience in the various dramatic modes should help us to see how the York dramatist has approached these problems in this final play. The ways are various. In part, this tableauesque play works like a statement: this is the way it will be. But for the force of this statement, for its urgency, the play draws upon all the ways in which the audience has been involved in the action so far, focusing the cumulative experience of the audience and, as it were testing it. Through most of the play the audience sees on the stage figures who are themselves as they will be, and they are figures who have or have not responded to precisely those appeals that the plays have made to the audience. In this context, the audience hears once again those appeals being made. For those on stage, there is no opportunity to respond to them. For the audience, there is, and the ending of the cycle leaves them with both the encouragement to reflect their experience of the plays in their own lives, and the warning that they must.

The York Last Judgment play prepares its audience for the cycle's final scene through a lengthy prologue spoken by God, at the end of which He summons the Angels "Tọ blawe þer bemys, þat all may here / The tyme is comen I will make ende" (63–64). The ending which has been in sight since God announced Himself as "*Alpha et O*" at the very beginning of the cycle is about to be acted out. Those opening moments are recalled at the start of the Judgment play as God looks back to the time when He first made the world and thought it good, when He created men in His own likeness only to find that "man to greve me gaffe he noght" (7). Therefore, God now announces, "me rewis þat I þe worlde began" (8). Once before in the cycle man's sinfulness had caused God to repent having made the world, and specific verbal parallels echo that moment at the end of the

Noah plays; but the ending God prepares for here is the final ending He had then prophesied through Noah.

Elaborating on His opening announcement, God proceeds to survey the significant stages in the process that has led to this moment. Two stanzas are given to an account of the Fall of man. The first tells how God set man in Paradise with the sole warning that if he ate of the tree of good and evil he would be "broght oute of all blisse" (16). The second tells what happened, the carry over of the alliterating 'b' sound suggesting its sad inevitability:

> Belyve brak manne my bidding:
> He wende have bene a god þerby,
> He wende have wittyne of all-kynne thyng
> In worlde to have bene als wise as I. (17–20)

It is worth pointing to some of the poetic details in these lines, for while the play is composed throughout in the straightforward double quatrain stanza, the verse is among the finest in the cycle, formal yet flexible, subtly varied in its sounds and rhythms. So here, for instance, the alliteration on 'b' and 'w' in all four lines, against which the word 'god' stands out reproachfully (alliteration in this play is ornamental rather than structural); the repeated phrase "He wende . . ." that draws attention to the plain statement of man's vain presumption; the changing rhythms of the lines, slowed by the repetition, quickened by the increase in syllables, building from the clipped first line that establishes the definitive act of disobedience God explains. The quatrains themselves are usually carefully used: the second quatrain of this stanza defines the Fall in more concrete terms before God describes how He punished man's sinfulness. Beguiled by "glotony" (22)—one of the sins which Christ had resisted in the play of His Temptation by Satan—Adam and his offspring were put "to pyne" (24).

With a symmetry that is to become the formal characteristic of this play, the next two stanzas are given over to an account of the second stage in the history God ordains, the Incarnation and the Redemption of man. One quatrain describes the Incarnation; the next, linked by the rhyme scheme, the Passion of Christ:

> For rewþe of þame he reste on roode,
> And boughte þame with his body bare;
> For þame he shedde his harte and bloode–
> What kyndinesse myght I do þame mare?
> (29–32)

The reproachful question, borrowed from a lyric motif to be offered in more extended form later in the play, is well placed, not just because it breaks up the rhythms of the direct statements, nor just for its potential for arousing in the audience an appropriate feeling of guilty wonder as they hear God rehearse His plan for their redemption, but also for the way it prepares for the next stanza. For God in Christ did do more: Christ harrowed hell, and overcame the devil "For þame þat ware sounkyn for synne" (36). Moreover, having redeemed man's sinfulness, Christ also established the Gospel and the example by which each man could be restored to the "blisse þat nevere may blynne" (40).

So far, what God has described is the sum of what the drama has presented to its audience, the Fall, the Redemption, the teachings and the example of Christ. But as God continues to describe the third stage in the action of salvation, the time He refers to opens up to span a time not dramatized within the plays, the time between the Ascension of Christ and that from which God speaks in the play, the time that is most significantly that of the audience. During this time, God explains, He has shown Himself full of "mercye," "grace," and "forgiffenesse" (41–42). Yet men have continued to live their lives in wickedness:

> Men seis þe worlde but vanite,
> Ȝitt will no-manne be ware þer-by;
> Ilke a day þer mirroure may þei se,
> Ȝitt thynke þei noȝt þat þei schall dye.
> All þat evere I saide schulde be
> Is nowe fulfillid thurgh prophicie,

Ther-fore nowe is it tyme to me
To make endyng of mannes folie.

I have tholed mankynde many a ȝere
In luste and likyng for to lende,
And unethis fynde I ferre or nere
A man þat will his misse amende.
In erthe I see butte synnes seere—
Therfore myne aungellis will I sende
To blawe þer bemys, þat all may here
The tyme is comen I will make ende.

(49–64)

The homiletic commonplace of the vanity of the world takes on a new persuasiveness in this context—God is preparing to show in the play that the world itself is impermanent, not just the things of the world which the warning usually refers to. It would strike a familiar note to the audience, briefly bringing home to them the imminence in their own lives of the Judgment they are being prepared to see. The dramatist takes advantage of the expectations aroused to force home the homiletic point: the judgment is not just the fulfillment of a process ordained by God; it is also the result of "mannes folie." That "folie" is universal. Earlier, God had found Noah; now there is no one "þat will his misse amende." Implicit in God's words is the call to repentance traditionally a feature of homiletic and meditative versions of the Last Judgment scenes.[41] That it remains implicit is part of the impact of God's speech, for as the audience watches the plays draw to their anticipated and inevitable end, there is, for the moment, no time to repent—even though the audience hears itself described as the most immediate cause of God's decision "to make endyng."

"Aungellis! blawes youre bemys belyve!" (65)—the pace quickens as God gives the instructions which will bring about the end. The Angels are to summon everyone to judgment, "Leerid and lewde, both man and wiffe," "Ilke a leede þat evere hadde liffe: / Bese none for-getyn, grete ne small" (67, 69–70). Here the formulaic phrases—the first of many in this play—express the comprehensiveness of God's judgment. But they also contain the antithetical structure which the rest of the play is to be built upon and which is immediately realized in God's final words:

> Mi blissed childre, as I have hight,
> On my right hande I schall þame see:
> Sethen schall ilke a weried wight
> On my lifte side for ferdnesse flee.
> Þis day þer domys þus have I dight
> To ilke a man as he hath served me.
>
> (75–80)

This prologue, then, prepares in a number of ways for the event it leads up to—it is more than the "last recapitulation of the story of the creation, fall, and salvation of man" that Rosemary Woolf has described it as being.[47] Like the other prologues that have introduced significant events—the Flood, the Annunciation, the Harrowing—it draws together moments from throughout the play to establish the process enacted as one ordained by God. At the same time it sets up expectations of the event to be acted out so that the audience's experience will confirm the expository emphasis. But there is a difference, for in these expectations the time of the drama briefly coincides completely with the actual time in which the audience exists. What they are led to anticipate is their own future, not just a future dramatic event. It is an uncomfortable coincidence, for the audience is unmistakably aligned with those who will find themselves exiled from God. In some ways the prologue summarizes the audience's experience of the drama as it summarizes the dramatic action, holding both up reproachfully for the audience to contemplate. They have rejected the saving grace of God in Christ which the drama has once again involved them in. But they are not yet being summoned to judgment; and as they are now allowed to contemplate those who are, they will find themselves encouraged to amend their lives through hope and love as well as through fear.

Singing the praises of the "lorde of myghtis moste" (81), the Angels hasten to carry out God's instructions. The souls are ordered to join themselves to the flesh from which they were separated at death and appear at "þis grete assise" (94) to give a reckoning of how they have served God. Whether or not the Souls were distinguished by their costumes,[43] their words clearly identify them from the start. The Good Souls speak first, their opening formulae of loving praise echoing those of the Angels; then two Bad Souls, both lamenting, the first in a phrase that epitomizes the despair of the damned: "Allas! allas! þat we were borne" (113). As each of the two Angels had been given a one-stanza speech, so with the two Good Souls. This is the first Soul's:

> Loved be þou lorde þat is so schene
> Þat on þis manere made us to rise
> Body and sawle to-gedir clene
> To come before þe high justise.
> Of oure ill dedis, lorde, þou not mene,
> That we have wroght uppon sere wise,
> But graunte us for thy grace be-dene
> Þat we may wonne in paradise.
>
> (97–104)

The Good Soul knows he has nothing to fear from the Judgment, and his prayer of penitent humility confirms him in virtue by avoiding all sense of presumption.

When the Bad Soul speaks, he is just as surely revealed and defined by his words:

> Allas! allas! þat we were borne,
> So may we synfull kaytiffis say;
> I here wele be þis hydous horne
> Itt drawes full nere to domesday.
> Allas! we wrecchis þat ar for-lorne
> Þat never ȝitt served God to paye,
> But ofte we have his flessh for-sworne—
> Allas! allas! and welaway!
>
> (113–120)

His lamentations are those first heard in the Creation play from the devils in hell; though since the damned soul acknowledges his sin the echo is rather of Judas (XXXII, 127–315). Upsetting the symmetry in order to exploit the warning for the audience contained in the figure of the damned, the dramatist gives extended speeches to the Bad Souls. The first is filled with despair by the knowledge of his damnation:

> To aske mercy us is no nede
> For wele I wotte dampned be we.
> Allas! þat we swilke liffe schulde lede,
> Þat dight us has þis destonye.
>
> (125–128)

He knows that the "wikked werkis" of the Souls for whom he speaks, no longer capable of being concealed, must now be met with "wikked peynes" everlasting, and describes the consequences of their sinfulness with theological precision:

> We mon be sette for oure synnes sake
> For evere fro oure salvacioune,
> In helle to dwelle with feendes blake
> Wher never schall be redempcioune.
>
> (141–144)

The Second Bad Soul is just as sure of his fate, and this knowledge fills him with fear:

> Allas! now wakens all oure were,
> Oure wikkid werkis may we not hide,
> But on oure bakkis us muste þem bere:
> Thei will us wreye on ilke a side.
> I see foule feendis þat will us feere
> And all for pompe of wikkid pride.
> Wepe we may with many a terre—
> Allas! þat we þis day schulde bide.
>
> (153–160)

The self-exposition of the Bad Souls is sanctioned by the doctrine that the Last Judgment will be the "final and public ratification of the divine decision made for each man at the personal judgment."[44] The souls rightly know their fate when they are summoned, perhaps confirming the justice of God's judgment as well as allowing the dramatist the opportunity for the homiletic commentary. Yet however noticeable the homiletic impulse behind this scene and its characterizations, it is both qualified and enriched by the restrained lyric impulse that images the quiet joy of the saved and the fear and regret of the damned. These figures are not remote abstractions—they are given life in their speeches to make them moving as well as instructive objects for contemplation by the audience. Moreover, they are also characters in the action of the drama as well as didactic 'types.' To see the figures of the souls, as David Leigh has done, as illustrating a "nonliteral representation of the human race" and hence as characterizations different from those in preceding plays, is misleading for two reasons.[45] First, they are 'literal'—they are souls rejoined to the body summoned to judgment as part of the literal action of the drama. The reference in their speeches is first of all to the situation on the stage, to "þe high justise" (100), to the Angels who summon them from the grave (107), to "þis hydous horne" (115), or, in the last speech quoted, to the "foule feendis" waiting to receive the damned (157). And second, while their importance as types is stressed—they speak as representatives—they are to be seen as the definitive focus for the exemplary mode that has informed the characterizations throughout the plays. To be sure, they do not enact in speech and gesture the humility or willfulness of earlier characters. The deeds are done by which they are judged. But their generalized expressions of penitence or despair sustain the paradigmatic oppositions displayed in previous plays even as, in the context of the Judgment, they give it its most meaningful definition: some men are saved and some are damned. If this truth is reductive, it is also everything. And if this ending emphasizes the paradigmatic at the expense of the circumstantial, it does not deny the latter. On the contrary, it depends upon it, for what the drama shows is that all the events and actions it contains, explicitly those of Biblical history, implicitly those of the audience, are part of a process that leads inexorably to the fulfillment of God's will in the Last Judgment when the saved and the damned will be parted.

As the Second *anima mala* cries for all the damned, "Allas! unborne and we hadde bene" (168), the Angel of God appears to separate the Good from the Bad in preparation for the final Judgment. He echoes God's words as he carries out His commandment, most noticeably in the verbal antitheses that accomplish the separation even as they explain it:

> Þe goode on his right hande ȝe goe,
> Þe way till hevene he will you wisse;
> Ȝe weryed wightis, ȝe flee hym froo
> On his left hande as none of his.
>
> (173–176)

Into the space created on the stage by this separation, Christ now comes "to deme my domes" (181), descending to earth in His flesh marked with the signs of His redemptive Passion for "All mankynde" to see (184). We cannot be sure how this play was staged, but it creates the opportunities for some spectacular effects. I have already pointed out that the Mercers Guild at York owned a pageant-wagon with an elaborately decorated superstructure to represent heaven, complete with an iron swing on which Christ could move from heaven to earth; they also list among their properties "Array for god þat ys to say a Sirke wounded a diademe with a veserne gilted."[46] No doubt these properties would have been used in the performance of the Judgment play—the visual spectacle offered by the play must have been full of movement and colorful detail. In contrast to the Creation play where the poetry works to enhance the stage spectacle, in the Judgment play the poetry is used primarily to sustain the dignity and quiet solemnity of the action, to order and focus the effects of staging. Christ's descent is verbally subdued. Setting the Apostles beside the Judgment seat "To here þe dome of gode and ill" (203), He explains that, as He had promised them, those who have listened to the disciples' message and have repented their sinfulness will go with them and "wynly wake" (196—a beautifully elliptical phrase to describe the state of everlasting joy), while those who have rejected the disciples' teaching "Shulde fare to fyre with fendis blake" (198). The Apostles take their places (they, too, are represented by two spokesmen who are aligned with the Good Souls and with the Angels by their prayerful exclamations, "I love þe, lord god all myghty" [204; cf. 209, 212]), the first with an extended prayer of loving obedience to the will of Christ, the second with the undisguised explanation of Christ's actions that "here is it sene / Þou will fulfille þi forward right / And all þi sawes þou will maynteyne" (209–211). The playwrights who reworked the York Last Judgment play for the Towneley cycle—among them, the Wakefield Master—seem to have found this scene between Christ and the Apostles unimpressive or unnecessary. They replace it with an energetic scene in which the devils in hell, notably Tutivillus, rejoice at the sins of men which will bring so many to them, a scene that allows for lively and pointed social satire. Though it is an impressive scene, the play loses much by the change. Most crucially, I think, it loses the lyrical intimacy, even tenderness, of the York scene, so crucial to the balance between serenity and admonition which the play as a whole achieves. Moreover, the scene also reflects and resolves some motifs developed throughout the cycle. The fact that Christ descends in fulfillment of the promises He made to the disciples and to men is stated four times in the short scene (11. 188, 201, 210, 216), thus confirming in the awesome context of Last Judgment that aspect of the narrative which has extended the movement of the plot to the audience. And that the Apostles are present with Christ, and do speak, confirms the exemplary modes of the drama which have encouraged the audience to make themselves disciples of Christ: even as the Apostles are placed in glory, the first Apostle's words present a final verbal image of that humble obedience which the plays have offered the audience as a way to win the bliss of heaven at the Last Judgment. The

Second Apostle acknowledges with gratitude that they "þat has erthely bene" are granted such dignity (213–214); in the midst of Angels and Devils, and Good and Bad Souls, the Apostles provide a warming image of men.[47]

"Cum cantu angelorum," Christ now moves to the seat of Judgment. But the Judgment so long expected is further delayed, first to allow the audience a timely glimpse of the devils gleefully awaiting the "full grete partie" (224) that will accompany them to hell since God "schall do right to foo and frende" (225); and second, to allow Christ in a lengthy and powerful speech to announce the Day of Judgment and to display the marks of His Passion. In this speech as throughout the play, the basic homiletic motive is rendered less obtrusive and yet more compelling by the lyricism of the verse and by the appeal made to the audience. Christ's opening demand for attention, "Ilke a creature, takes entent" (229) recalls that of His earlier appeals from the cross; now, however, the appeal is made to those on the stage, specifically to the damned who have rejected the offer of mercy and the demand for compassion made by His Passion. For them, the summons is full of terror. For them, this is "The day of kaydyfnes," "þe day of bale and bittirnes," "The day of drede to more and less, / Of care, of trymbeling, and of tene" (237, 239, 241–242). The copyist first wrote "ire" instead of "care" in this last phrase, no doubt hearing in this cumulatively imposing description of the Judgment Day echoes of the awesome liturgical hymn *Dies irae*.[48]

The Christ who speaks here is the Judge who comes "as crouned kynge" (232) from God. But in a paradox from which pictorial representations had drawn a moving intensity (no doubt paralleled in Christ's visual appearance in the play), Christ also comes as the man who suffered death on the cross. Fulfilling His promise to the disciples in the Ascension play, Christ now displays the marks of His suffering:[49]

Here may ȝe see my woundes wide
Þe whilke I tholed for youre mysdede,
Thurghe harte and heed, foote, hande, and hide,

Nought for my gilte, butt for youre nede.
Beholdis both body, bak, and side,
How dere I bought youre brotherhede:
Þes bittir peynes I wolde abide
To bye you blisse, þus wolde I bleede.

(245–252)

As in God's opening prologue, the changing rhythms of the lines and the pointing of alliteration are the basis of the poetry's effectiveness—the slow detailing of the wounds in the third line of this stanza, the antithesis of the fourth, the enjambement in the last two lines to stress the wonderful nature of Christ's grace that made Him suffer to bring men to bliss. Christ goes on to recount how He was scourged, crucified, crowned with thorns, pierced with the spear, and spat upon—all for love of mankind. Finally, He makes this appeal:

Behalde, mankynde, þis ilke is I
Þat for þe suffered swilke mischeve;
Þus was I dight for thy folye,
Man, loke, thy liffe was to me full leffe.
Þus was I dight þi sorowe to slake;
Manne, þus behoved þe to borowed be,
In all my woo toke I no wrake,
Mi will itt was for þe love of þe.
Man, sore aught þe for to quake
Þis dredfull day þis sight to see;
All þis I suffered for þi sake—
Say, man, what suffered þou for me?

(265–276)

Disturbing enough in the context of the Passion, Christ's question is here overwhelming in its reproachfulness. While the speech at every point recalls the Passion and the appeals then made, its effect is more complicated in the context of the Judgment. There the effect had been to elicit loving compassion—from both the figures on the stage and from the audience. Here, instead of providing a communion through love, Christ's speech becomes a means of measuring the distance between man and Christ. For the souls on the stage, that distance is terrifyingly definitive. But for the audience—and it is impossible not to hear the audience addressed in the repeated exclamation, "Manne"—the lyric form is still a powerful way of bringing them to an awareness of the love of God for man that allows repentance to be efficacious, even though its primary effect is to reproach them too for their failure to respond with love to the demonstration of love which Christ's wounds give witness to. There is, then, a difference in meaning for those on the stage and for the audience; but whereas in earlier plays similar discrepancies had produced an irony directed against those on stage for their refusal to listen to Christ's appeal, here the irony is turned against the audience.

The tableau is set: Christ in glory surrounded by His "darlyngis dere," with the blessed on His right hand and the damned on His left. The rest of the play explains this tableau for an audience inevitably excluded from it, but explains it in such a way that its urgent relevance to the audience is also made clear. In precisely parallel speeches based on the words of Christ in Matthew xxv, 34–46, Christ welcomes the blessed and rejects the damned. The following stanzas are representative of this moving sequence:

Mi blissid childre on my right hande
Youre dome þis day ȝe thar not drede,
For all youre comforte is command:
Youre liffe in likyng schall ȝe lede.
Commes to þe kyngdome ay lastand
Þat ȝou is dight for youre goode dede,
Full blithe may ȝe be where ȝe stande
For mekill in hevene schall be youre mede.

Whenne I was hungery ȝe me fedde,
To slake my thirste youre harte was free,
Whanne I was clothles ȝe me cledde,
Ȝe wolde no sorowe uppon me see.
In harde presse[50] whan I was stedde

Of my paynes ȝe hadde pitee,
Full seke whan I was brought in bedde
Kyndely ȝe come to coumforte me. . . .

Ȝe cursid caytiffis of Kaymes kynne,
Þat nevere me comforte in my care,
I and ȝe for ever will twynne
In dole to dwelle for evermare.
Youre bittir bales schall never blynne
Þat ȝe schall have whan ȝe come þare.
Þus have ȝe served for youre synne
For derffe dedis ȝe have done are.

Whanne I had mistir of mete and drynke,
Caytiffis, ȝe cacched me fro youre ȝate,
Whanne ȝe were sette as sirs on benke
I stode þer-oute, werie and wette,
Was none of yowe wolde on me thynke
Pyte to have of my poure state;
Þer-fore till hell I schall you synke
Weele are ȝe worthy to go þat gate.

(277–292; 317–332)

That this is the just God who judges is neatly conveyed in the perfect symmetry of Christ's speeches. But with an unostentatious delicateness, the dramatist has avoided making Christ harsh or His judgments repellent. The impact of the scene lies mainly in the discrepancy between the situation of the characters on the stage, for whom these words seal their fate, and that of the audience who, with the loving assurance that the good will be saved as well as the warning that the bad will be damned, still have time to change the actions by which they will be judged.

The works that Christ describes and explains belong to the Seven Works of Mercy familiar to the audience from their frequent formulation in contemporary handbooks and sermons used to instruct the laity. The formulation is paradigmatic—all acts are to be located within this paradigm through which they are recognized to be an imitation or rejection of Christ. That is what the Souls on the stage cannot understand. The Bad Souls plaintively wonder how the Almighty God can ever have been in a position to need their help and pity:

> Whan had þou, lorde þat all thyng has,
> Hungir or thirste? sen þou god is,
> Whan was [that][14] þou in prisonne was?
> Whan was þou naked or herberles?
>
> (349–353)

The answer comes: "To leste or moste whan ȝe it did / To me ȝe did þe selve and þe same" (363–364). It transcends the limits of the play as surely as it transcends the historical identity of Christ. Having witnessed how Christ comes to men to save them and judge them, having been urged to follow the example of Christ and heed His teachings, the audience is finally told and shown how they can enact in their own lives what they have learned and so join those who will be taken to Christ at the Last Judgment.

To Christ are given the last words of the play:

> Mi chosen childir, comes unto me,
> With me to wonne nowe schall ȝe wende,
> Þere joie and blisse schall ever be
> Youre liffe in lyking schall ȝe lende.
> Ȝe cursed kaitiffis, fro me ȝe flee
> In helle to dwelle with-outen ende;
> Þer ȝe schall nevere butt sorowe see
> And sitte be Satanas þe fende.
> Nowe is fulfillid all my for-þoght
> For endid is all erthely thyng;
> All worldly wightis þat I have wroght
> Aftir þer werkis have nowe wonnyng.
> Thei þat wolde synne and sessid noght
> Of sorowes sere now schall þei syng,
> And þei þat mendid þame whils þei moght
> Schall belde and bide in my blissyng.
>
> (365–380)

The plan of God, like the action of the cycle, is fulfilled, and all earthly things, like the cycle itself, are brought to an end. Behind the formulation in these last words lies the cumulative force of the play's enactment of the controlling will of God and of the options available to men, an enactment which at every point has revealed that the will of God must and can be fulfilled in the lives of those who watch this image of the ending of the world and sense its immanence in their present moment. In the inclusive and conclusive antithesis of the last stanza of the play lie all the actions of men, and between the past and future tenses of the final quatrain lies all of time as an eternal presentness which, now the play is ended, is the presentness of the audience.

We have no idea of what the devils do to the damned at the end of the play. A stage direction tells us what Christ does: *Et sic facit finem cum melodia angelorum transiens a loco ad locum.* Amidst the singing of the Angels, Christ returns to heaven where the play had begun. He leaves behind the audience: it is now for them to determine whether or not they will join Him when they are summoned to Judgment.

Conclusion

Vastness and variety—these are perhaps the most lasting impressions left by the York Corpus Christi Play. In simple statistical terms its size is remarkable: forty-eight separate plays, over three hundred speaking parts, more than thirteen thousand lines of dialogue. At least fourteen hours would be needed to perform the complete cycle just at a single location.[1] Unconcerned with the effects aimed at by the classical dramatic unities, this drama boldly takes the whole cosmos as its place, the whole of history as its time, and, as the basis of its action, the most comprehensive and significant story the playwrights and their audiences knew. No less remarkable is the variety offered by the plays, a variety which must be in part the result of the drama's historical development but which should also be seen as the result of an artistic responsiveness to the potential of the inclusive action. Many scenes are crowded with incidents and figures, rich in details which can easily be overlooked when there is so much to see—Pilate's wife swaying off to bed after a glass of wine (XXX, 126), Joseph sheepishly letting Mary go before him to confront the intimidating Doctors in the temple (XX, 233–248). Other scenes stand out in sharp relief as familiar tableaux—the Creation, the Nativity, Doomsday. Brutality and tenderness, dignity and confusion, grandeur and simplicity all find a place in this drama. The comparison with medieval cathedrals comes to mind: in both we can sense the variety of the world and the fullness of God in the world.

Yet in all their variety, the York plays, again like the cathedrals, create a strong sense of the marvelous coherence of all they contain. No single dramatic principle seems capable of explaining this coherence, just as no single theme can include the drama's variety of emphasis. The playwrights clearly felt free to work in piecemeal fashion on the collection of plays, shaping and developing the individual play rather than the whole cycle. And yet it seems just as clear that what allowed this freedom was the firmness of the whole and some shared understanding of its significance, as well as a sure and un-selfconscious sense of what the purpose of the drama was. That last point is what this study has been stressing—that the coherence of the York Corpus Christi Play is as much a rhetorical as a dramatic coherence.

In a study that did much to reinstate the medieval religious drama as a rewarding object of critical attention, O. B. Hardison, Jr. claimed that the "most imperative challenge" for the early Middle Ages was "the need to achieve outward and visible expression of the forms of union between the human and the divine."[2] Though Hardison is pointing to the liturgy as an expression that met this challenge, his words aptly describe the most general terms in which we should see the aims and the achievement of the Corpus Christi drama. The cycle plays show that union in order to create it. Our attention, then, is properly on both the dramatic image offered by the plays and the ways in which the audience is brought to see and respond to that image. As the chapters of this study have tried to show, these two dimensions of the York plays are hardly separable. Internal motifs and patterns that give coherence to the dramatic action are consistently the intensification of concerns derived from the drama's address of the audience—we have seen, for example, how the thematic motif of the true versus the false teacher internalizes the drama's purpose to instruct its audience, or how the structuring of episodes around a movement from sorrow to joy reflects the experience of the audience to define their emotional involvement with the action. At other moments—when Christ speaks from the cross or when John the Baptist preaches to the audience—the explicit acknowledgment of the audience becomes a way of extending the action to include the audience and to assure their awareness of their involvement in the action as it moves toward its fulfillment in God.

Especially in performance, every aspect of the drama participates in creating this constant interaction between the world of the plays and the audience. To the extent that the stage is a place separate from the space occupied by the audience (and it is clear that during most of the action it *is* a separate place), it images heaven, earth, and hell in their proper relationship and shows earth to be the place where God and man come together in anticipation of their reunion in heaven. But to the extent that the stage is extended to include the audience (and it is, both when characters appear among the audience and when they address the audience from the stage) it is also the place where the audience and God come together as they will again, the plays make clear, when Christ descends "till erþe" at the Last Judgment (XLVIII, 179).

Similarly the temporal dimension of the plays comes to mediate between the audience's time and the eternity in which God exists. The fact that drama takes place in a perpetual present makes it a superbly appropriate medium for presenting a history which is also understood to be perpetually present, but that coincidence is given more precise definition in the plays. The unfolding of the plays becomes, I have suggested, an analogue of the process of history which incorporates the audience in it. And that the time of the drama comes to an end does not in any way compromise its meaningfulness for the audience in their extradramatic time. On the contrary, as an experience taking place in time, the drama becomes a precise analogue of the process of history, as precise as the Incarnation itself. Both are events complete and real in time, yet still to be fulfilled in time, events in which past, present, and future are contained, events which image the whole action of God in terms of man's understanding so that men might be brought to fulfill that action in their own lives and for the time being in anticipation of the time when it will be fulfilled finally and for eternity. Both the literal reality of the drama's time, like the literal reality of the stage, and its figural meaning, like that of the stage, are important to the drama's effect.

That effect, I have been arguing, we recognize most clearly in the poetry of the plays, in what the audience hears during performance, as its interplay of dramatic and rhetorical effects works to include the audience within the design of God which it helps to show forth. Like all dramatic poetry, that of the York plays is called upon first of all to give life and definition to the dramatic image presented to the audience. And it does—in the liveliness of its details as well as the variety of its styles and textures. There may be isolated plays from other cycles in which the poetry is more imaginatively handled, such as the Wakefield Master's plays or the play of the Woman taken in Adultery in the *Ludus Coventriae* cycle. But none of the other cycles rivals York for the consistent assuredness with which the poetry brings characters and incidents to life or establishes the tone of the action. Moreover, while the Chester cycle in its uniformity of style and verse form might seem the most homogeneous of the cycles, the variety of style and meter in the York plays does not in any way disrupt the cycle's coherence. On the contrary, that coherence, as we have seen, is in large part the result of patterns sustained in the poetry, patterns of style, of traditional forms, of repeated images or phrases. Even the poetry of the York Realist, so dramatically powerful, derives its force in part from patterns established in surrounding plays of whose significance he, and the audience, remain aware. In the creation and ordering of the dramatic world of the plays, the poetry plays an impressive part, supple enough in its language and rhythms to image both God and men.

But the appropriateness of the poetry of the York plays

cannot be judged on the basis of dramatic criteria alone. In the Corpus Christi drama, the audience and their place in the action are still of crucial concern, so we should expect to find poetry that justifies itself by the appeal it makes to the audience outside the play. Poetry of exposition and poetry of devotion have a rightful place in a drama that aims at explaining and moving. But granting that, we can also recognize how unobtrusively the rhetorical aims are accomplished without compromising the fictive life of the drama, how thoroughly the rhetorical and the dramatic merge in the poetry of the York plays. The traditions of poetry and the possibilities of drama reinforce each other. The needs of the dramatic form impose a discipline on the poetry and demand a flexibility of it which revitalize the traditional modes from which it is made; at the same time, the strategic handling of these traditional modes creates that interpenetration of the world of the plays and the world of the audience which is the basis of the drama's effectiveness, and of its purpose.

The remarkable achievement of the York Corpus Christi Play—one that some twentieth-century dramatists such as Brecht and Eliot have worked for—is that it is so completely dramatic and rhetorical. What allows this achievement, and makes it so difficult for modern dramatists to imitate, is that there is as yet in the drama no distinction between the "reality" constituted by the plays and the "reality" constituted by the audience. However actual both might be, both are made incomplete and tentative by the fact that behind both, manifested in both, is the only reality of God. The lives of the people in the audience and the world they inhabit are finally as insubstantial as the play itself:

> Men seis þe worlde but vanite
> ȝitt will no-manne be ware þer-by
> Ilke a day þer mirroure may þei se
> ȝitt thynke þei noȝt þat þei schall dye,

God says as He prepares to bring the world, and the cycle of plays, to an end (XLVIII, 49–52). Given the familiarity of the metaphor, it is tempting to describe the York plays as themselves a "mirroure." But they are neither just the Shakespearean mirror held up to reflect the reality of the audience, nor are they just, as Anne Righter has described them, "a glass held up towards the Absolute, reflecting the 'age and body of the time' only incidentally."[3] They are both. As a *speculum humanae salvationis*, the drama is an image in which the action of God is revealed in terms of the actions of men and in which the actions of men are reflected in terms of the action of God. From its insistence on the here and now, the drama derives its vitality. But by leading from the contemporary to the eternal, from the particular to the universal, from man to God, it achieves its distinctive effectiveness—it fulfills, for the moment, the design of God.

Notes

Introduction

1. Homer A. Watt, "The Dramatic Unity of the *Secunda Pastorum*," in *Essays and Studies in Honor of Carleton Brown* (New York, 1940), p. 158; A. P. Rossiter, *English Drama from Early Times to the Elizabethans* (London, 1950), p. 66; V. A. Kolve, *The Play Called Corpus Christi* (Stanford, 1966), p. 272.

2. See John R. Elliott, Jr., "A Checklist of Modern Productions of the Medieval Mystery Cycles in England," *Research Opportunities in Renaissance Drama* 13–14 (1970–1971): 259–266.

3. For examinations of the assumptions behind early criticism of the medieval religious drama, see O. B. Hardison, Jr., *Christian Rite and Christian Drama in the Middle Ages* (Baltimore, 1965), pp. 1–34; Jerome Taylor, "Critics, Mutations, and Historians of Medieval English Drama," in *Medieval English Drama: Essays Critical and Contextual*, ed. Jerome Taylor and Alan Nelson (Chicago, 1972), pp. 1–27.

4. The most direct influence of the Corpus Christi drama on modern dramatists is found in the religious verse plays of T. S. Eliot, Charles Williams, Dorothy Sayers, and others. See the excellent study by William V. Spanos, *The Christian Tradition in Modern British Verse Drama* (New Brunswick, 1967).

5. *Play Called Corpus Christi*, p. 1.

6. *The English Mystery Plays* (Berkeley and Los Angeles, 1972).

7. John Gardner has addressed himself to these questions in his

recent study of the Wakefield cycle, *The Construction of the Wakefield Cycle* (Carbondale and Edwardsville, Illinois, 1974). My study of the York plays was complete before this book became available to me.

8. For a description of the manuscript of the York plays, see *York Plays,* ed. Lucy Toulmin Smith (Oxford, 1885; reissued New York, 1963), pp. xi–xviii.

9. Rossiter, *English Drama from Early Times,* p. 54; Eleanor Prosser, *Drama and Religion in the English Mystery Plays* (Stanford, 1961), p. 62.

10. *English Religious Drama of the Middle Ages* (Oxford, 1955), p. 62.

11. Arnold Williams, *The Drama of Medieval England* (East Lansing, Michigan, 1961), p. 141.

12. "Style in the English Mystery Plays," *JEGP* 38 (1938): 496–524.

13. *Drama and Religion,* p. 63.

14. See Charles Davidson, *Studies in the English Mystery Plays* (New Haven, 1892), pp. 102–147; W. W. Greg, *Bibliographical and Textual Problems of the English Mystery Plays* (London, 1914); E. K. Chambers, *English Literature at the Close of the Middle Ages* (Oxford, 1943), pp. 28–33; Craig, *English Religious Drama,* pp. 151–256.

15. Williams, *Drama of Medieval England,* p. 141.

16. *The Chester Plays,* ed. Hermann Deimling and J. Matthews, EETS e.s. 62, p. 1 (from Ms. Harl. 2013). Paul Strohm stresses the rhetorical aims of the Chester plays in his valuable unpublished dissertation "The Dramatic and Rhetorical Techniques of the Chester Mystery Plays" (University of California, Berkeley, 1966).

17. *English Mystery Plays,* p. 100.

I. The Poetry of the Play

1. A. M. Kinghorn, *Mediaeval Drama* (London, 1968), p. 19; cf. Wells, "Style in the English Mystery Plays," 54. Woolf, *English Mystery Plays,* p. 106, has more generously observed that "the splendor of the thought is sustained by the measured stanza form made weighty by alliteration."

2. Kinghorn, *Mediaeval Drama,* p. 16.

3. The technical description of the stanza form is: $abab_4cddc_3$. This form is used in two other plays in the cycle (Plays XL and XLV). Though variations in the rhyme scheme occur in the last four lines, the specific variation I point to here occurs in only one other stanza, when Jesus speaks to the Virgin Mary in the play of

the Death of Mary (XLV, 151–158). There too there is some appropriateness in the effect, for it joins the pronouns "me" and "þe" precisely at the point when Jesus summons Mary to Him.

4. The four extant cycles all open with some version of the formula, "Ego sum Alpha et O, primus et novissimus." The words are from Revelations xxii, 13, where they are spoken by Christ. But whereas the other cycles justify the application of these words to the Creator by having God explain the nature of the Trinity, the York play foregoes such an exposition. It seems to insist, in fact, that it is the Second Person of the Trinity who is the Creator, for the words from Revelations are supported by the equally familiar words of Christ from John xiv, 5: "I am the Way, the Truth, and the Life." In this connection it is interesting that when God speaks later in the play a later hand has inserted the abbreviation "Ihc" before the word "Deus" that identifies the speaker. The idea that "the thought of the Father was realized in the Son through whom it passed from potentiality to act, and thus the Son is the true Creator" is thoroughly traditional (Emile Mâle, *The Gothic Image*, tr. Dora Nussey [London, 1961] p. 29; cf. Ruth M. Ames, *The Fulfillment of the Scriptures: Abraham, Moses and Piers* [Evanston, 1970] pp. 53–72, esp. 66–68). The theological implications of this opening formula would perhaps not be apparent to many members of the audience, but its implications for the drama are substantial: Christ introduces the action which He will conclude in the play of the Last Judgment. The formula thus anticipates and includes the end of the action it introduces and at the same time points to the means by which the action will be fulfilled.

5. *Cursor Mundi*, ed. Richard Morris, EETS o.s. (1874), Trinity Ms., ll. 271–288.

6. See Stanley J. Kahrl, *Traditions of Medieval English Drama* (London, 1974), pp. 27–52.

7. For useful collections of records concerning the Corpus Christi procession and the play at York, see Smith, *York Plays*, pp. xvii–xlii; E. K. Chambers, *The Medieval Stage* (2 vv., Oxford, 1902), II, pp. 399–406; Arthur Brown, "York and Its Plays in the Middle Ages," in *Chaucer under seine Zeit*, ed. Arno Esch (Tübingen, 1968), pp. 407–418; Canon S. J. Purvis, *From Minster to Market Place* (York, 1969); and Alan H. Nelson, *The Medieval English Stage* (Chicago and London, 1974). Nelson's fresh, though controversial, interpretation of some of the relevant records has encouraged us to see that York had both a nondramatic Corpus Christi Play—a procession of pageants—and the dramatic Corpus Christi Play recorded in the Register. Though Nelson seems to argue that the plays were not presented on the wagons used in the liturgical procession, his argument is not conclusive.

8. Kahrl, *Traditions of Medieval English Drama*, pp. 38–39; cf. Williams, *Drama of Medieval England*, pp. 97–98.

9. See Alexandra F. Johnston and Margaret Dorrell, "The Doomsday Pageant of the York Mercers, 1433," *Leeds Studies in English*, n.s., 5 (1973): 29–34.

10. See, e.g., E. Martin Browne, "Producing the Mystery Plays for Modern Audiences," *Drama Survey* 3 (1963): 5–15.

11. *Ludus Coventriae or The Plaie Called Corpus Christi*, ed. K. S. Block EETS e.s. 120 (1922), p. 17, 11. 29–30.

12. Guild records from other cities, and pictorial traditions, suggest that the Angels would have been brightly dressed, perhaps in feathered costumes of different colors, with painted wings and jeweled belts and collars, and might have carried symbolic attributes to identify the various orders: see Glynne Wickham, *Early English Stages, 1300–1660* (2 vv., London, 1959, 1963), I, pp. 106–107, and M. D. Anderson, *Drama and Imagery in English Medieval Churches* (Cambridge, 1963), pp. 167–168. For discussions of the nature and function of music in the Corpus Christi plays, see Fletcher Collins, Jr., "Music in the Craft Cycles," *PMLA* 47 (1932): 613–621; R. W. Ingram, "The Use of Music in English Miracle Plays," *Anglia* 75 (1957): 55–76; John R. Moore, "The Tradition of Angelic Singing in English Drama," *JEGP* 22 (1923): 89–99; and John Stevens, "Music in Medieval Drama," *Proceedings of the Royal Musical Association* 84 (1958): 81–95. Stevens has suggested the symbolic function of music: "It is there, like God's beard of gold or the horned animal heads of the devils, because it signifies something. It is easy to be misled by the directions which require music to be played, or sung, at some of the great dramatic moments. The point was not to increase dramatic tension or to 'soften up' the audience, but *representation*. 'Heaven is music,' so at the crises in the drama when heaven directly intervenes, music too intervenes" (83).

13. The idea dramatically realized here is traditional. In *The City of God*, Book XI, ch. 19, St. Augustine interprets the words from Genesis, "God divided the light from the darkness; and God called the light Day and the darkness he called Night," as describing also the separation of the Good and the Bad Angels. For him, light is "the society of holy angels whose minds are aglow with the illumination of Truth," and darkness is "the society of evil angels whose darkened minds turned away from the light of justice" (tr. Demetrius Zema *et al.* [New York, 1950–1952]).

14. *Early English Stages*, I, p. xxvii.

15. See Hans-Jürgen Diller, "The Craftsmanship of the Wakefield Master," *Anglia* 83 (1965): 271–288, reprinted in *Medieval English Drama*, ed. Taylor and Nelson, pp. 245–259.

16. *Traditions of Medieval English Drama*, pp. 53–55. For an excellent commentary on this play, see J. W. Robinson, "A Commentary on the York Play of the Birth of Jesus," *JEGP* 70 (1971): 241–254.

17. "The Theater of the World: A Study in Medieval Dramatic Form," *The Chaucer Review* 7 (1974), 244.

18. From a complaint by Friar William Melton against the York plays, 1426. The translation is that of Francis Drake in *Eboracum, or the History and Antiquities of the City of York* (London, 1736), pp. xxix–xxx. Some interesting illustrations of how preachers thought their congregations behaved are given by G. R. Owst, *Preaching in Medieval England* (Cambridge, 1926), pp. 331–333, and Homer G. Pfander, *The Popular Sermon of the Medieval Friar in England* (New York, 1937), p. 8.

19. The twelfth-century Anglo-Norman play *Le Mystère d'Adam* contains the following instruction: "Adam shall be well-trained not to answer too quickly nor too slowly when he has to answer. Not only Adam, but all the actors, shall be instructed to control their speech and to make their actions appropriate to the matter they speak of; and in speaking the verse, not to add a syllable, nor to take one away, but to enunciate everything distinctly, and to say everything in the order laid down": *Medieval French Plays,* ed. and tr. Richard Axton and John Stevens (Oxford, 1971), p. 7. See also J. W. Robinson, "Medieval English Acting," *Theatre Notebook* 13 (1959): 83–88.

20. From the *Proclamacio ludi corporis cristi facienda in vigilia corporis cristi* in Smith, *York Plays,* p. xxxiv.

21. Smith, *York Plays,* p. xxxvii.

22. E.g., E. Martin Browne, "Producing the Mystery Plays," 7: "The plays are written in a verse sometimes elaborately decorated with alliteration and often quite complex in pattern. Its value lies not only in its flavor, but in its aid to the actor. The amateur who has to sustain a big part finds that the verse structure holds him up and enables him to stretch himself to the size of his material. He may take some time to master the verse so that he can speak it in a free and real manner; but he will be repaid. These writers, writing for amateur players, knew what they were doing."

23. Owst, *Preaching in Medieval England,* p. 273.

24. E.g., "The Cambridge Prologue" in *Non-Cycle Plays and Fragments,* ed. Norman Davis, EETS s.s. 1 (1970), pp. 114–115.

25. Grace Frank's study of French medieval drama, *The Medieval French Drama* (Oxford, 1954), contains useful descriptions of the verse forms of the French plays and comments on their effects. See also Richard Axton and John Stevens, eds., *Medieval French Plays.*

26. The text of the *Sponsus* play is printed in Karl Young, *The Drama of the Medieval Church* (2 vv., Oxford, 1933), II, pp. 362–364.

27. *Le Mystère d'Adam,* ed. Paul Studer (Manchester, 1918).

28. "Franciscan Spirituality and the Rise of Early English Drama," *Mosaic* 8 (1975), 19.

29. For an excellent study of the Franciscan aesthetic especially as it affects vernacular lyric verse in England and Europe, see David Jeffrey, *The Early English Lyric and Franciscan Spirituality* (Lincoln, Nebraska, 1975).

30. "Poetry and Drama," in *On Poetry and Poets* (New York, 1957), p. 75.

31. Smith, *York Plays*, pp. li–lii, provides a "Sketch-Analysis of Metres" for the plays.

32. See especially Craig, *English Religious Drama*, pp. 220–233, where the findings of previous investigators are evaluated.

33. The most thorough technical study of the alliterative verse of the York plays is Jesse Byers Reese, "Alliterative Verse in the York Cycle," *SP* 48 (1951): 639–668.

34. Smith, *York Plays*, p. 102.

35. *English Literature at the Close of the Middle Ages* (Oxford, 1945), p. 30.

36. Plays X, XI, XII, XV, XVII, XX, XXIII, XXIV, XXVII, XXXV, XXXVII, XLIV.

37. Craig, *English Religious Drama*, pp. 223–224. The influence of the Middle English Gospel of Nichodemus on the York plays was first proposed by W. A. Craigie, "The 'Gospel of Nicodemus' and the York Play," in *An English Miscellany Presented to Dr. Furnivall* (Oxford, 1911), pp. 52–61.

38. H. J. Chaytor, *The Troubadours in England* (Cambridge, 1923). The most comprehensive manual of verse forms in Middle English poetry is John L. Cutler, "A Manual of Middle English Stanzaic Patterns," (unpublished dissertation, Ohio State University, 1949).

39. For extensive analysis of both the music and the stanza form of this play, see Sister Catherine Louise Wall, "A Study of 'The Appearance of Our Lady to Thomas': Pageant XLVI in the York Cycle of Mystery Plays" (unpublished dissertation, Catholic University of America, 1965). A similar stanza form, though with ornamental rather than structural alliteration, is used by John Audelay: see *The Poems of John Audelay*, ed. Ella Keats Whiting, EETS o.s. 184 (1931), pp. xxi–xxii.

40. Allardyce Nicoll, *British Drama* (5th ed., New York, 1962), p. 36.

41. *Christian Rite and Christian Drama*, p. 276.

42. Moody E. Prior, *The Language of Tragedy* (New York, 1947), p. 14.

43. Ibid., p. 15.

44. Katherine Lee Bates, *The English Religious Drama* (New York, 1921), p. 169.

45. "The Relationship of Chaucer to the English and European Traditions," in *Chaucer and Chaucerians*, ed. Brewer (London, 1966), pp. 1–2.

46. See Hardison, *Christian Rite and Christian Drama,* pp. 1–34, 178–283. Cf. Kolve, *Play Called Corpus Christi,* pp. 33–42, and Woolf, *English Mystery Plays,* pp. 3–24, 39–76. Richard Axton, *European Drama of the Early Middle Ages* (London, 1974) has recently studied the two traditions, emphasizing the popular nature of the traditions of representation reflected in the vernacular plays.

47. *European Drama,* p. 104.

48. Ibid., p. 100.

49. Cf. Axton, ibid., pp. 112–130. See also Erich Auerbach, "Adam and Eve," in *Mimesis,* tr. Willard Trask (Princeton, 1953), pp. 143–173.

50. For the fullest surveys of drama in England before the cycle plays, see Axton, *European Drama,* pp. 161–168, and Woolf, *English Mystery Plays,* pp. 3–101, *passim.*

51. See "The Cambridge Prologue" and "The Rickinghall (Bury St. Edmunds) Fragment" in *Non-Cycle Plays and Fragments,* ed. Davis, pp. 114–115, 116–117. Cf. Rossell Hope Robbins, "An English Mystery Play Fragment Ante 1300," *MLN* 65 (1950): 30–35.

52. See Carleton Brown, "An Early Mention of a St. Nicholas Play in England," *SP* 28 (1931): 594–601. See also "The Durham Prologue" in *Non-Cycle Plays and Fragments,* ed. Davis, pp. 118–119.

53. Woolf, *English Mystery Plays,* p. 58. For the English verses see Carleton Brown, "Sermons and Miracle Plays: Merton College Ms 248" *MLN* 49 (1934): 394–396.

54. Printed in *Non-Cycle Plays and Fragments,* ed. Davis, pp. 90–105. A brief commentary on the play is offered by Axton, *European Drama,* pp. 166–168. I have omitted from this list of precycle drama the Shrewsbury Fragments which were once thought to be a link between the liturgical plays and the cycle plays because they contain translations of Latin lines which bear a close resemblance to parallel speeches in the York plays. More recent opinion sees the Fragments not as preceding the cycle plays but as representing "the reworking of earlier Latin offices under the influence of the cycles" (Woolf, *English Mystery Plays,* p. 331); cf. *Non-Cycle Plays and Fragments,* ed. Davis, pp. xiv–xxi, 1–7; Axton, *European Drama,* p. 163.

55. Cf. Raymond Oliver, *Poems Without Names: The English Lyric 1200–1500* (Berkeley and Los Angeles, 1970), pp. 41–73, who analyzes and stresses the "public and practical" language of the English lyric. The plays (and, I think, the lyrics) show a far wider range of effect than Oliver indicates, but his analysis gives useful terms for understanding the basic language of popular poetry of the late Middle Ages in England.

56. I am using the term "formulaic" not in the precise technical

sense developed by linguistic studies of oral poetry, but in a more general sense to describe a language characterized by stock phrases, verbal repetition, and general, abstract terms. A very useful essay surveying the linguistic studies of "oral-formulaic" poetry and their application to Old and Middle English poetry is R. F. Lawrence, "The Formulaic Theory and Its Application to English Alliterative Poetry," in *Essays on Style and Language*, ed. Roger Fowler (London, 1966), pp. 166–183. Brewer, "The Relationship of Chaucer to the English and European Traditions," and J. A. Burrow, *Ricardian Poetry* (London, 1971), pp. 11–46, examine the handling of formulaic phrases in the poetry of Chaucer and his contemporaries; Marie Borroff, *Sir Gawain and the Green Knight: A Stylistic and Metrical Study* (New Haven, 1962), and Larry D. Benson, *Art and Tradition in Sir Gawain and the Green Knight* (New Brunswick, 1965), offer full and valuable analyses of the formulaic study of an alliterative poem. Though there is much alliterative verse in York plays, it is not as intellectually or metrically sophisticated as that in *Sir Gawain*, and the comments of Borroff and Benson are, as a result, only generally of relevance.

57. The "lament of an old man" is a form found in contemporary vernacular lyrics. See George C. Taylor, "The Relation of the English Corpus Christi Play to the Middle English Religious Lyric," *MP* 5 (1907): 6–7. Stephen Manning, *Wisdom and Number* (Lincoln, Nebraska, 1962), pp. 50–55, comments on the lyric *topos* and analyzes the Harley lyric "Heȝe Louerd, þou here my bone" which is a particularly fine version of it. Manning notes the strategic use of formulaic phrases in the lyrics, and notes that "The poets . . . characterize their speakers with intensity rather than depth" (p. 50).

58. *Mimesis*, p. 158.

59. "The Aims of Poetic Drama," *Adam International Review* 200 (1949), 12. Cf. Eliot, *Religious Drama, Medieval and Modern* (New York, 1954).

II. Poetry and Instruction

1. "Dan Jon Gaytryge's Sermon," in *Religious Pieces in Prose and Verse*, ed. George Perry, EETS o.s. 26 (rev. ed. 1889), pp. 1–2.

2. Useful surveys of the vernacular homiletic works of the fourteenth century are provided by W. A. Pantin, *The English Church in the Fourteenth Century* (Cambridge, 1955), pp. 189–262, and by Owst, *Preaching in Medieval England*, pp. 222–308. The connections between these works and the Corpus Christi

plays have been explored by Prosser, *Drama and Religion,* pp. 19–42; G. R. Owst, *Literature and Pulpit in Medieval England* (2nd ed., Oxford, 1961), pp. 471–547; and Axton, *European Drama of the Early Middle Ages,* pp. 159–168.

3. *Chester Plays,* pp. 83–84.

4. *Ludus Coventriae,* pp. 192–193; *Towneley Plays,* ed. George England and Alfred W. Pollard, EETS e.s. 71 (1897), pp. 390–392.

5. The figure is not named in the Register. There is a reference in Roger Burton's descriptions of the Corpus Christi pageants at York (1415) to a "Doctor declarans dicta prophetarum de nativitate Christi futura" in the Annunciation pageant (Smith, *York Plays,* p. xx).

6. Cf. E. Catherine Dunn, "The Literary Style of the Towneley Plays," *American Benedictine Review* 20 (1969): 481–504. In a valuable essay, Dunn argues for the presence in all the Corpus Christi cycles of "a basic voice ... the voice of the Church ... This denotes an authoritative commentator, recognized by medieval men for interpretation of Scripture ... Since much of the commentary is interpretative, its function is essentially expository" (483–484). I would agree with Dunn's interesting argument that the role of expositor derives ultimately from the liturgical drama; but it has been inevitably influenced by the more readily available image of the preacher, and the poetic style of the voice is derived from the popular homiletic tradition.

7. Comments on the appropriateness of a given verse form are very rare in Middle English literature. However, Robert Mannyng of Brunne, in the prologue to his translation of Peter Langcroft's Chronicle (c. 1340) says that since he is writing for "lewed menn" he will avoid writing "in ryme couwee or in strangere or in enterlace," preferring instead "lighte ryme" (i.e., couplets). Cf. H. J. Chaytor, *The Troubadours in England* (Cambridge, 1923), pp. 5–17. Most of the lengthy treatises and sermons in verse are in couplets.

8. *English Metrical Homilies from MSS of the Fourteenth Century,* ed. John Small (Edinburgh, 1862), pp. 3–5.

9. *English Religious Drama,* p. 220.

10. MS. Bodl 2325, f. 68^b contains a metrical version, in English, of the Gospel "In die Ascensionis" which is very close to the paraphrase in the York play: see W. Heuser, "Eine Vergessene Handschrift Der Surteespsalters und die Dort Eingeschalteten Mittelenglischen Gedichte," *Anglia* 29 (1906): 385–412.

11. Quoted from MS. Worc. Cath. Libr. F. 10, fols. 49b–50, in Owst, *Literature and Pulpit,* p. 374. For their enemies, the Lollards came to be the epitome of hypocrisy: e.g., the author of *Jacob's Well,* in his instructions to priests, says, "if þou feyne þe holy, þat þou myȝt þerby dysseyve þe peple be þi fals techyng as

lollardys don, þanne synnest þou dedly": ed. Arthur Brandeis, EETS o.s. 115 (1900), pp. 164–165.

12. *Chester Plays*, pp. 224–225.

13. Cf. Peter S. Macaulay, "The Play of the Harrowing of Hell as a Climax in the English Mysteries," *Studia Germanica Gandensia* 8 (1966): 115–134. See also the discussion of the Harrowing of Hell plays in Woolf, *English Mystery Plays*, pp. 269–274.

14. Woolf, ibid., p. 271.

15. Ibid., pp. 271–272.

16. Behind the characterizations of the "Bisschopes," Annas and Caiphas, there is an extensive tradition of attacks on the abuses of priests. See, e.g., Owst, *Literature and Pulpit*, pp. 242–286. The author of the *Speculum Christiani* makes these distinctions: "Foure maner or kyndes be founden of presthode. Fyrste kynde felowes glotonye. Secunde kynde swes lechory. Therde kynde swes covetyse or veyn-glorye. Fourte kynde of preste felowes ryhghtwysnes": ed. Gustaf Holmstedt, EETS o.s. 182 (1933), pp. 174–176.

17. Cf. Strohm, "The Dramatic and Rhetorical Technique of the Chester Mystery Plays," pp. 53–82.

18. Used with reference to Hennig Brinkmann, "Zum Ursprung des Liturgischen Spieles," by Mary Hatch Marshall, "Aesthetic Values of the Liturgical Drama," reprinted in *Medieval Drama*, ed. Taylor and Nelson, p. 31.

19. The use of Thomas' doubts as a way of reinforcing the faith of a congregation is traditional in homiletic works. See, e.g., John Mirk, *Festial*, ed. Theodor Erbe, EETS e.s. 96 (1905), p. 18, who explains that one reason the Day of St. Thomas is celebrated is his "hegh prevyng of our fay . . . This holy apostoll prevet so our fay þat he lafte no scrypull yn no parte þerin." Cf. *Middle English Sermons*, ed. Woodburn O. Ross, EETS o. s. 209 (1940), p. 134.

20. *English Mystery Plays*, p. 172.

21. Ibid., p. 173. Prosser, *Drama and Religion*, pp. 92 ff., reads the York Joseph play as a (very unsatisfactory) demonstration of the doctrine of repentance, but repentance does not seem to be an issue in the play.

22. *Festial*, p. 108. There is an interesting contemporary lyric in *Religious Lyrics of the XIVth Century*, ed. Carleton Brown (rev. ed. G. V. Smithers, Oxford, 1952) #58, pp. 78–80, in which Joseph, a grey-haired and wrinkled "sergant / Þat sadlie seide his sawe," explains the mystery of the Virgin birth—a presentation analogous to that in the York play.

23. *The Play Called Corpus Christi*, p. 247.

24. Ibid., pp. 239–240.

25. Woolf, *English Mystery Plays*, p. 277.

26. Cf. Kolve, *Play Called Corpus Christi*, pp. 107–109, for a brief

discussion of the historiographical basis of the drama's concern to find moral lessons in the events it presents. For an excellent discussion of the exemplary or "illustrative" tendency of medieval narrative in general, see Robert Scholes and Robert Kellogg, *The Nature of Narrative* (Oxford, 1966), esp. pp. 82–159.

27. *Non-Cycle Plays and Fragments*, ed. Davis, pp. 56–57.

28. *Chester Plays*, p. 84, 11. 477–484 (from Mss. B, W, h).

29. Cf. the comments of Eleanor Prosser on this episode, *Drama and Religion*, pp. 104–105. She sees the dramatist as "caught between two themes," those of repentance and 'let not the guilty condemn,' arguing that the repentance theme "is forced in." I think it is she who does the forcing. At least in the episode as we have it (one leaf is missing from the Register), repentance is not the concern; Christ's meekness, as it has been in the plays of the Baptism and the Temptation, is. Prosser notes in connection with this episode in the various cycles that the dramatists "knew that the audience was so trained by the Church to respond to any story, whether recounted or enacted, as an *exemplum*" (pp. 103–104). I agree; but the York playwright's verbal emphasis on meekness shows a determination to direct that response.

30. See e.g., *Metrical Homilies*, ed. Small, pp. 154–159.

31. From *Timber, or Discoveries* in *Ben Jonson*, ed. C. M. Herford and Percy and Evelyn Simpson (Oxford, 1947), v. 8, p. 625.

32. *Middle English Sermons*, p. 120.

33. Ibid., p. 233.

34. See, e.g., Chaucer's "Manciple's Tale," where Cato, Seneca, and, most extensively, the Bible, are referred to in warnings against "janglyng": *The Works of Geoffrey Chaucer*, ed. F. N. Robinson (2nd ed., London, 1957), pp. 224–233, esp. 11. 310–362.

35. A passage in *Jacob's Well*, pp. 228–229, illustrates the kind of homiletic significance that might be associated with the verbal images of heaven and hell in the Creation play: "Crisostomus seyth: wo! wo! to ydel & wycked spekerys. Ȝif þou haddyst openyd þi tunge & stynkyng mowth to have praysed þi god, þou schuldyst have sungyn wyth aungellys in heven, wyth-outen ende, 'Sanctus! sanctus! sanctus! dominus deus omnipotens,' holy! holy! holy! almiȝty god! & for þou hast noȝt openyd þi mouthe to prayse þi god, but spekyn ydell woordys & iapys, lesynges & oþere slaundre, þerfore ȝellyng, roryng, & wepyng, þou schalt cryin with feendys in helle, wythouten ende, "ve! ve! ve! quante sunt tenebrae,' wo! wo! wo! grete arn my therknessis in peyne. Þe mouth þat lyeth in ydel woordys sleeth þe soule . . . wycked & ydell woordys corruptyn gode manerys."

36. Rosemary Woolf describes the differences in treatment of the Fall of Lucifer in the cycle plays, arguing that the York version is the most successful: *English Mystery Plays*, pp. 105–112. Robert

Brawer, on the other hand, argues for the superiority of the Towneley version in its dramatization of a conflict amongst the Angels: "Dramatic Technique in the Corpus Christi Creation and Fall," *MLQ* 32 (1971): 357–358. I prefer the York dramatist's handling of the episode. Since Lucifer is not addressed by the other Angels, his isolation—which he sees as his glory but which is his sin *and* its punishment—is emphasized. In Lucifer's speeches there is a gradual increase in his self-glorification; his fall is inevitable—there is no other agency. And the antiphonal arrangement achieves a paradigmatic clarity which subsequent plays can draw upon. Brawer does note that in the opening plays of the cycles "diction is essential in illustrating the patterns of response which the divine sovereignty elicits from mankind through-out salvation history" (354), but his concern is with specific words and phrases rather than with the styles of the speeches.

37. *Jacob's Well*, pp. 266–267.

38. E.g., Woolf, *English Mystery Plays*, p. 112.

39. *Ludus Coventriae*, p. 55, 11. 135–138.

40. The speech is given to Christ during His Trials in the *Gospel of Nicodemus*, which, it has been suggested, the York playwright was following as he composed these plays. But even there, the speech occurs much earlier in the sequence of Trials: *The Middle English Harrowing of Hell and Gospel of Nicodemus*, ed. William Henry Hulme, EETS e.s. 100 (1908), p. 36, 11. 221–224. The speech is based on Matthew 12: 34–37.

41. See e.g., J. W. Robinson, "The Art of the York Realist," *MP* 60 (1962): 241–251; Clifford Davidson, "The Realism of the York Realist and the York Passion," *Speculum* 50 (1975): 270–283.

42. Cf. Robert Brawer, "The Characterization of Pilate in the York Cycle Play," *SP* 69 (1972): 289–303.

43. The most extensive treatments of the "sins of the mouth" occur in the English treatises derived from the French *Somme le Roi.* In the fifteenth-century *Book of Vices and Virtue*, for example, the discussion of the Seven Deadly Sins is interrupted to allow a separate discussion of the Sins of the Tongue. There are ten, each taking many forms: idle words, boasting, flattery, backbiting, lying, swearing, causing strife through one's words, complaining, rebelling, blasphemy: ed. W. Nelson Francis, EETS o.s. 217 (1942), pp. 54–58. Cf. *Speculum Christiani*, ed. Gustaf Holmstedt, EETS o.s. 182 (1933), pp. 82–87, which lists thirty-three sins of the mouth.

44. *Middle English Sermons*, pp. 69–71; cf. *English Metrical Homilies*, pp. 34–59.

45. See e.g., in connection with the York plays, Purvis, *From Minster to Market-Place* pp. 18–24.

46. Ed. Edward Peacock, rev. F. J. Furnivall, EETS o.s. 31

(1902), pp. 1–2. Cf. Mirk's *Festial,* p. 192; *Middle English Sermons,* p. 53.

47. The hypocrisy of priests is a constant topic for satire and complaint. See, e.g., *Piers Plowman* Passus XV (B-text), and Owst, *Literature and Pulpit,* pp. 210–286.

48. *Middle English Sermons,* p. 279.

49. See J. A. Mosher, *The Exemplum in the Early Religious and Didactic Literature of England* (New York, 1911).

50. The exhortation to cleanse the temple of the body in preparation for the coming of God is a commonplace most frequently associated with Pentecost: see, e.g., Mirk's *Festial,* pp. 155–158; *Middle English Sermons,* pp. 103–110; *Speculum Sacerdotale,* pp. 157–161. But behind John's exhortation to "be clene haly" lies also the traditional understanding that the sacrament of baptism cleanses man of original sin "and alkyn othir syn, . . / that we er filed with ar we take it": *The Lay Folk's Catechism,* ed. Thomas F. Simmons and H. E. Nolloth, EETS o.s. 118 (1901), p. 62. At the opening of the Towneley and *Ludus Coventriae* Baptism plays, John makes a similar appeal to the audience: *Towneley Plays,* pp. 195–203, *Ludus Coventriae,* pp. 188–193.

51. See, e.g., Mirk's *Festial,* p. 48; *Stanzaic Life of Christ,* ed. Frances A. Foster, EETS o.s. 166 (1926), ll. 2309–2312.

52. *English Mystery Plays,* p. 219.

53. For a contemporary explanation of the reasons for Christ's baptism that contains striking verbal similarities to Christ's speech in the York play, see "Religious Poem by William of Nassington," in *Religious Pieces in Prose and Verse,* p. 65, ll. 173–186. An extended discussion of the exemplary humility that Christ shows at His baptism is found in *Meditations on the Life of Christ,* ed. Isa Ragusa and Rosalie B. Green (Princeton, 1961) pp. 102–116. In the *Ludus Coventriae* Baptism play, Christ, John, and God the Father all point to Christ's act as "exaumple of lowly mekenes" (ll. 73–87, 94–96).

54. The contemporary popular sermon provides close analogues to the lessons drawn from the Baptism in the York play. See, e.g., Mirk's *Festial,* pp. 47–52: "Wherfor he þat byleveth and doth þe werkes of þe byleve wythout dowte, he shall be savet; and he þat byleveth not, he schall be dampnet." Cf. *Speculum Sacerdotale,* p. 158: "We oweþ to trowe þat yche man takeþ the Holy Ghost in baptym, and he bydeþ as longe with hym as he lasteþ in riȝt beleve and good werkis." The Towneley Baptism play ends with an explicit exhortation to the audience to "Thynk how in baptym ye ar sworne / To be godis servandis withoutten nay; / let never his luf from you be lorne / God bryng you to his blys for ay" (ll. 285–288).

III. Poetry and Communion

1. Quoted from *Orologium Sapientie* (Ms. Douce 114, fol. 90), by Owst, *Preaching in Medieval England*, p. 279.

2. I had completed this chapter before having access to David L. Jeffrey's *The Early English Lyric and Franciscan Spirituality* (Lincoln, Nebraska, 1975). In this valuable study, Jeffrey offers a full account of the devotional and aesthetic aspects of English lyric verse before the mid-fourteenth century in the historical context of the Franciscan movement. His comments are always relevant to a consideration of the devotional aspects of the Corpus Christi plays and the spiritual and poetic traditions from which they are derived. Jeffrey has begun to explore the relationship between the drama and the Franciscan movement in "Franciscan Spirituality and the Rise of Early English Drama," *Mosaic* 8 (1975): 17–46.

3. Waldo F. McNeir, "The Corpus Christi Passion Plays as Dramatic Art," *SP* 48 (1951): 622.

4. *Meditations on the Supper of Our Lord, and the Hours of the Passion,* ed. J. Meadows Cowper, EETS o.s. 60 (1875), 11. 607–08, 299–300. This version of the *Meditations* is a partial translation by Robert Mannyng of the most popular of medieval devotional works, the *Meditationes Vitae Christi* attributed to St. John of Bonaventura.

5. The most notable examples are those of the Resurrection monologues of Christ in the Towneley and *Ludus Coventriae* cycles. That in Towneley is a shortened version of a lyric printed in *Religious Lyrics of the XVth Century,* ed. Carleton Brown (Oxford, 1939), pp. 151–156. That in the *Ludus Coventriae* cycle is closely related to a complaint spoken by Christ at the start of the Middle English *Harrowing of Hell,* ed. Hulme, EETS e.s. 100 (1907), 11. 27–30. For a comparison of the Towneley monologue with its nondramatic analogue, see Rosemary Woolf, *English Religious Lyric in the Middle Ages* (Oxford, 1968), pp. 202–205.

6. See George C. Taylor, "The Relation of the English Corpus Christi Play to the Middle English Religious Lyric," *MP* 5 (1907): 1–38.

7. *English Religious Lyric,* p. 19.

8. See especially Lu Emily Pearson, "Isolable Lyrics of the Mystery Plays," *ELH* 3 (1936): 228–252.

9. Cf. J. W. Robinson, "The Late Medieval Cult of Jesus and the Mystery Plays," *PMLA* 80 (1965): 511, n. 21; and Woolf, *English Mystery Plays,* p. 275 and p. 407, n. 19.

10. *Middle English Sermons,* p. 111.

11. The fullest treatment of the English lyrics of "the Complaints of Christ" is in Rosemary Woolf, *English Religious Lyric,*

esp. pp. 35–44. See also George Kane, *Middle English Literature* (London, 1951), pp. 144–146. The relationship between these independent lyrics and the speeches of Christ in the Corpus Christi plays has often been noted: see especially Taylor, "Relation of Corpus Christi Play to M. E. Religious Lyrics": 8; Pearson, "Isolable Lyrics": 246; and Woolf, *op. cit.*, p. 44.

12. *Religious Lyrics of the XIVth Century*, ed. Brown, #46, pp. 59–60.

13. From *Religious Lyrics of the XVth Century*, #108, pp. 168–169. In the Ms. the words of Christ are labeled "Querela divina" and the words of man "Responsio humana" as if to stress the paradigmatic quality of the lyric.

14. For studies which include extensive discussion of the traditions of formal meditation, see Etienne Gilson, *La Théologie Mystique de Saint Bernard* (Paris, 1947), and *History of Christian Philosophy in the Middle Ages* (New York, 1955); P. Pourrat, *La Spiritualité Chrétienne* (rev. ed., Paris, 1951), v. II; Louis L. Martz, *The Poetry of Meditation* (rev. ed., New Haven, 1962).

15. Walter Hilton, *The Scale of Perfection,* ed Evelyn Underhill (London, 1923), Book I, ch. v, p. 9. For a useful study of this work which sets it in the context of contemporary mystical and homiletic traditions, see Joseph E. Milosh, *'The Scale of Perfection' and the English Mystical Tradition* (Madison, 1966).

16. Hilton, *Scale of Perfection,* Book I, ch. xxxv, pp. 80–81.

17. Ms. St. Albans Cath. fol. 20 (MS. Laud Misc. 23), quoted in Owst, *Literature and Pulpit,* p. 508.

18. *Meditations on the Life of Christ,* ed. Ragusa and Green, p. 15.

19. Hilton, *Scale of Perfection,* Book I, ch. v, p. 10.

20. "A Sermon Against Miracle-Plays," in *Reliquiae Antiquae,* ed. Thomas Wright and James O. Halliwell (London, 1845), vol. II, p. 45.

21. Ibid., p. 48.

22. E.g., E. K. Chambers, *The Medieval Stage,* II, pp. 39–40, 75–76, 129; George C. Taylor, "The English 'Planctus Mariae,'" *MP* 4 (1907): 605–637; Paul Kretzmann, *Liturgical Element in the Earliest Forms of the Medieval Drama* (Minneapolis, 1916), esp. 89–113; Woolf, *English Mystery Plays,* pp. 263–266.

23. See the discussion, and rejection, of this long-held view by Sandro Sticca, *The Latin Passion Play: Its Origins and Development* (Albany, 1970), pp. 122–131. Cf. Young, *The Drama of the Medieval Church,* I, 492–539.

24. See especially, Taylor, "English 'Planctus Mariae,'" *passim,* and Woolf, *English Religious Lyrics,*pp. 239–273, for discussions of the *planctus* and related lyric forms in English.

25. Woolf, *English Religious Lyric,* p. 154.

26. Mirk, *Festial,* p. 113.

27. Ibid., p. 113. One fourteenth-century lyric makes particularly effective use of this devotional *topos:* see Brown, *Religious Lyrics of the XIVth Century,* #126, pp. 225–226, and cf. *A Stanzaic Life of Christ,* pp. 200–201, 11. 5921–5948.

28. "The Late Medieval Cult of Jesus," 512.

29. Taylor, "Relation of English Corpus Christi Play to Middle English Religious Lyric," 4–5, notes the obvious connection between the "Hail" lyrics of the drama and independent versions.

30. Cf. Woolf, *English Religious Lyric,* pp. 283–293; Manning, *Wisdom and Number,* pp. 62–72. For examples of such hymns to Mary see *The Poems of John Audelay,* ed. Ella Keats Whiting, EETS o.s., 184 (1931), #19,20.

31. *The Poems of John Audelay,* ed. Whiting, #8, 11. 55–62. Cf. *Worcestershire Miscellany,* ed. Nita Scudder Baugh (Philadelphia, 1956), pp. 149–150; *Speculum Christiani,* ed. Holmstedt, p. 160.

32. *Early English Stages,* I, pp. 63–81; cf. Purvis, *From Minster to Market-Place,* pp. 75–80 for examples from York.

33. See especially O. B. Hardison, Jr., *Christian Rite and Christian Drama,* pp. 35–177, and Sarah Appleton Weber, *Theology and Poetry in the Middle English Lyric* (Columbus, Ohio, 1969), pp. 1–27.

34. "In ipsa quinta feria devote turbe fidelium propter hoc ad ecclesias affectuose concurrant, ut tunc cleri et populi pariter congaudentes in cantica laudis surgant, tunc omnium corda et vota, ora et labia ymnos personent letitie salutaris": quoted and translated Kolve, *Play Called Corpus Christi,* p. 45.

35. Mary Hatch Marshall, "Aesthetic Values of the Liturgical Drama," in *Medieval Drama,* ed., Taylor and Nelson, p. 34; cf. Hardison, *Christian Rite and Christian Drama,* pp. 178–252.

36. *English Mystery Plays,* p. 278.

37. "Exultamus nimirum nostrum rememorando liberationem et recolendo passionem dominican, per quam liberati sumus, vix lacrimas continemus . . . et gaudemus pie lacrimantes et lacrimamus devote gaudentes, letas habendo lacrimas et letitiam lacrimantem": quoted and translated Kolve, *Play Called Corpus Christi,* p. 45. Note how crucial the syntax of the Latin is to the expression of balance and fusion: as I will be suggesting, the characteristic syntax in which the emotions of grief and joy are held together in the York plays is *contentio,* a syntactic structure which enacts a transformation rather than expresses a balance.

38. Pearson, "Isolable Lyrics," 234.

39. Woolf, *English Mystery Plays,* p. 120.

40. Cf. Taylor, "Relation of Corpus Christi Play to Middle English Religious Lyric," 6–7; Catherine Dunn, "Lyrical Form and the Prophetic Principle in the Towneley Plays," *Medieval Studies,* 23 (1961): 80–90. For a brief but useful analysis of this lyric form, see Manning, *Wisdom and Number,* pp. 50–54.

41. Macauley, "The Play of the Harrowing of Hell as a Climax in the English Mystery Cycles," *Studia Germanica Gandensia* 8 (1966): 115–134.

42. Woolf, *English Mystery Plays*, p. 280. The play as a whole is praised as "a beautiful lyric handling of the themes of loss, recognition, and recovery" (ibid.).

43. For the lyric, which survives in at least ten manuscripts, see Brown, *Religious Lyrics of the XIVth Century*, #91, pp. 114–119; and for a discussion of the lyric, see Woolf, *English Religious Lyric*, pp. 163–165.

44. See Rosemary Woolf, "The Theme of Christ the Lover-Knight," *RES* n.s., 12 (1962): 1–16 and *English Religious Lyric*, pp. 44–60.

45. For relevant discussions of independent lyrics on the Passion based on a dialogue between Christ and His mother, see Manning, *Wisdom and Number*, pp. 77–80, and Weber, *Theology and Poetry*, pp. 125–145.

46. Cf. Woolf, *English Mystery Plays*, pp. 289–291. The sequence of plays makes extensive use of lyric forms in praise of Mary which have been most fully discussed by Woolf, *English Religious Lyric*, pp. 114–158, 274–308.

47. See Catherine Wall, "York Pageant XLVI and its Music," *Speculum* 46 (1971): 687–712. The article is based on her unpublished dissertation which is devoted to a study of this one play from the York cycle and includes an exhaustive and suggestive examination of the lyrical aspects of this play and of the Corpus Christi drama in general: "A Study of 'The Appearance of Our Lady to Thomas': Pageant XLVI in the York Cycle of Mystery Plays" (unpublished dissertation, Catholic University of America, 1965).

48. For discussions of independent lyrics in English on the theme of the Joys of Mary, see Manning, *Wisdom and Number*, pp. 74–77; Woolf, *English Religious Lyric*, pp. 134–143, 297–302; Weber, *Theology and Poetry*, pp. 147–193.

49. *Chester Plays*, pp. 309–317 (Play XVI, 11. 689–892); *Towneley Plays*, pp. 275–278 (Play XXIII, 11. 545–666); *Ludus Coventriae*, pp. 301–305 (Play 32, 11. 846–970).

50. Smith, *York Plays*, p. xxvi.

51. I imagine the staging of the play to be thus: the crucified Christ is at the center of the stage, perhaps slightly elevated, from the start of the play. The two thieves on their crosses are on either side of Christ, perhaps toward the edges of the stage. John and the three Marys form a group at the foot of Christ's cross on His right hand. Pilate, Annas, and Caiphas, with Garcio, Longeus, and the Centurion in attendance, are, at least at the start of the play, standing apart from the crosses and below them on Christ's left hand. Such a tableau is found in many contemporary pictorial representa-

tions of the Crucifixion: see, e.g., G. McNeil Rushworth, *Medieval Christian Imagery as Illustrated by the Painted Windows of Great Malvern Priory Church, Worcestershire* (Oxford, 1936), pp. 192–193. As this tableau is brought to life in the play, Christ remains almost to the end the central visual focus, the point of reference for all the movements of the other figures, with the traditional associations of Christ's right hand with salvation and His left hand with damnation, specifically realized in the placing of the two thieves, thus adding a familiar symbolic dimension to the movements on the stage.

52. J. W. Robinson, "The Late Medieval Cult of Jesus," 513, similarly assesses the effects of this opening speech.

53. Cf. Woolf, *English Mystery Plays*, p. 265.

54. Cf. Woolf, ibid., p. 260.

55. *Northern Passion*, p. 211, 11. 1804e–1640 (Harleian Ms.).

56. Ibid., p. 211, 1. 1804a. In her comments on the connections between the York plays and the *Northern Passion*, Frances Foster points to this parallel displacement as showing that the playwright "was here following the *Passion* and not rearranging the Bible independently" EETS o.s. 147 (1916), p. 83. But there are many differences in the arrangement of the two versions; the dramatist's handling of the episode is far superior to any of its possible sources, and argues great independence.

57. Cf. Kolve, *Play Called Corpus Christi*, pp. 218–221, for a brief discussion of the characterization of Longinus (Longeus) in the various cycles. Kolve is concerned with the strictly dramatic effects of the characterization, and seems to miss the important effect in the York play that makes Longeus an exemplary fulfillment of the action which the audience is also encouraged to participate in.

IV. Poetry and Fulfillment: The Narrative Modes

1. See Smith, *York Plays*, p. xxviii; cf. Woolf, *English Mystery Plays*, p. 290.

2. Craig, *English Religious Drama*, and Hardison, *Christian Rite and Christian Drama*, for example, associate the cycle structure with the liturgy and liturgical drama; Jerome Taylor, "The Dramatic Structure of the English Corpus Christi, or Cycle, Plays," reprinted in *Medieval Drama*, ed. Taylor and Nelson, pp. 148–156, claims that the Corpus Christi Feast holds the key to the structural unity of the cycles; Kolve, *Play Called Corpus Christi*, pp. 33–100, also claims the Corpus Christi Feast as the definitive basis for the cycle structure, and argues for the principles of typology and the Seven Ages of the World as accounting for the selection of epi-

sodes in the cycles; E. Catherine Dunn, "The Medieval 'Cycle' as History Play: An Approach to the Wakefield Plays," *Studies in the Renaissance* 7 (1960): 76–89, derives the structure of the cycles from traditional theological concepts of salvation history; Woolf, *English Mystery Plays,* pp. 54–76, stresses the influence of pictorial analogues on the structure of the cycles, an influence more fully described in Patrick Collins, "Narrative Bible Cycles in Medieval Art and Drama," *Comparative Drama* 9 (1975): 125–146; Nelson, *Medieval English Stage,* argues that the form and theme of the cycle plays was provided by civic processions; Woolf, *English Mystery Plays,* pp. 336–338, summarizes views on the influence of French plays on the English cycles.

3. *Chester Plays,* p. 87, 11. 69–72.

4. Tom F. Driver, *The Sense of History in Greek and Shakespearean Drama* (New York, 1960), p. 5.

5. For discussions of borrowings from narrative poems in the York plays, see e.g., Frances A. Foster, ed., *The Northern Passion,* EETS o.s. 147 (1916), 81–86; Craigie, "The 'Gospel of Nicodemus' and the York Mystery Plays," in *An English Miscellany,* pp. 52–61; Eleanor G. Clark, "The York Plays and the "Gospel of Nicodemus,'" *PMLA* 43 (1928): 153–161. See also Kolve, *Play Called Corpus Christi,* pp. 176–180, for brief but valuable comments on the problems faced by the playwrights in working from narrative accounts of the Passion of Christ.

6. "The Late Medieval Cult of Jesus and the Mystery Plays," *PMLA* 80 (1965): 512.

7. *Play Called Corpus Christi,* p. 122. Kolve's chapter, "Medieval Time and English Place," pp. 101–123, offers a very useful discussion of anachronism in the Corpus Christi drama in support of his general argument that "it is possible that these cycles felt no need to stage actions from present time because they staged all past actions as if they were of the present. The Corpus Christi drama managed to hold a mirror to the times while imitating the structure of human time" (p. 104).

8. *Early English Stages,* I, pp. 103, 108–109. Cf. Kolve, *Play Called Corpus Christi,* p. 106 and p. 295 n. 15.

9. Cf. Spanos, *The Christian Tradition in Modern British Verse Drama,* p. 57.

10. *English Mystery Plays,* p. 136.

11. Cf. Kolve's discussion of the Noah Plays, *Play Called Corpus Christi,* pp. 146–151; Alan H. Nelson, "'Sacred' and 'Secular' Currents in 'The Towneley Play of Noah,'" *Drama Survey* 3 (1964): 393–401; and Woolf, *English Mystery Plays,* pp. 132–145.

12. See, e.g., Erich Auerbach, *Mimesis,* tr. Willard R. Trask (Princeton, 1953), esp. pp. 143–202; Auerbach, "Figura," in *Scenes from the Drama of European Literature,* tr. Ralph Manheim (New

York, 1959), pp. 11–76; George Poulet, *Studies in Human Time,* tr. Elliott Coleman (Baltimore, 1956). Cf. Kolve, *Play Called Corpus Christi,* pp. 116–123; Spanos, *The Christian Tradition,* pp. 25–29.

13. *Play Called Corpus Christi,* p. 84.

14. Although Kolve acknowledges that the anachronism of the drama's representations of events is prompted by the Christian understanding of time, he does not make any explicit connection between this anachronism and the figural aspects of the drama's narrative which he discusses. In his study of the Towneley cycle, Walter E. Meyers does argue that the anachronism is an aspect of the "typological outlook" which he analyzes in the plays: *A Figure Given: Typology in the Wakefield Plays* (Pittsburgh, n.d.).

15. A. J. Maas, "Types in Scriptures," *Catholic Encyclopedia,* XV (1913). Cf. Kolve, *Play Called Corpus Christi,* pp. 63–84; Meyers, *A Figure Given,* pp. 1–20.

16. "Medieval Poetry and the Figural View of Reality," *Proceedings of the British Academy* 54 (1968): 78.

17. Nelson, *The Medieval Stage,* p. 4, and Woolf, *English Mystery Plays,* p. 69, both refer to Lydgate's "ordenaunce of a processyoun of the feste of corpus cristi made in london" which emphasizes typological meaning through its arrangement of Biblical scenes. Woolf, *ibid.,* pp. 69–70, also discusses continental plays arranged on a typological principle.

18. *Chester Plays,* pp. 68–69, 11. 113–114.

19. Cf. Woolf, *English Mystery Plays,* p. 61: "It is clear that the main principle was historical, not typological: that is the events were chosen for their importance in a historical sequence, and not in the first place because they foreshadowed the Redemption." Paul Strohm, "The Dramatic and Rhetorical Technique of the Chester Mystery Plays," pp. 15–34, after a valuable analysis of the Chester Old Testament plays, concludes that typology is only sporadically evident in them. He too offers the principle of prophecy and fulfillment as the basis of the narrative of the Chester plays.

20. *Festial,* p. 77.

21. The *Northern Metrical Homilies* precisely makes the traditional association between the Presentation of Christ, the Crucifixion, and the Eucharist: "In tempel first offered was he / And sithen on the rod tre / And ilke day in prestes hand / May we se Crist be made offerend" (ed. Small, pp. 157–158).

22. *Ludus Coventriae,* pp. 254–257, 11. 670–769.

23. *Chester Plays,* p. 268, 11. 65–80.

24. See A. J. Mill, "The York Bakers' Play of the Last Supper," *MLR* 30 (1935): 132.

25. Arnold Williams, "Typology and the Cycle Plays: Some Criteria," *Speculum* 43 (1968): 680–681 has insisted that any typological meaning that is not made explicit, "must be conveyed by theat-

rical means": "If any suggested typology is capable of representation on a stage, and if it enhances and deepens the meaning of the piece, let us accept it" (681).

26. Meyers, *A Figure Given,* has emphasized that the "typological outlook" is "a mode of looking at history in which discrete events are ordered, not by their sequential arrangement, but by congruities of pattern" (p. 18). I have found his examination of repeated patterns in the Towneley Plays useful; but I do not agree with his claim that "congruities of pattern" are the main principles of organization in the cycle plays.

27. *English Mystery Plays,* p. 154.

28. Ibid.

29. *Play Called Corpus Christi,* pp. 62–63. Cf. Reginald Pecock, *The Reule of Crysten Religioun,* ed. William C. Greet, EETS o.s. #171 (1927), 209.

30. Cf. Catherine Dunn's discussion of a similar pattern in the Towneley plays, "The Medieval 'Cycle' as History Play": 81–85. God's intervention in the events of history is more explicitly acknowledged in the Towneley plays than in the York plays.

31. Strohm, "The Dramatic and Rhetorical Technique of the Chester Plays," pp. 35–52, discusses the plot of the Chester plays in similar terms. The idea that Christ is the fulfillment of prophecy is, of course, one of the basic tenets of the Christian faith, founded in the words of Christ Himself and extended by the Apostles and by patristic commentators. For a discussion of this idea with reference to Middle English literature, see Ames, *The Fulfillment of the Scriptures: Abraham, Moses, and Piers.*

32. *Chester Plays,* pp. 101–102, 11. 401–432.

33. Cf. Dunn, "The Literary Style of the Towneley Plays," 496–504, who traces the role and the style of speech of the Towneley Shepherds to the liturgical drama.

34. In the York Register, this play has been copied out of sequence (it is Play XLI in Smith's edition). A note in the Register indicates that the play should follow Play XVII, The Adoration: Smith, *York Plays,* p. 433, n. 1.

35. *A Stanzaic Life of Christ,* 11. 2629–2636.

36. Homer A. Watt, "The Dramatic Unity of the *Secunda Pastorum,*" in *Essays and Studies in Honor of Carleton Brown* (New York, 1940), p. 158.

37. See Macauley, "The Play of the Harrowing of Hell." Cf. Dunn, "The Medieval 'Cycle' as History Play," 85–86; Woolf, *English Mystery Plays,* pp. 269–274.

38. Though scholars have tried to explain the choice of this ending in terms of liturgical or doctrinal concerns, it was in all probability most immediately determined by the form of the Corpus

Christi festival procession, itself derived from pictorial representation of the scheme of salvation history: see the discussions of the cycle form in Kolve, *Play Called Corpus Christi,* pp. 33–56; Woolf, *English Mystery Plays,* pp. 54–76; and Nelson, *The Medieval English Stage,* pp. 1–14. Woolf's brief comparative study of the four Last Judgment plays (ibid., pp. 294–299) is very helpful.

39. Cf. Woolf, ibid., pp. 295–299. David J. Leigh, "The Doomsday Mystery Play: An Eschatological Morality," reprinted in *Medieval English Drama,* ed. Taylor and Nelson, pp. 260–278, has discussed what he sees as "the problematic features of the Doomsday play," arguing that in these features and in the ways in which the dramatists handle them are to be found the origins of the Morality play. The connections Leigh draws with the Morality plays are instructive, but I think he exaggerates the problems inherent in the Doomsday scene and the differences between the Judgment plays and other cycle plays.

40. Cf. Leigh, ibid., pp. 265–266.

41. See, e.g., the moving sermon in *Middle English Sermons,* pp. 110–114, which combines a meditation on Christ's Passion with one on the Judgment to exhort the congregation to repentance. A number of sermons in this collection involve treatments of the Last Judgment: see pp. 18–19, 26–30, 102–103, 173–175, and 317–318.

42. *English Mystery Plays,* p. 294.

43. The list of properties owned by the Mercers' Guild responsible for the Last Judgment play mentions only "Array for ij euell saules þat ys to say ij Sirkes ij paire hoses ij vesenes and ij Chauelers Array for ij gode saules þat ys to say ij Sirkes ij paire hoses ij vesernes and ij cheuelers": see Johnston and Dorrell, "The Doomsday Pageant of the York Mercers, 1433," 29.

44. Woolf, *English Mystery Plays,* p. 294.

45. "The Doomsday Mystery Play," 264.

46. Johnston and Dorrell, "The Doomsday Pageant of the York Mercers, 1433," 29.

47. Leigh is clearly mistaken when he says of the Apostles in the York play that "none of them is given lines to speak": "The Doomsday Mystery Play," 263–264. The Apostles are precisely the image of "historical" men which Leigh forces out of the Judgment plays.

48. See, Smith, *York Plays,* p. 506.

49. The "Reproaches of Christ," of which this speech is a version, were originally developed in the context of the Last Judgment, though especially in the vernacular lyric tradition, they were usually associated with the Crucifixion: see Woolf, *The English Religious Lyric,* p. 36 ff., cf. p. 218. See also Robinson, "The Late Medieval Cult of Jesus and the Mystery Plays," 510–511.

50. Woolf is probably correct in emending "presse" to "prison" (the reading of the closely parallel Towneley play): *English Mystery Plays*, p. 297 and p. 414, n. 104.

51. This is the syntactically and rhythmically superior reading of the Towneley play.

Conclusion

1. See Nelson, *Medieval English Stage*, p. 24, Table 3.

2. *Christian Rite and Christian Drama*, p. 176.

3. *Shakespeare and the Idea of the Play* (Harmondsworth, 1967), p. 16.

Bibliography

Editions of Plays

The Chester Plays. Edited by Hermann Deimling and J. Matthews. Early English Text Society, extra series, 62, 115. London, 1892, 1916.

Ludus Coventriae, or The Plaie Called Corpus Christi. Edited by Katherine S. Block. EETS e.s. 120. London, 1922.

Medieval French Plays. Edited and translated by Richard Axton and John Stevens. Oxford: Basil Blackwell, 1971.

Le Mystère d'Adam. Edited by Paul Studer. Manchester: Manchester University Press, 1918.

Non-Cycle Plays and Fragments. Edited by Norman Davis. EETS, supplementary series, 1. London, 1970.

The Towneley Plays. Edited by George England and Alfred W. Pollard. EETS e.s. 71. London, 1897.

York Plays. Edited by Lucy Toulmin Smith. Oxford, 1885. Reissued New York: Russell and Russell, 1963.

Other Primary Sources

St. Augustine. *The City of God.* Translated by Demetrius Zema *et al.* New York: Fathers of the Church, Inc., 1950–1952.

Book of Vices and Virtues. Edited by W. Nelson Francis. EETS, original series, 217. London, 1942.

Chaucer, Geoffrey. *The Works of Geoffrey Chaucer.* Edited by F. N. Robinson. 2nd ed. Cambridge, Massachusetts, 1957.

Cursor Mundi. Edited by Richard Morris. EETS o.s. 57, 59, 62, 68, 69. London, 1874–1892.

English Metrical Homilies from Mss of the Fourteenth Century. Edited by John Small. Edinburgh, 1862.

Hilton, Walter. *The Scale of Perfection.* Edited by Evelyn Underhill. London: Watkins, 1923.

Jacob's Well. Edited by Arthur Brandeis. EETS o.s 115. London, 1900.

Jonson, Ben. *Timber, or Discoveries.* In *Ben Jonson,* edited by C. M. Herford and Percy and Evelyn Simpson. 12 volumes. Oxford: Oxford University Press, 1947.

The Lay Folks' Catechism. Edited by Thomas F. Simmons and Henry E. Nolloth. EETS o.s. 118. London, 1901.

The Lay Folks' Mass Book. Edited by Thomas F. Simmons. EETS o.s. 71. London, 1879.

Meditations on the Life and Passion of Christ. Edited by Charlotte d'Evelyn. EETS o.s. 158. London, 1921.

Meditations on the Life of Christ. Edited and translated by Isa Ragusa and Rosalie B. Green. Princeton: Princeton University Press, 1961.

Meditations on the Supper of Our Lord, and the Hours of the Passion. Edited by J. Meadows Cooper. EETS o.s. 60. London, 1875.

The Middle English Harrowing of Hell and Gospel of Nicodemus. Edited by William H. Hulme. EETS e.s. 100. London, 1908.

Middle English Sermons. Edited by Woodburn O. Ross. EETS o.s. 209. London, 1940.

Mirk, John. *Festial: A Collection of Homilies.* Edited by Theodor Erbe. EETS e.s. 96. London, 1905.

Mirk, John. *Instructions for Parish Priests.* Edited by Edward Peacock, revised by F. J. Furnivall. EETS o.s. 31. London, 1902.

The Northern Passion. Edited by Frances A. Foster. EETS o.s. 145, 147. London, 1913, 1916.

Pecock, Reginald. *The Reule of Crysten Religioun.* Edited by William C. Greet. EETS o.s. 171. London, 1927.

The Poems of John Audelay. Edited by Ella Keats Whiting. EETS o.s. 184. London, 1931.

Religious Lyrics of the XIVth Century. Edited by Carleton Brown. Oxford, 1924. 2nd edition revised by G. V. Smithers. Oxford: Clarendon Press, 1952.

Religious Lyrics of the XVth Century. Edited by Carleton Brown. Oxford: Clarendon Press, 1939.

Religious Pieces in Prose and Verse (Thornton Ms.). Edited by George G. Perry. EETS o.s. 26. London, 1867. Revised edition, London, 1889.

Reliquiae Antiquae. Edited by Thomas Wright and James O. Halliwell. 2 volumes. London, 1845.

Speculum Christiani: A Middle English Religious Treatise of the 14th Century. Edited by Gustaf Holmstedt. EETS o.s. 182. London, 1933.

Speculum Sacerdotale. Edited by Edward H. Weatherly. EETS o.s. 200. London, 1936.

A Stanzaic Life of Christ. Edited by Frances A. Foster. EETS o.s. 166. London, 1926.

A Worcestershire Miscellany Compiled by John Northwood, c. 1400. Edited by Nita Scudder Baugh. Philadelphia, 1956.

Secondary Sources

Anderson, M. D. *Drama and Imagery in English Medieval Churches.* Cambridge: Cambridge University Press, 1963.

Ames, Ruth M. *The Fulfillment of the Scriptures: Abraham, Moses, and Piers.* Evanston, Illinois: Northwestern University Press, 1970.

Auerbach, Erich. "Figura." In *Scenes from the Drama of European Literature.* Translated by Ralph Manheim, pp. 11–76. New York: Meridian Books, 1959.

Auerbach, Erich. *Mimesis: The Representation of Reality in Western Literature.* Translated by Willard R. Trask. Princeton: Princeton University Press, 1968.

Axton, Richard. *European Drama of the Early Middle Ages.* London: Hutchinson & Co. Ltd., 1974.

Bates, Katherine Lee. *The English Religious Drama.* New York: The Macmillan Company, 1921.

Benson, Larry D. *Art and Tradition in 'Sir Gawain and the Green Knight'.* New Brunswick: Rutgers University Press, 1965.

Borroff, Marie. *'Sir Gawain and the Green Knight': A Stylistic and Metrical Study.* New Haven: Yale University Press, 1962.

Brawer, Robert S. "The Characterization of Pilate in the York Cycle Play," *Studies in Philology* 69 (1972): 289–303.

Brawer, Robert S. "Dramatic Technique in the Corpus Christi Creation and Fall," *Modern Language Quarterly* 32 (1971): 347–364.

Brewer, Derek S. "The Relationship of Chaucer to the English and European Traditions." In *Chaucer and Chaucerians,* edited by D. S. Brewer, pp. 1–38. London: Thomas Nelson & Sons, Ltd., 1966.

Brown, Arthur. "York and Its Plays in the Middle Ages." In *Chaucer und seine Zeit: Symposium für Walter F. Schirmer,* edited by Arno Esch, pp. 407–418. Tübingen, 1968.

Brown, Carleton. "An Early Mention of a St. Nicholas Play in England," *Studies in Philology* 28 (1931): 594–601.

Brown, Carleton. "Sermons and Miracle Plays: Merton College Ms. 248," *MLN* 49 (1934): 394–396.

Browne, E. Martin. "Producing the Mystery Plays for Modern Audiences," *Drama Survey* 3 (1963): 5–15.

Burrow, J. A. *Ricardian Poetry*. London: Routledge & Kegan Paul, 1971.

The Catholic Encyclopedia. Edited by Charles G. Herbermann *et al.* 15 volumes and Index. New York, 1907–1914.

Chambers, E. K. *English Literature at the Close of the Middle Ages*. Oxford: Clarendon Press, 1945.

Chambers, E. K. *The Medieval Stage*. 2 volumes. Oxford: Clarendon Press, 1903.

Chaytor, H. J. *The Troubadours and England*. Cambridge: Cambridge University Press, 1923.

Clark, Eleanor Grace. "The York Plays and the 'Gospel of Nicodemus'," *PMLA* 43 (1928): 153–161.

Collins, Fletcher Jr. "Music in the Craft Cycles," *PMLA* 47 (1932): 613–621.

Collins, Patrick J. "Narrative Bible Cycles in Medieval Art and Drama," *Comparative Drama* 9 (1975): 125–146.

Craig, Hardin. *English Religious Drama of the Middle Ages*. Oxford: Clarendon Press, 1955.

Craigie, W. A. "The 'Gospel of Nicodemus' and the York Mystery Plays." In *An English Miscellany Presented to Dr. Furnivall*, pp. 52–61. Oxford, 1901.

Cutler, John L. "A Manual of Middle English Stanzaic Patterns." Unpublished Dissertation: Ohio State University, 1949.

Davidson, Charles. *Studies in the English Mystery Plays*. New Haven: Yale University Press, 1892.

Davidson, Clifford. "The Realism of the York Realist and the York Passion," *Speculum* 50 (1975): 270–283.

Diller, Hans-Jürgen. "The Craftsmanship of the Wakefield Master," *Anglia* 83 (1965): 271–288. Reprinted in *Medieval English Drama*, edited by Taylor and Nelson (q.v.), pp. 245–259.

Drake, Francis. *Eboracum; or the History and Antiquities of the City of York, from its Original to the Present Times*. London, 1736.

Driver, Tom F. *The Sense of History in Greek and Shakespearean Drama*. New York: Columbia University Press, 1960.

Dunn, E. Catherine. "Lyrical Form and the Prophetic Principle in the Towneley Plays," *Mediaeval Studies* 23 (1961): 80–90.

Dunn, E. Catherine. "The Medieval 'Cycle' as History Play: An Approach to the Wakefield Plays," *Studies in the Renaissance* 7 (1960): 76–89.

Dunn, E. Catherine. "The Literary Style of the Towneley Plays," *American Benedictine Review* 20 (1969): 481–504.

Eliot, T. S. "The Aims of Poetic Drama," *Adam International Review* 200 (1949): 10–16.

Eliot, T. S. "Poetry and Drama." In *On Poetry and Poets*, pp. 75–95. New York: Farrar, Strauss, and Cudahy, 1957.

Eliot, T. S. *Religious Drama, Medieval and Modern*. New York: House of Books, 1954.

Elliott, John R., Jr. "A Checklist of Modern Productions of the Medieval Mystery Cycles in England," *Research Opportunities in Renaissance Drama* 13–14 (1970–1971): 259–266.

Frank, Grace. *The Medieval French Drama*. Oxford: Oxford University Press, 1954.

Gardner, John. *The Construction of the Wakefield Cycle*. Carbondale and Edwardsville: Southern Illinois University Press, 1974.

Gilson, Etienne. *History of Christian Philosophy in the Middle Ages*. New York: Random House, 1955.

Gilson, Etienne. *La Théologie Mystique de Saint Bernard*. Paris: J. Vrin, 1947.

Greg, W. W. *Bibliographical and Textual Problems of the English Mystery Plays*. London: A. Morning, 1914.

Hardison, O. B., Jr. *Christian Rite and Christian Drama in the Middle Ages: Essays in the Origin and Early*

History of Modern Drama. Baltimore: The Johns Hopkins Press, 1965.

Heuser, W. "Eine Vergessene Handsschrift Der Surteespsalters und die Dort Eingeschalteten Mittelenglischen Gedichte," *Anglia* 29 (1906): 385–412.

Ingram, R. W. "The Use of Music In English Miracle Plays," *Anglia* 75 (1957): 55–76.

Jeffrey, David L. *The Early English Lyric and Franciscan Spirituality.* Lincoln: University of Nebraska Press, 1975.

Jeffrey, David L. "Franciscan Spirituality and the Rise of Early English Drama," *Mosaic* 8 (1975): 17–46.

Johnston, Alexandra F. and Dorrell, Margaret. "The Doomsday Pageant of the York Mercers, 1433," *Leeds Studies in English* n.s., 5 (1971): 29–34.

Kahrl, Stanley. *Traditions of Medieval English Drama.* London: Hutchinson & Co., Ltd., 1974.

Kane, George. *Middle English Literature: A Critical Study of the Romances, the Religious Lyrics, 'Piers Plowman'.* London: Methuen & Co. Ltd., 1951.

Kinghorn, A. M. *Mediaeval Drama.* London: Evans Brothers Limited, 1968.

Kolve, V. A. *The Play Called Corpus Christi.* Stanford: Stanford University Press, 1966.

Kretzmann, Paul. *Liturgical Element in the Earliest Forms of the Medieval Drama.* Minneapolis: University of Minnesota Press, 1916.

Lawrence, R. F. "The Formulaic Theory and Its Application to English Alliterative Poetry," in *Essays on Style and Language.* Edited by Roger Fowler. London: Routledge and Kegan Paul, 1966, pp. 166–183.

Leigh, David J. "The Doomsday Mystery Play: An Eschatological Morality," *Modern Philology* 67 (1970): 211–223. Reprinted in *Medieval English Drama,* ed. Taylor and Nelson (q.v.), pp. 260–278.

McNeir, Waldo F. "The Corpus Christi Passion Plays as Dramatic Art," *Studies in Philology* 48 (1951): 601–628.

Macauley, Peter Stuart. "The Play of the Harrowing of Hell as a Climax in the English Mystery Cycles," *Studia Germanica Gandensia* 8 (1966): 115–134.

Mâle, Emile. *The Gothic Image: Religious Art in France of the Thirteenth Century.* Translated from the third edition by Dora Nussey. London: Collins, 1961.

Manning, Stephen. *Wisdom and Number: Toward a Critical Appraisal of the Middle English Religious Lyric.* Lincoln: University of Nebraska Press, 1962.

Marshall, Mary Hatch. "Aesthetic Values of the Liturgical Drama." In *English Institute Essays,* ed. Alan S. Downer, 1950, pp. 89–115. Reprinted in *Medieval English Drama,* ed. Taylor and Nelson (q.v.), pp. 28–43.

Martz, Louis L. *The Poetry of Meditation.* Revised edition. New Haven: Yale University Press, 1962.

Meyers, Walter E. *A Figure Given: Typology in the Wakefield Plays.* Pittsburgh: Duquesne University Press, n.d.

Mill, Anna J. "The York Bakers' Play of the Last Supper," *Modern Language Review* 30 (1935): 145–158.

Milosh, Joseph E. *'The Scale of Perfection' and the English Mystical Tradition.* Madison: University of Wisconsin Press, 1966.

Moore, John R. "The Tradition of Angelic Singing in English Drama," *JEGP* 22 (1923): 89–99.

Mosher, J. A. *The Exemplum in the Early Religious and Didactic Literature of England.* New York: Columbia University Press, 1911.

Nelson, Alan H. *The Medieval English Stage: Corpus Christi Pageants and Plays.* Chicago and London: University of Chicago Press, 1974.

Nelson, Alan H. " 'Sacred' and 'Secular' Currents in 'The Towneley Play of Noah'," *Drama Survey* 3 (1964): 393–401.

Nicoll, Allardyce. *British Drama.* 5th edition. New York: Barnes & Noble, 1962.

Oliver, Raymond. *Poems Without Names: The English Lyric 1200–1500.* Berkeley: University of California Press, 1970.

Owst, G. R. *Literature and Pulpit in Medieval England.* 2nd edition. New York: Barnes & Noble, 1961.

Owst, G. R. *Preaching in Medieval England.* Cambridge: Cambridge University Press, 1926.

Pantin, W. A. *The English Church in the Fourteenth Century.* Cambridge: Cambridge University Press, 1955.

Pearson, Lu Emily. "Isolable Lyrics of the Mystery Plays," *ELH* 3 (1936): 228–252.

Pfander, Homer G. *The Popular Sermon of the Medieval Friar in England.* New York, 1937.

Poulet, George. *Studies in Human Time.* Translated by Elliot Coleman. Baltimore: The Johns Hopkins University Press, 1956.

Pourrat, P. *La Spiritualité Chrétienne.* Paris: Librairie Lecoffre, 1951.

Prior, Moody E. *The Language of Tragedy.* New York: Columbia University Press, 1947.

Prosser, Eleanor. *Drama and Religion in the English Mystery Plays: A Re-Evaluation.* Stanford: Stanford University Press, 1961 (Stanford Studies in Language and Literature, 23).

Purvis, Canon J. S. *From Minster to Market-Place.* York: St. Anthony's Press, 1969.

Reese, Jesse Byers. "Alliterative Verse in the York Cycle," *Studies in Philology* 48 (1951): 639–668.

Righter, Anne. *Shakespeare and the Idea of the Play.* Harmondsworth: Penguin Books, 1967.

Robbins, Rossell Hope. "An English Mystery Play Fragment Ante 1300," *MLN* 65 (1950): 30–35.

Robinson, J. W. "The Art of the York Realist," *MP* 60 (1963): 241–251. Reprinted in *Medieval English Drama,* ed. Taylor and Nelson (q.v.), pp. 230–244.

Robinson, J. W. "A Commentary on the York Play of the Birth of Jesus," *JEGP* 70 (1971): 241–254.

Robinson, J. W. "The Late Medieval Cult of Jesus and the Mystery Plays," *PMLA* 80 (1965): 508–514.

Robinson, J. W. "Medieval English Acting," *Theatre Notebook* 13 (1959): 83–88.

Rossiter, A. P. *English Drama from Early Times to the*

Elizabethans. London: Hutchinson and Co., 1950.

Rushworth, G. McNeil. *Medieval Christian Imagery as Illustrated by the Painted Windows of Great Malvern Priory Church, Worcestershire.* Oxford: Clarendon Press, 1936.

Salter, Elizabeth. "Medieval Poetry and the Figural View of Reality," *Proceedings of the British Academy* 54 (1968): 73–92.

Scholes, Robert and Robert Kellogg. *The Nature of Narrative.* Oxford: Oxford University Press, 1966.

Spanos, William V. *The Christian Tradition in Modern British Drama: The Poetics of Sacramental Time.* New Brunswick: Rutgers University Press, 1967.

Stevens, John. "Music in Mediaeval Drama," *Proceedings of the Royal Musical Association* 84 (1958): 81–95.

Stevens, Martin. "The Theater of the World: A Study in Medieval Dramatic Form," *The Chaucer Review* 7 (1974): 234–249.

Sticca, Sandro. *The Latin Passion Play: Its Origins and Development.* Albany: State University of New York Press, 1970.

Strohm, Paul. "The Dramatic and Rhetorical Technique of the Chester Mystery Plays." Unpublished dissertation: University of California, Berkeley, 1966.

Taylor, George C. "The English 'Planctus Mariae'," *Modern Philology* 4 (1907): 605–637.

Taylor, George C. "The Relation of the English Corpus Christi Play to the Middle English Religious Lyric," *Modern Philology* 5 (1907): 1–38.

Taylor, Jerome. "Critics, Mutations, and Historians of Medieval English Drama: An Introduction to the Essays that Follow." In *Medieval English Drama,* ed. Taylor and Nelson (q.v.), pp. 1–27.

Taylor, Jerome. "The Dramatic Structure of the English Corpus Christi, or Cycle, Plays." In *Literature and Society,* ed. Bernice Slote, pp. 175–186, Lincoln: University of Nebraska Press, 1963. Reprinted in *Medieval English Drama,* ed. Taylor and Nelson (q.v.), pp. 148–156.

Taylor, Jerome and Nelson, Alan H., eds. *Medieval English Drama: Essays Critical and Contextual.* Chicago and London: University of Chicago Press, 1972.

Wall, Catherine. "A Study of 'The Appearance of Our Lady to Thomas': Pageant XLVI in the York Cycle of Mystery Plays." Unpublished Dissertation: Catholic University of America, 1965.

Wall, Carolyn. "York Pageant XLVI and its Music," *Speculum* 46 (1971): 687–712.

Watt, Homer A. "The Dramatic Unity of the *Secunda Pastorum.*" In *Essays and Studies in Honor of Carleton Brown,* pp. 158–166. New York: Oxford University Press, 1940.

Weber, Sarah Appleton. *Theology and Poetry in the Middle English Lyric: A Study of Sacred History and Aesthetic Form.* Columbus, Ohio: Ohio State University Press, 1969.

Wells, Henry W. "Style in the English Mystery Plays," *JEGP* 38 (1938): 496–524.

Wickham, Glynne. *Early English Stages 1300–1660.* 2 volumes. London: Routledge & Kegan Paul, 1959, 1963.

Williams, Arnold. *The Drama of Medieval England.* East Lansing: Michigan State University Press, 1961.

Williams, Arnold. "Typology and the Cycle Plays: Some Criteria," *Speculum* 43 (1969): 676–684.

Woolf, Rosemary. "The Theme of Christ the Lover-Knight," *Review of English Studies* n.s. 13 (1962): 1–16.

Woolf, Rosemary. *The English Mystery Plays.* Berkeley and Los Angeles: University of California Press, 1972.

Woolf, Rosemary. *English Religious Lyric in the Middle Ages.* Oxford: Oxford University Press, 1968.

Young, Karl. *The Drama of the Medieval Church.* 2 volumes. Oxford: Clarendon Press, 1933.

INDEX